SETTING THE TONE FROM THE TOP

How leaders' conversations shape a positive culture

Melinda Muth
Bob Selden

Book production and text design by Publish Central
Cover design by Ben Odering

Disclaimer

CONTENTS

ACKNOWLEDGEMENTS

From Bob Selden

I was fortunate to undertake my formal psychology studies in my early 30s by which time I'd had both some life and work experiences and reached a certain level of maturity. One of the early writers that fascinated me was D.C. McClelland who is famous for his work on the need for achievement. However, it was his research into the impact of words on developing this drive for achievement that really got my attention. For example, he posited that a society's future may be predicated on the words the society currently uses in day-to-day conversations, books (particularly children's books), stories, films, plays, cartoons and the popular press.

Around that time, I started working for my long-term mentor, Dennis Pratt, one of Australia's foremost organisational development consultants and author of *Aspiring to Greatness: Above and Beyond Total Quality Management*. Dennis was instrumental in fostering my interest in all things to do with motivation and has been an inspiration in my consulting work over many years. Dennis and I used to run training programs for managers, teaching them how to use McClelland's theory to develop a greater need for achievement. The key underpinning of this training was training people how to write achievement-oriented stories (rather than negative ones). And although I didn't realise it at the time, this was a good example of priming and in many cases, reframing the words and phrases we use to gain a more positive outcome.

I'd like to thank my co-author Melinda, who has inspired me during our writing of *Setting the Tone from the Top* with her vast experience, executive stories (some that we couldn't print!) and quotes around the topic of senior executive conversations. I've tremendously enjoyed our collaboration during this process.

Finally, I'd like to thank my number one fan, my wife Anita, whose constant encouragement makes me want to succeed at everything I do.

From Melinda Muth

I've had a lot of variety in my career and the thread that ties it all together is a deep interest in people, teams and ways to manage group dynamics to make better decisions. One of my career moves was to train as a psychologist. While I was studying, a wise friend called to my attention that rather than doing a Bachelor's degree in psychology, I should consider a PhD in organisational behaviour in order to build on my interest in that subject during my MBA years at Harvard. I then ended up making an application to the PhD program at AGSM/UNSW thinking I would research effective group leadership at the executive level and ended up doing research on boards and directors. This led to a dissertation supervised by Professor Lex Donaldson on the topic of board structure and its impact on company performance.

I joined the organisational behaviour faculty at AGSM which led to many opportunities to work with executive groups. Here, I observed firsthand the impact of positive behaviour, and not so positive behaviour on group performance. During my time at AGSM, I was very fortunate to meet John Colvin who was working as an Adjunct Professor. He later became the CEO of AICD and invited me to join the AICD facilitation team. I will be forever grateful to John for that invitation and for his leadership. Working with AICD has allowed me to utilise all the skills I've developed over the years and to build on the work I did during my PhD years.

In addition to meeting John, during my time with the executive education team at AGSM, I met my co-author, Bob Selden. We have kept in touch over the years and after the success of his first book *What To Do When You Become The Boss*, I was delighted to hear about the publication of his second book *Don't: How using the right words will change your life*. Bob kindly gave me an advance copy and when I read it, I instantly thought about how the content could be applied to the impact of conversation on company culture. In my work with executives, one of the questions I am most often asked is how to deal with difficult group dynamics. I thought the practical advice in Bob's second book could be tailored for executives who want to build healthy workplace culture. The result is *Setting the Tone from Top*.

I want to thank my co-author Bob for being such a collaborative, and of course, positive colleague. He does indeed 'practice what he preaches' and I have experienced firsthand how well his recommendations work.

Finally, I would like to the two people who inspire me most, my daughter, Jilly Pfifferling, and my husband, Ian Hill. Their support and optimism about what I can achieve keeps me going.

From Bob and Melinda

We are grateful to those writers who permitted us to quote from their work, such as Spiro Zavos, Sports Journalist from the *Sydney Morning Herald*, who piqued our interest in the notion of locus of control; Professor Marianne Schmid Mast from the Université de Lausanne whose study of the impact of words on young male drivers fascinated us; M K Chen, Associate Professor Economics, at UCLA Anderson School of Management whose ongoing work on futured languages will, we believe, have major implications for our positivity; Penny Tompkins and James Lawley who first introduced us to the importance of metaphors and the use of 'clean language'; Bud Hennekes, blog owner of

"A Boundless World" http://www.aboundlessworld.com/about/ for his great feedback story; Louise Sedgwick from Campbell Page and her colleagues who jumped at the opportunity to tell their positivity story, and many others too numerous to name but who are catalogued in the footnotes throughout the book.

INTRODUCTION

War over words erupts as World Bank star economist loses management duties

The World Bank's Chief Economist, Paul Romer has been stripped of his management duties after researchers rebelled against his efforts to make them communicate more clearly, including curbs on the written use of the word "and".

Romer will remain chief economist, providing management with "timely thought leadership on trends directly affecting our client countries, including the 'future of work'," World Bank president Jim Yong Kim said in the note to staff dated May 9.

Romer said he met resistance from staff when he tried to refine the way they communicate. "I was in the position of being the bearer of bad news," he said in an interview.

"It's possible that I was focusing too much on the precision of the communications and not enough on the feelings my messages would invoke" Romer, 61, explained.[1]

Imagine someone at such a senior level being stripped of his or her seniority, or even losing their job, over the words they have used? Unlikely? Yet it happened in this case. Read again that last statement

---

1   A Mayeda, 2017, "War over words erupts as World Bank start economist loses management duties", *Sydney Morning Herald*, 26 May, https://www.smh.com.au/business/the-economy/war-over-words-erupts-as-world-bankd-start-economist-loses-management-duties-20170526gwdj97.html, (accessed 26 May 2017).

of Romer's: "It's possible that I was focusing too much on the precision of the communications and not enough on the feelings my messages would invoke."

The impact?

Every statement we make, either verbal or written, has both an intent—what we want to achieve—and an impact—how it is received by the recipient. Sometimes intent and impact are in sync, sometimes not. Human beings transfer information (and feelings) from one person to another by putting thoughts into words. This includes thoughts about everything from the values we hold dear, to our thoughts about strategies, goals, and views on risk. Those in positions of authority with a clear understanding of the impact of their words and their thoughts on the behaviour of those they wish to lead, are in a better position to ensure their impact is what they mean it to be.

However, our intent doesn't always result in the impact we intend. For example, in Paul Romer's case he was reported to have been frustrated with what he saw as the dense, convoluted style of many of the department's reports. His intent was to have researchers write more clearly, using the active voice to be more direct. In particular, he had a distaste for the conjunction 'and'. In doing so, his emails became short and terse. The impact? It was quite different from his intent. Staff reportedly said they were upset by his tone and as a result, felt they were not being listened to. "They felt under-appreciated," Romer said. "It reflected a kind of siege mentality that I can't quite understand."[2] Notice here, that Romer's intention of improving the quality of reports (his logic and reasoning about data and information) resulted in an impact on the recipients' feelings. Often when there is a mismatch between intent and impact, what seems like a logical, reasoned communique to the sender, produces an impactful and unexpected arousal of the negative feelings in the recipient.

---

2   ibid.

Therefore, for leaders facing the task of driving cultural change and building organisational trust, the importance of aligning intent and impact is critically important. For it's how people 'feel' about the message that will gain their commitment, not necessarily the 'reason and logic' behind the message, no matter how sound the reasons may appear to executive team and the board.

Our intent in *Setting the Tone from the Top* is to demonstrate how something so simple as words, can have so much impact. If something someone does or says in a particular way, sets the tone for an event or activity, it establishes the way that event or activity will continue, and this is especially the case for the mood of the people involved. Words are the building blocks of effective communication, both verbal and written. Effective communication impacts the way people interact with each other and whether those interactions are positive and open, or negative and possibly harmful. In short, words are the most basic building blocks for setting the tone in terms of the 'way we do things around here'. Words shape behaviours, which impact decisions and actions, and in turn, form the culture of an organisation. Frances Frei and Anne Morriss explain the formation of culture like this:

"Culture guides discretionary behaviour and it picks up where the employee handbook leaves off. Culture tells us how to respond to an unprecedented service request. It tells us whether to risk telling our bosses about our new ideas, and whether to surface or hide problems. Employees make hundreds of decisions on their own every day, and culture is our guide. Culture tells us what to do when the CEO isn't in the room, which is of course most of the time."[3]

---

3   Frances Frei and Anne Morriss, 2012, "Culture Takes Over When the CEO Leaves the Room", *Harvard Business Review*, 10 May, https://hbr.org/2012/05/culture-takes-over-when-the-ce, (accessed 13 July 2022).

It all begins with words

The aim of this book is to examine what the words 'setting the tone' really mean, and indeed how words create the conversations that 'set the tone' in actual practice, and why this is so important for leaders, those who are in the highest position of authority in organisations of every kind—from family businesses, to non-profit organisations and major listed companies. The words leaders use have power. Senior executive conversations with management (and in boardrooms) shape the behaviour and decisions, which influence employees, suppliers, creditors and the community.

The evolution of attitudes in the community about the conduct of companies has heightened expectations of the role leaders at all levels play in shaping culture. According to the Edelman Trust Barometer 2022 survey a 'failure of leadership makes distrust the default'.[4] We are in a low trust moment in society and employees are looking at their own organisations and asking questions about conduct and behaviour. And then there is the phenomenon of people quitting jobs at higher rates than usual resulting in the term coined by Professor Anthony Klotz: 'the Great Resignation'.[5] Pandemic experiences, the way employees were treated during the pandemic, and a host of other factors tied to the pandemic have created staff shortages. All of which makes the subject of workplace culture an important agenda item for organisations who want to retain staff and sustain performance.

The aim of this book is to provide leaders at all levels with tools and processes for shaping a healthy workplace culture through effective conversation with each other, with executives and stakeholders, to ensure all views on key topics such as conduct, risk and strategy,

---

4   2022 Edelman Trust Barometer, https://www.edelman.com/trust/2022-trust-barometer, (accessed 11 July 2022).

5   Amy Fontineelle, 2002, "The Great Resignation", *Investopedia—Economy*, 05 May, https://www.investopedia.com/the-great-resignation-5199074, (accessed 11 July, 2022).

are canvassed, heard and evaluated so that the tone being set, i.e. the culture being transmitted and maintained, is positive, healthy, and meets the expectations of all stakeholders.

Using encouraging and affirmative language, having effective conversations, and developing beneficial relationships, at the top (where this approach starts) and externally with other stakeholders, are often described by social scientists and communication experts as 'process management' skills. These skills distil into three elements—words, language, and conversations—that are essential for developing the important relationships that enable leaders to set the tone from the top. **Figure 1: The three building blocks of effective tone are relationships, conversation and words** depict how 'words' are the

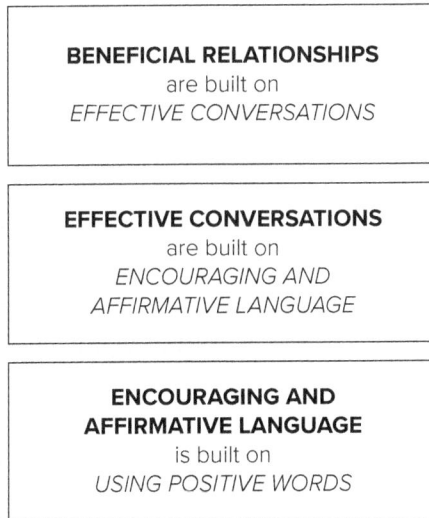

```
┌─────────────────────────────────────┐
│      BENEFICIAL RELATIONSHIPS        │
│             are built on             │
│      EFFECTIVE CONVERSATIONS         │
└─────────────────────────────────────┘

┌─────────────────────────────────────┐
│      EFFECTIVE CONVERSATIONS         │
│             are built on             │
│        ENCOURAGING AND               │
│        AFFIRMATIVE LANGUAGE          │
└─────────────────────────────────────┘

┌─────────────────────────────────────┐
│        ENCOURAGING AND               │
│        AFFIRMATIVE LANGUAGE          │
│             is built on              │
│       USING POSITIVE WORDS           │
└─────────────────────────────────────┘
```

Figure 1: The three building blocks that set the tone and shape a healthy workplace culture.

building blocks that construct 'effective conversations', which in turn build 'effective relationships' that ultimately set the tone from the top.

In various conversations as a leader and manager, the topics being discussed, for example, strategy, technology, finance and operational issues, are the 'content' of the conversations. The way these topics are discussed—the communication skills used, such as questioning, listening, using positive words, reframing, triangulating, managing the agenda and so on—are the process management skills leaders need to apply to be at their best in role modelling 'the way we do things around here'.

It's our experience, that few leaders take the time to manage and evaluate their process management skills. Accordingly, each of the Parts in *Setting the Tone from The Top* covers these key process management fundamentals.

Part 1 covers the setting and shaping of culture—how is it originally formed? What impact do founders, CEOs and executive leaders have on the culture of the organisation? What are the 'levers' the CEO and senior management use in developing an appropriate culture? And particularly, what part does language, both verbal and written, play in setting the tone from the top?

This leads us to **discussing 'conversation' in Part 2**—the key process through which leaders harness the knowledge of the senior management and all staff in their organisation. Whilst Part 1 is principally about the 'why?' (why leaders should be concerned with culture), in Part 2 we commence the 'how?'—how leaders play their part in setting the tone at the top, by understanding the impact their words and language have on tone through their conversations inside and outside the organisation.

In Part 3, we introduce specific strategies, techniques and tactics for leaders. These techniques and tactics can be used in day-to-day conversations that model the behaviour leaders expect everyone to follow. We also examine how choosing particular words in conversation, can cause either a positive or negative impact on others. Part 3 concludes with a chapter on how using certain language in conversation over periods of time, impacts how the brain functions—either positively or negatively.

The book concludes with **Part 4 showing how leaders can apply the conversational processes we cover in Parts 2 and 3, to specific, challenging conversations** such as 'giving critical feedback to a direct report' or 'handling a difficult media conversation', and even 'managing difficult conversations with directors in the boardroom'. We suggest reading Parts 1 to 3 in their entirety as each builds on the other. Part 4 contains stand-alone chapters and may be read as and when needed—however, we do encourage leaders to read at least the Introduction to Part 4, as it covers the six-step process that a conversation follows in greater detail. It also provides specific examples that will assist in assimilating this important process management strategy.

In addition to the footnotes throughout the book, highlighting the research that underpins these key process management fundamentals, we've included a short list of further reading on a range of topics like the brain, words and conversation, for those who are interested in developing their knowledge in these areas.

We trust you'll enjoy our conversation about words and language and how they impact organisational culture. We'd love to have you join the conversation, you may do so by contacting us on: www.melindamuth.com and www.bobselden.com.

PART 1

SETTING THE TONE AT THE TOP

1.1 How leaders set and shape culture

We begin with a discussion of the word 'culture' and what it means. The definition we hear most often is 'the way we do things around here.' It's all about conforming and aligning behaviour with the values and objectives of the organisation, and leadership behaviour is a critical element.

For example, 3M is recognised as having a corporate culture that has seen them become and remain, one of the most successfully innovative companies in the world. And yet probably apart from their world famous *Post It Note* and being the inventors of sand paper, most of us are unaware that we all use at least one of their products every day—in fact Simon Sinek in his book "Leaders Eat Last" suggests that figure is closer to 60 or 70![6]

We had the pleasure of working with the Asia Pacific Division of 3M over a three year period helping them design and implement their Leadership Development Process, so we can attest to the underpinnings of their innovative culture—in a word, "inclusiveness".

---

6   S Sinek, *Leaders Eat Last*, 2017, Penguin Press, New York.

Fred J Palensky, 3M's former Chief Technology Officer, put it this way, "Every single technical employee in the company has dual citizenship—they're part of a particular business, lab, or country, and part of the 3M global technical community."

"We don't restrict people from moving from one business to another, from one industry to another, or across country boundaries," he said. And our experience with 3M and their developing leaders supports that view as a great example of how culture, in this case one of "innovation", is set by the senior leaders. "We believe that no one business has everything it needs to conduct business in its marketplace without leveraging the rest of the company," said Palensky.

Another example of a leader setting the tone is James Sinegal, found of Costco. In a 2009 interview[7] he talked about why Costco was the only major retailers without layoffs. He said "we knew how nervous everyone was. It's certainly one of the first times in my life I can recall fear in people relative to economics … and our employees … deserve our loyalty. They needed it just as much then as they ever did, or more. So we said, let's see how we can get through this thing without having layoffs." His tone was reinforcing the "family" oriented culture he developed in Costco.

Both of these examples illustrate the focus of this book: examining the ways leaders influence and shape behaviours, policies, and performance goals in organisations. That is, how do leaders of an organisation, set the tone that shapes the culture?

What levers are leaders able to use?

The following diagram, **Figure 2: Elements of culture creation and maintenance**, shows the 'factors' that relate to how culture is originally created and subsequently, shaped. It also depicts the key levers

---

7   https://www.seattletimes.com/business/qa-costco-ceo-jim-sinegal-talks-about-recession-succession/, (accessed 17 July 2022).

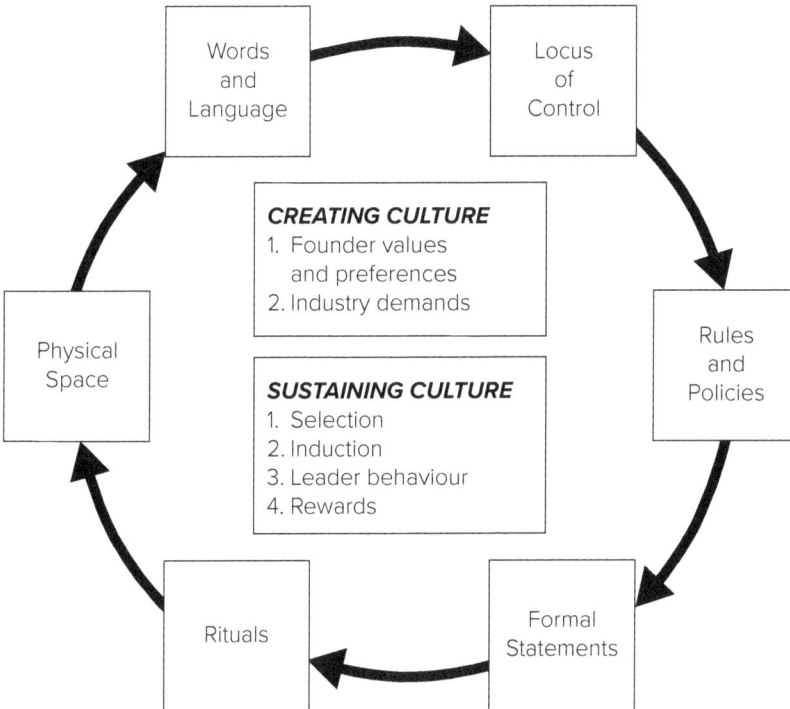

Figure 2: Elements of culture creation and maintenance.

which impact culture over which leaders have influence. We'll discuss these in detail and demonstrate the part conversation plays in each, as we progress through this chapter and chapter **1.2 How leaders shape culture**.

How are cultures created?

Where do cultures come from in the first place? An understanding of this question is essential for those wanting to influence, change or sustain culture. What happens inside an organisation is influenced by both internal and external challenges and how the people in the organisation decide to deal with those challenges. When their decisions result in success (i.e. rewards earned, recognition received, status achieved, threats overcome), the values and behaviours perceived as central to that success are retained.

How is a company's culture created? The founders' values and preferences, and the demands of the industry are critical elements. Culture is shaped by the founder together with the demands of the industry and the initial successes (and failures) experienced as the organisation grows.[8]

For example, 3M was mentioned at the start of this chapter. When 3M was founded in 1902, it was remarkably unsuccessful in its first three years (due to mining for the wrong product). Today it has become a global phenomenon with over 90,000 employees across 129 countries and producing 55,000 products. What is their recipe for success? A culture that fosters innovation—their website exclaims; "3M is a global innovation company that never stops inventing. Over the years, our innovations have improved daily life for hundreds of millions of people all over the world. We have made driving at night easier, made buildings safer, and made consumer electronics lighter, less energy-intensive and less harmful to the environment. We even helped put a man on the moon. Every day at 3M, one idea always leads to the next, igniting momentum to make progress possible around the world."[9]

In the case of 3M, initial industry demands for a different product and the founders' desire to be successful through continuous innovation, have shaped the way the company and the people in it behave and perform today. Indeed, it has a culture that could be summed up as 'promoting innovation'.

---

8   M Carpenter, B Bauer and B Erdogan, 2009, *Principles of Management*, v. 1.1, p 359–361, open textbook, https://2012books.lardbucket.org/pdfs/management-principles-v1.0.pdf, (accessed 29 March 2018).

9   3M—*Company Information—Who We Are*, http://solutions.3m.com/wps/portal/3M/en_US/3M-Company/Information/AboutUs/WhoWeAre/, (accessed 29 March 2018).

1. *The founder and their values*

An organisation's culture in its early years is inevitably tied to the values and personality of its founder. For example, Mark Zuckerberg is the founder, Chair, CEO of Meta and the culture of the company is tied to his thinking and behaviour. Similarly, Steve Jobs shaped the culture and values of Apple. When a person starts a business, or founds a non-profit organisation, it is their vision, their goals, rules and the people they hire that determine the behaviours and standards of performance that are expected and acceptable.

Another example is Atlassian, a company which has grown to earn its name (from the mythical Greek God, Atlas). It's valued at around $30 billion today, a far cry from the $10,000 credit card debt of its beginnings. Atlassian now employs 8,100 people worldwide, and despite this, the founders, Scott Farquhar and Mike Cannon-Brookes, haven't let it change them or their company or their values. In the early days of their company, they individually hired everyone who joined their company. When they started delegating the hiring, they ran into problems—in their words "we did it without specifically knowing what we should look for and what types of people fit with Atlassian."[10] Following this realisation, they ran a process with their management team and long-standing staff to identify the values that matter at Atlassian. They subsequently aligned their hiring practices with those values. Farquhar and Cannon-Brookes attribute much of their success to those values and the culture that has been created because of those values. Their story illustrates how founder values become part of the organisation culture to the extent they help the company become successful.

---

10 B Rogers, 2017, "How culture drives Atlassian's ambitions to be the collaboration platform for all companies", *Forbes*, 20 January, p 1, https://www.forbes.com/sites/brucerogers/2017/01/20/how-culture-drives-atlassians-ambitions-to-be-the-collaboration-platform-for-all-companies/#1c63a9316f41, (accessed 29 March 2018).

2. Industry demands

The influence of founders is powerful, but industry characteristics also play a significant role. For instance, banking and insurance companies are stable and rule-oriented; technology companies tend to be more visibly innovative; and non-profit organisations more people focused. If an industry is highly regulated, such as banking or healthcare, then the presence of more regulation and compliance requirements can be expected. It is important therefore to recognise the influence of industry on culture formation—it may not be possible to imitate the culture of a company in a different industry even though it may appear to be admirable to outsiders who have high expectations for the capacity of the CEO to change culture. For example, General Electric (GE) under the leadership of Jack Welch was lauded for its leadership development, preparing dozens of executives for senior roles inside and outside GE. Yet many of the disciples of GE style leadership did not prosper outside GE. What GE needed was different from what was needed in the companies taken over by the 'disciples'.[11] Bob Nardelli left GE to head up Home Depot to turn it around. While some of his initiatives worked, in the end he was pushed out of the company because of his lack of retail experience, a very different industry sector to that of GE.

Another case in point is the failure of major Australian retailer Woolworths, when it launched its Masters hardware chain in a venture with major backing from American hardware company, Lowes. On the surface, moving from one industry sector to another might seem an appropriate strategic move for a successful grocery retailer. However, as Masters CEO Melinda Smith said when addressing analysts in the wake of Woolworths being forced to blow out its projected losses

---

11   Daniel Gross, 2003, "Do They Know Jack", *Slate*, 4 March, https://slate.com/business/2003/03/why-jack-welch-s-proteges-are-failing.html, (accessed 11 July 2022).

for Masters in its first five years, "The company failed to grasp the seasonality of hardware." She acknowledged that she didn't know a lot about the structure of the business when it began "We didn't know a lot about this business when we set the budget for financial 2013," Smith said.[12]

The Masters case demonstrates some of the industry demands that may differ, even within sectors. And in the case of Masters, there's an even greater pressure on success—culture. As pointed out in an article[13] on the topic comparing Masters to the success of its competitor Bunnings:

Bunnings has successfully developed a strong organisational culture where workers feel empowered. Bunnings Head of Human Resources, Willem Pruys championed a workplace where challenging the boss was expected and feedback and ideas welcomed. 'The culture has produced a number of outcomes,' Mr Lake said. Team members by and large love working at Bunnings. The staff churn is incredibly low. Customers who know nothing of the culture notice eye contact, smiles, willingness and enthusiasm not often experienced in Australian retail.

It also results in rapid feedback of market information to those making far ranging decisions. For a huge retailer, Bunnings is amazingly nimble. Woolworths is a very top-down company.

Masters had a written policy of insisting staff park their cars tail-in to the kerb, which is symptomatic of their rigid workplace culture.

---

12 E Greenblat, 2013, "Woolworths 'failed to understand' hardware", *Sydney Morning Herald*, 18 July, https://www.smh.com.au/.../woolworths-failed-to-understand-hardware-20130718-2q5if, (accessed 29 March 2018).

13 E Stewart, 2016, "Masters: Five reasons Woolworths is pulling the plug on struggling hardware chain", *ABC News*, January 16, www.abc.net.au/news/2015-05-06/five-reasons-woolworths-is...hardware/6450364, (accessed 29 March 2018).

This relationship between culture and industry demands is well summarised in an insightful open letter to Woolworths' CEO Grant O'Brien, by financial analyst Sam Ferraro who wrote at the time: "Perhaps your greatest legacy to the company you have worked at since a teenager will be to have the courage to admit to past failures and exit home improvement, while re-assessing the synergies that exist between general merchandise and supermarkets."[14]

And it is likely to be more than an assessment of the synergies between general merchandise and supermarkets that is required to understand what went wrong. It can be argued that another aspect of culture played a role in the failure of Masters. Woolworths would have executed its strategy with the participation of its key venture partner, Lowes, a successful player in the US retail hardware market. The beliefs of a culture shaped by success in one country do not easily translate across national borders.

How are cultures sustained?

As a company grows and matures, values and behaviours are refined and reinforced. Early values, those shaped by the founder and reinforced by their association with success, influence the development of future values. Existing organisational culture influences hiring decisions. Indeed, a talented person can be rejected on the basis of being 'not a good cultural fit'. Once new people join an organisation, they quickly observe what is acceptable and what is not acceptable and they respond to the behaviour that is rewarded. Cultures are maintained by reinforcing behaviours through the selection of who is in the company. This includes group membership; how the rules are transmitted to new members; how they are rewarded (or punished); and the behaviour of leaders.

---

14 S Ferraro, 2015, *Livewire*, n.d., https://www.livewiremarkets.com/wires/an-open-letter-to-grant-o-brien, (accessed 29 March 2018).

It's widely known, for instance, that there's one thing that will make or break you at Apple; cultural fit. In 2013, Apple CEO Tim Cook fired John Browett just one month after the European electronics executive had been appointed Apple's head of retail. Browett, according to Apple executives, didn't fit in at Apple, and frequently upset store employees by changing their schedules. "After being fired from Apple, Browett said in a speech that he was shocked that he was let go due to not fitting in with company culture, even though he was qualified for the position."[15]

1. Attraction and selection—who is on the team?

People are attracted to organisations for a variety of reasons and the belief that they will fit in is an important one. Research shows that employees with different personalities find different cultures attractive. For example, out of the 'Big Five' personality traits,[16] people who demonstrate high rigidity and anxiety are less likely to be attracted to innovative cultures, whereas those with high openness to experience are more likely to be attracted to innovative cultures.[17]

'Values similarity' is only one reason a person may be attracted to a particular company. High salaries, bonuses and benefits are other powerful attractors. And the door swings both ways—companies are also looking for people who will fit in and often they hire for fit in attitude rather than specific skills which can be taught on the job. Companies use different techniques to weed out candidates who do not fit with corporate values. For example, Google uses a process of multiple interviews with future peers to learn what potential co-workers

---

15 J Linshi, 2015, "This surprising trait can get you fired at Apple", *Time*, 26 March, http://time.com/3760114/apple-tim-cook-fired/, (accessed 29 March 2018).

16 R McCrae and O John, 1992, "An introduction to the five-factor model and its applications", *Journal of Personality*, Vol 60, No 2, p 175–215.

17 T Judge and D Cable, 1997, "Applicant personality, organizational culture, and organization attraction", *Personnel Psychology*, Vol 50, No 2, p 359–94.

think of a candidate in order to make an assessment of fit. And similarly, returning to the Atlassian story:

> *When we hire someone, it's not enough to have a great resume and experience. You have to value the same things we do: transparency, customer service, work-life balance, initiative, and fun.*
>
> *In other words, if we passed each other on the sidewalk some sunny Sunday afternoon, we'd actually want to stop and talk with you. Why is this so important? Because if you like the people you work with and value the same things, you'll spend more time with them and collaborate more.*
>
> *This* doesn't *mean you should just hire a bunch of people that look and sound and think like you. That leads to a homogeneous, workforce, which can actually stifle innovation. Hiring for "values fit" leaves plenty of room for hiring people of diverse backgrounds, interests, ages, etc. while ensuring that what you have in common are the things that really matter.*[18]

The words 'values fit' along with 'diversity', 'innovation' and 'experience' clearly illustrate what matters at Atlassian. From sporting teams to orchestras, management teams to boards, it matters who is selected to be in the group. If there is a lack of clarity or consistency about who is accepted into a company, it can be argued that maintaining the culture by insisting on adherence to the values is even more important for shaping behaviour when new members join.

While management is responsible for the hiring of staff, we would argue it is the CEO, the person whose behaviour and words will be in the spotlight, who is the 'chief culture officer'.

---

18 D Garfield, 2015, "Inside Atlassian: building a culture of innovation", 23 November, https://www.atlassian.com/blog/inside-atlassian/how-atlassian-builds-innovation-culture, (accessed 29 March 2018).

2. Induction—what are the 'rules of the game'?

Another way in which an organisation's values and patterns of behaviour are transmitted to employees is the induction process. Formal induction programs are helpful in teaching employees about the goals and history of a company, as well as communicating the power structure and smoothing the way for integration into a team. Face-to-face orientation has been shown to demonstrate these benefits more fully than computer-based programs,[19] again demonstrating the power of words delivered in face-to-face conversation. And now due to the pandemic, organisations face the phenomenon of job hoppers, people moving from job to job never physically meeting their colleagues. This illustrates how emotional and personal attachments to jobs have been weakened, creating uncertainty among employers over how to induct and then retain people they barely know.[20] Even in the 'new normal' with virtual and hybrid working arrangements, we would argue that it's important for new hires to meet face-to-face with the people they will be working most closely with, to get to know people as people not only faces on a screen."

Management is responsible for developing and implementing appropriate induction processes for staff. The quality of the working relationships and conversation with management in formal, informal and virtual settings, is of the strongest influences on culture. In fact, we would suggest that induction programs and training, because of their relevance to the development and maintenance of organisation culture, are the most important development processes in which organisations should invest.

---

19 M Wesson and C Gogus, 2005, "Shaking hands with a computer: an examination of two methods of organizational newcomer orientation", *Journal of Applied Psychology*, Vol 90, No 5, Sep, p 1018–26.

20 K Browning and E Griffith, 2021, "If you never met your co-workers in person, did you even work there?", 29 October, *New York Times*, https://www.nytimes.com/2021/09/08/business/remote-office-co-workers-working-from-home.html, (accessed 11 July 2022).

Setting the groundwork for a clear understanding of how relationships can work best from the start, is an important way to set the tone at the top. Two contrasting examples illustrate the difference 'tone at the top' can set when new CEO's enter the induction phase of their careers.

First, consider the words used to describe Arvind Krishna's appointment as CEO of IBM: "Arvind is the right CEO for the next era at IBM ... through his multiple experiences running businesses in IBM, Arvind has built an outstanding track record of bold transformations and proven business results, and is an authentic, values-driven leader. He is well-positioned to lead IBM and its clients into the cloud and cognitive era."[21]

Then compare the tone of the words of the board of investment company Vanguard on the appointment of CEO, Mortimer J 'Tim' Buckley: "... the company has chosen its most hard-driving combative CEO yet ... Buckley has already shown a willingness to bend Vanguard's culture in pursuit of more assets."[22] What culture is portrayed by adopting such a tone? What are the particular words that 'jump out' from this statement that indicate the culture the organisation is endeavouring to set? What is the likely outcome for future relationships between the CEO and staff members at Vanguard vs IBM?

3. Leadership behaviour—who sets the tone?

Leaders are instrumental in creating, maintaining and shaping organisational culture. There is a direct correlation between leadership style and culture. When leaders provide motivation for employees through

---

21 "Arvind Krishna Elected IBM Chief Executive Officer", *IBM Newsroom*, https://newsroom.ibm.com/2020-01-30-Arvind-Krishna-Elected-IBM-Chief-Executive-Officer, (accessed 11 July 2022).

22 S Gandel, 2018, "Vanguard's CEO's big challenge is dealing with success", *Australian Financial Review*, 7 January, http://www.afr.com/markets/vanguard-ceos-big-challenge-is-dealing-with-success-20180107-h0em2u, (accessed 24 May 2018).

vision, clarity and inspiration, culture tends to be more supportive and open. When leaders endeavour to motivate employees by making rewards contingent on performance, the culture tends to be more performance oriented and competitive.[23]

Leaders set the tone through role modelling and describing what is important. In 2021, Facebook (now known as "Meta") had a tough year, PR wise. Frances Haugen, a former Facebook employee turned whistle blower, blasted the company's leadership in interviews with news outlets and before Congress. Her claim that the company consistently puts profits before people sparked increased scrutiny of the company, which has had a rash of crises since the Cambridge Analytica scandal after the 2016 U.S. election.

At every opportunity where Facebook (Meta), has had a chance to deepen audience trust or build reputational goodwill, the company seems to choose the path of most resistance," says Andrew Moyer, executive vice president and general manager with Reputation Partners. "They retreat into a 'bunker mentality,' which has them positioned to fight, deny or shift any blame or responsibility, instead of using those moments to build reputational credit by demonstrating genuine awareness, concern and compassion." The takeaway for Moyer—as for many—has been poor leadership from the top of the organization.[24]

Research suggests that leader behaviour, the consistency between organisational policy and leader actions, along with leader role modelling, determines the degree to which the organisation's culture

---

23   J Sarros, J Gray and I Densten, 2002, "Leadership and its impact on organizational culture", *International Journal of Business Studies*, Vol 10, No 2, p 1–26.

24   T Kitterman, 2021, https://www.prdaily.com/5-top-crises-from-2021-and-the-warnings-they-offer-for-the-year-ahead/, *PR Daily*, https://www.prdaily.com/5-top-crises-from-2021-and-the-warnings-they-offer-for-the-year-ahead/, (accessed 17 July 2022).

emphasises ethics and positive behaviour.[25] In practical terms for modelling positive cultural behaviour, one piece of advice we would offer to senior executives is to live the adage, 'the standard you walk past, is the standard you accept.'

Leader behaviour will signal to individuals what is acceptable behaviour and what is unacceptable. The signals sent by leaders guide the actions of those around them and so, shape culture. For example:

- Do they praise a job well done or do they say nothing?
- How do they react when someone admits to making an honest mistake?
- Do they want to know what caused a mistake so that it can be prevented from happening again, or do they seem more concerned about how much money was lost because of the mistake?
- In meetings, what types of questions do they ask? Are they (in general) open and inquisitive, or closed and directive (e.g. "Don't you think that …?")?
- Do they seem outraged when an employee is disrespectful to a colleague, or does their reaction depend on whether the harasser has status and is well liked?

The answers to these questions are important not only in relation to the CEO, the organisation, and its stakeholders, but also for the relationships throughout the organisation. When the answers are positive, demonstrated in positive affirming language and effective conversation, then the tone shows commitment to openness, honesty and ethical behaviour and indicates a positive corporate culture.

For example, in 2015 the US marketing software company Moz was working on a large project (which had been running for two years) to rebuild the systems behind the company's web index. Some of Moz's

---

25 K Driscoll and M McKee, 2007, "Restoring a culture of ethical and spiritual values: a role for leader storytelling", *Journal of Business Ethics*, Vol 73, No 2, p 205–17.

engineers had privately expressed their worries about the progress and lack of results to CEO, Sarah Bird. In any other company, even a private conversation would have been tough, and the whole episode may well have resulted in a failure of the project and a dent in morale. Instead, Moz founder Rand Fishkin says they took the concern public. During a two-hour meeting, senior staff were invited to ask the big-data team questions. He told *Fast Company*: "It was a great session, and I think everyone walked away feeling more confident in the team and project, as well as more trusting of the individuals involved."[26]

In this company, there are obviously open, honest and affirming conversations among senior staff and with the CEO, which filters down throughout the organisation.

4. *Rewards—what gets recognised and rewarded, gets done!*

Culture is ultimately shaped through success, and reward and recognition systems have a significant impact on the definition of success in any organisation. Rewards and recognition focus behaviours and a key element is whether their emphasis is on results or behaviours, or both!

For instance, some organisations have reward systems that include intangible elements of performance as well as metrics that are easily quantified. Whereas in companies in which goal achievement is the only criterion for reward, there is often a focus on measuring the results without regard for the process (and consequently behaviour), and it is likely the culture will be outcome-oriented and competitive.

Whether the organisation rewards performance or seniority can also make a difference in culture. When promotions are based on seniority, it can be difficult to establish a culture of outcome orientation.

---

26 L Dishman, 2015, "Beyond Transparency: Can A Culture of 100% Honesty Work?", *Fast Company*, March 19, https://www.fastcompany.com/3043826/beyond-transparency-can-a-culture-of-100-honesty-work, (accessed 29 March 2018).

And if we return to our experience with 3M they have one of the most unusual promotional systems we have seen. 3M have a two stream basis of career progression. One is the traditional promotion via team and staff management roles; the other, is via technical expertise. So, one can rise through the ranks as a manager or as a technical expert—the latter illustrating a real commitment to their culture of innovation.

So, the types of behaviours that are rewarded, ignored or punished are what sets the tone and determines how the culture will evolve. And these decisions are critical for both the short and long-term viability of the company.

Decisions about how the CEO and senior team are remunerated and evaluated will most likely affect how others in the company are rewarded and recognised. At the very least, it will flag to all employees 'what's recognised around here'. There needs to be a clear understanding of the structure of the reward system in place in the organisation. Not only will organisation success depend on it, the CEO must be held accountable for the reward system. For example, the Federal Reserve Bank in the United States recently censured Wells Fargo Bank by placing restrictions on its growth and blasted its board for failing to oversee the bank.[27] Wells Fargo had been showered with praise and its reward process had been copied by others for appearing to perfect the art of 'cross-selling'—selling new financial products to existing customers. It turned out that the incentive system in place for 'cross-selling' resulted in abusive sales practices and the creation of millions of fake accounts and inappropriate charges.

---

27 E Flitter, B Appelbaum and S Cowley, 2018, "Federal Reserve shackles Wells Fargo after fraud scandal", *New York Times*, 2 February, https://www.nytimes.com/2018/02/02/business/wells-fargo-federal-reserve.html, (accessed 29 March 2018).

The bottom line ...

CREATING CULTURE
1. Founder values
   and preferences
2. Industry demands

Culture is created when the organisation is formed and comes about through the founders' values and preferences together with industry demands at the time.

Being aware of this, leaders should ask "How do we sustain such culture, and is there a need for changing or shaping it further?"

SUSTAINING CULTURE
1. Selection
2. Induction
3. Leader behaviour
4. Rewards

Culture is sustained through processes such as selection, induction, rewards and the behaviour of leaders. Processes are indicative of the culture that will sustain the success of the organisation. The CEO is the 'Chief Culture Officer.'

1.2 How leaders shape and sustain culture

The significant elements of culture—values, rules, leadership behaviour and rewards—influence the way employees think, behave and interact with one another. However, one of the major challenges for leaders is that they are often sitting on top of larger hierarchical structures. What they see and hear on a daily basis is likely to be filtered and too distant from the frontline. Leaders are not often in a position to consistently observe all employees and their interactions. If and when they do have the opportunity to observe, their presence may impact the dynamics of interactions and obscure reality.

So, with these limitations in mind, and provided that the CEO is the best fit for the job, how can the CEO and the top team ensure that a positive and ethical culture is being transmitted and maintained in the organisation? **Figure 3: Processes that indicate and shape culture**, shows the six visible aspects of organisational environment and leadership behaviour that provide signals about culture and whether the tone being set is positive or negative:

Words and language

A recent study aimed at identifying the norms and behaviour found in unethical companies, resulted in a number of patterns correlated with scandals.[28] One of the patterns was the language used by leaders, for

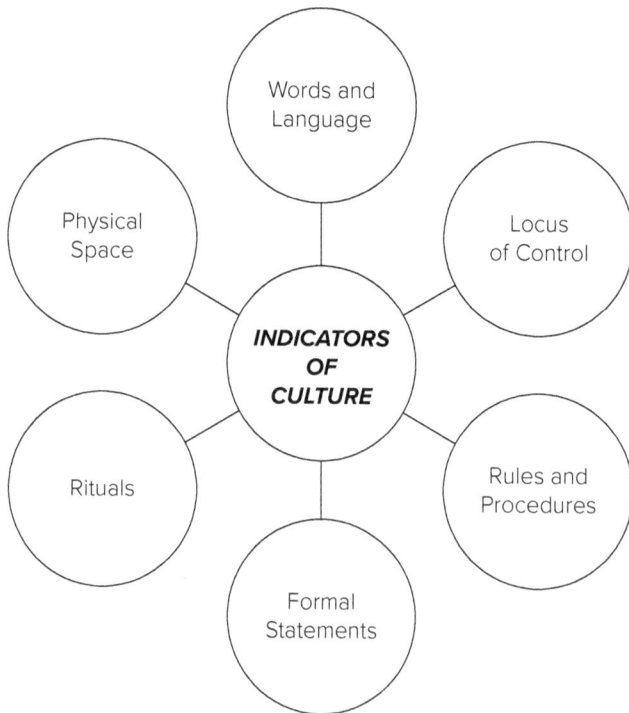

Figure 3: Processes that indicate and shape culture.

---

28 A Taylor, 2017, "5 signs your organisation may be headed for an ethics scandal", *Harvard Business Review*, 18 December, https://hbr.org/2017/12/5-signs-your-organization-might-be-headed-for-an-ethics-scandal, (accessed 29 March 2018).

example, describing events in terms of pressure, threat and the need to 'survive'. The language of threat then translates into justification for the use of toxic performance incentives and undermining efforts to raise concerns. When it comes to setting the tone, the use of words and language matters.

An inappropriate use of words was clearly indicated in an *Australian Financial Review* article about the tone being set at Domain (part of the Fairfax Media organisation): "While there was no sexual harassment, according to people who work there, there was a general tone of disrespect towards women and a permissive environment that encouraged heavy after-hours socialising among work colleagues. Women were referred to as 'babe' or 'doll' and urged to smile more by some male colleagues."[29]

The words used in the Domain example, 'babe' and 'doll', illustrate how words in combination can transmit a tone of disrespect and enable an environment which discounts the value of, for example, female staff members. Words are used to convey thoughts, interpret values and enable views to be shared. And as expressed in this example, they can impact how people feel about a situation or the organisation.

Words can also be used to convey status; whose views carry weight and who should be listened to—or not? It can be argued that words and language are the most important tools available to leaders and that their relationships are vital in terms of carrying out their duties. The quality of their conversation among senior team members is essential to setting a positive and ethical tone.

---

29 J Moullakis and A Patrick, 2018, "Antony Catalano: The fall of a party boy", *Australian Financial Review*, 8 February, https://www.afr.com/business/media-and-marketing/antony-catalano-the-fall-of-a-party-boy-20180206-h0v13z, (accessed 29 March 2018).

Organisational language—what does that mean?

Organisations have their own language—the jargon, acronyms and buzzwords that are clear to those inside and help set outsiders apart. Every profession and trade has its own specialised terms. Whole books have been devoted to the tyranny of jargon. For instance, Don Watson[30] describes official codes that we "must at least appear to understand or be excluded". He goes on to say: "Language has been made the machine of business and politics in the information age. But it cannot survive the experience and maintain its power to amuse, enchant, invent, comfort. It can't carry ideas and sentiments, bear the culture and be the culture's chief glory ... if it is machinery first and language second."[31]

One of the most effective ways in which leaders communicate culture and tone is through the skilful use of language in the form of stories and metaphors. Why are stories important? A story can be used to illustrate a critical event faced in an organisation and the sanctioned response to it—perhaps a heroic effort by a single employee—which illustrates the values of the organisation in action. Stories can engage emotions and generate identification with the organisation. A compelling story is a key mechanism through which leaders can motivate staff, give direction and energise people toward a goal. Stories shared in an induction process communicate an organisation's history and bring values and priorities to life, so it's important that they be 'told and retold'—some even take on a life of their own—for example, who hasn't heard the 3M Post-it Note story? Yes, that's right, it was nearly a failure after 10 years in development and almost written off until its inventor decided to send out free product to customers for trial—3M's 'promoting innovation'.

The power of stories (as opposed to relating facts and figures about similar situations) can be seen from recent research by the

---

30 D Watson, 2004, *Weasel Words*, Random House, Sydney, p 2.
31 ibid, p 3.

Communication Neuroscience Lab at Annenberg School who were studying people's preparedness to help others during the Covid pandemic. The researchers found that participants were much more immersed in the narrative messages (stories), where they felt a stronger relatable connection than in the fact-based messages. Moreover, those who felt this stronger connection were more likely to believe that the group they read about was more vulnerable to COVID-19, and more likely to believe that their own behaviours—such as staying home when feeling sick or engaging in physical distancing—could impact and protect these groups. These participants were also more likely to say they would donate to charities that could help the group they read about, or engage in behaviours to help other vulnerable groups."

Thinking about what this means for leaders, compare the difference in the following two examples of tone demonstrated in the language of the CEO of Enron, and then the CEO of Unilever.

The famous Enron story

Enron's advertising slogan in the early 2000s was "Ask Why?" It was supposed to suggest that Enron was an innovative company because it questioned conventional wisdom. However, employees in the company came up with an internal version of the slogan, "Ask Why, Ass … (expletive deleted)" following this famous encounter between fund manager, Richard Grubman and Enron CEO, Jeffrey Skilling:

Grubman: "You are the only financial institution that cannot produce a balance sheet or cash flow statement of their earnings."

Skilling: "Well, thank you very much, we appreciate that … 'A … expletive deleted'."[32]

---

32 "Jury hears ex-Enron CEO curse in Wall Street Call", 2006, *Houston Chronicle*, 2 February, https://www.chron.com/business/enron/article/ Jury-hears-ex-Enron-CEO-curse-in-Wall-Street-call-1637608.php, (accessed 19 June 2018).

Skilling's explanation for using vulgar language was: "The specific fellow that I was not real happy with, is a short seller in the market. I don't think it is fair to our shareholders to give someone a platform like that, they are using [it] for some personal vested interest related to their stock position."[33]

A few months later on 14 August 2001, the chair of Enron Kenneth Lay said: "There are no accounting issues, no trading issues, no reserve issues, no previously unknown problem issues. I think I can honestly say that the company is probably in the strongest and best shape that it has probably ever been in.[34]

Enron filed for Chapter 11 protection on 2 December, 2001.[35]

What did Skilling's language and tone suggest, not just to Grubman but to employees, shareholders and the general public? How would an employee or shareholder have felt?

The Unilever story

By contrast to Enron, in an interview in *The Guardian*, Paul Polman, CEO of Unilever, had this to say:

For us, it is very important that we can continue to show to everybody that in hell or high water, whatever the economic situation, we can continuously give competitive top line growth, improve our profitability, and do that in a responsible way. We can show that there is a different business model out there.

---

33   Enron CEO Uses Vulgarity in Attack on Fund Manager, *Fox News*, 13 January 2015, https://www.foxnews.com/story/enron-ceo-uses-vulgarity-in-attack-on-fund-manager, (accessed 19 June 2018).

34   Behr, P, 2004, "For Enron's Lay, a Day of Jarring Images", 9 July, *Washington Post*, https://www.washingtonpost.com/archive/business/2004/07/09/for-enrons-lay-a-day-of-jarring-images/4ae7cbce-38fe-4730-b040-ac48d0ac50c9, (accessed 22 June 2018).

35   M Perin, 2001, "Enron, subsidiaries file for Ch. 11 bankruptcy," *Houston Business Journal*, 3 December, https://www.bizjournals.com/houston/stories/2001/12/03/daily2.html, (accessed 23 June 2018).

We can hopefully start to address some of these major problems out there whilst at the same time satisfying the needs of our shareholders.[36]

What does Polman's language suggest at this point? What impact would Polman's tone have on employees, shareholders and the general public?

How is it that the tone and language of Unilever's Polman different to those of Enron's Skilling?

Notice that Polman used the words "major problems", and although 'problem' is often seen as a negative word (we'll discuss the impact of negative words such as 'problem' in a later chapter) here it was used in a positive way—Unilever is addressing the perception the public has of certain major corporations causing various types of problems (although not necessarily Unilever). Notice also that Polman used a very adept metaphor "hell or high water" to demonstrate the company's seriousness about their responsibilities (we'll also discuss the power of metaphor in detail in a later chapter).

Polman's response contained positive and affirming language. Are senior leaders more positive or more negative in their communication? Most leaders would like to think they are at the positive end of the continuum, but how do they know?

Locus of control

The positive or negative outlook projected by leaders can dramatically impact those around them. Often leaders are not aware of the messages they are sending through their language and role modelling.

---

36 Cited in G Ruddick, 2016, "Unilever CEO Paul Polman—the optimistic pessimist", *Guardian*, 26 January, https://www.theguardian.com/business/2016/jan/25/unilever-ceo-paul-polman-the-optimistic-pessimist, (accessed 21 May 2017).

The concept of locus of control, first developed by Julian Rotter,[37] gives insight into how tone is influenced by outlook and mindset.

Locus of control refers to an individual's perception of the main causes of the events in their life. For example, one CEO may believe that their destiny is within their control ("I did it myself"), while another believes that external forces such as fate or other people rule their performance ("It was someone else's fault", or "It was just a lucky break", or "the market took a dive at that time"). Put simply, if a person believes that behaviour is guided by personal decisions and efforts then they are more internally focused, that is they are said to have an internal locus of control. On the other hand, if a person believes that behaviour is guided by fate, luck, or other external circumstances (for example in the case of boards, by legislation, regulators, competition, industry demands or the market), that is an external locus of control.

Looking again at the words used by Jeffrey Skilling:[38] "The specific fellow that I was not real happy with, is a short seller in the market. I don't think it is fair to our shareholders to give someone a platform like that, they are using [it] for some personal vested interest related to their stock position." Skilling appears to demonstrate an external locus of control because rather than taking responsibility for his own actions, he blames 'the market' and makes it sound like short sellers are the reason for his company's poor performance.

Is an internal or external locus of control better? Psychologically, that's the $64,000 question. However, generally people with an internal locus of control tend to have greater influence on their motivation, expectations, self-esteem, risk-taking behaviour, and even on the outcome of their actions. Some studies also suggest that people with

---

37 J Rotter, 1966, "Generalized expectancies for internal versus external control of reinforcement", *Psychological Monographs*, Vol 80, No 1, p 1–28.
38 Enron CEO Uses Vulgarity in Attack on Fund Manager, *Fox News*, 13 January 2015, https://www.foxnews.com/story/enron-ceo-uses-vulgarity-in-attack-on-fund-manager, (accessed 13 July 2022).

an internal locus of control tend to be more positive in their behaviour and outlook.[39]

Are leaders likely to be aware of their own locus of control? There are a number of short tests freely available on the web that only take a few minutes to complete which lend insight into locus of control. There are some suggestions for these listed in the references section of this book.

A second and probably more important question is: Can an individual, a CEO or leader at any level, decide to be more internally focused—can locus of control be changed? The answer is an unequivocal "Yes".

Many studies[40] show that locus of control is something individuals learn and therefore can be changed. For example, experience with training athletics coaches by getting them to change their behaviour with their athletes improves the positive outlook the coaches display within 12 months. This approach has also been successful in the work environment with new and aspiring managers interested in improving the motivation of their teams.[41]

How does such training work? A simple method that can have a major impact and can be used immediately is to change the words used in everyday conversation. For instance, getting rid of the word 'don't' from one's vocabulary and replacing it with the positive image of what is being suggested begins to make for a far more positive outlook.

---

39 K Blankstein, in H M Lefcourt, (ed), 1984, *Research with the locus of control construct, Volume 3: Extensions and limitations*, Academic Press, Orlando, Florida, 1984, p 136.

40 See for example, T A Judge and J E Bono, 2001, "Relationship of core self-evaluations traits—self-esteem, generalized self-efficacy, locus of control, and emotional stability—with job satisfaction and job performance: A meta-analysis", *Journal of Applied Psychology*, Vol 86, No 1, p 80–92.

41 B Selden, 2016, "Don't: How using the right words will change your life", 1 May, *Bob Selden Pty Ltd*, Sydney, p 3.

We hear and see examples such as the following every day. What images come to mind when these words are read? The aim is to read the statement aloud and visualise what it is suggesting …

- Don't drop it.
- Don't walk on the grass.
- In case of fire do not use lifts.

In the first statement the image that comes to mind for most people is the picture of 'dropping something' and quite often, the negative consequences of doing so. This immediately reminds them of a previous negative experience of dropping something. The image that the second statement conjures up is of a person walking on the grass, not the footpath as the message intends. Note that 'footpath' is not mentioned. And in the third example, the only thing people tend to visualise is the lift. Studies show that when there is a fire emergency and the vestibule or foyer starts to fill with smoke, the only word that people recognise in these warning signs is the word 'lift' they immediately head straight for the lift, not the emergency exit as was intended. As a result, some authorities have now changed their signage to read 'In case of fire, use the emergency exit pictured in this diagram' (notice that in this new example the word 'lift' is not used at all and they've added a visual—'diagram').

Each of the original statements immediately has both the sender and the receiver visualising and thinking of exactly the opposite (and negative) action that should be taken. However, by eliminating the word 'don't' and replacing it with the positive action intended (as outlined below), thinking and behaviour tend to be more positive, resulting in a more positive impact on others, and thus becoming more internally focused. Look at the way a person with an internal locus of control, might express the three statements …

- Hold on to the glass very carefully.
- Walk on the footpath.
- In case of fire use the fire exit described in the diagram.

In these new statements, the receiver gets the positive, visual message immediately, words and impact are more likely to be in sync, and better results are achieved.

In most organisations there are plenty of rules and policies, and there are likely to be many 'don't' statements that produce negative images, such as:

- Don't take that approach.
- Don't tweet that.
- I don't understand what you're saying.
- I don't think we can discuss that.
- Don't discuss that with the media.

How could leaders change statements such as these, by eliminating 'don't' and making them more positive?

Setting the tone from the top, starts with just this simple change in words—there will be more on such simple word usage as we progress through the book.

Do organisations display a locus of control in their cultures?

Like people, do organisations develop a locus of control? It seems so.

Psychologists who studied this phenomenon in 14 companies over a 21-year period, found that organisations that made 'self-disserving' attributions for negative events (i.e. they took responsibility for their own poor performance and displayed an internal locus of control), had higher share prices a year later. The reason, they believe, is because those statements made the company seem more in control of its own performance.[42]

This result was also demonstrated in an interesting experiment where researchers produced two reports for two fictitious companies, and

---

42 T A Judge & J E Bono, Relationship of core self-evaluations traits— self-esteem, generalized self-efficacy, locus of control, and emotional stability—with job satisfaction and job performance: A meta-analysis. *Journal of Applied Psychology*, Vol 86(1), Feb 2001, p 80–92.

asked subjects to rate each company based on the reports. In the first report, the company held itself accountable by blaming strategic decisions for its poor showing (an internal locus of control). In the second report, the company deflected responsibility by pointing the finger at external factors, such as the economy and competition (external locus of control). At the end of the test, the company that took responsibility for the negative outcomes was rated more favourably by the participants.[43]

Rules and policies

Another way in which an observer may find out about a company's culture is to examine the words used to construct its rules and policies. Companies create rules to communicate acceptable and unacceptable behaviour and thus the rules that exist in a company will signal the values of an organisation. Sometimes the values are espoused rather than practiced. The way rules and policies are worded and role-modelled, has an impact on practice (the wording of policies will be covered later in the book).

Policies about issues such as decision rights, delegations, conduct and employee privacy, reveal what a company values and emphasises. For example, a company that has a policy such as 'all pricing decisions on merchandise will be made at corporate headquarters' is likely to have a centralised decision-making culture that is hierarchical, as opposed to decentralised and empowering.

The presence or absence of policies on sensitive issues such as bullying, unfair treatment of others, workplace surveillance, sexual harassment, workplace romances and corporate social responsibility, all make up pieces of the puzzle that identify a company's culture. The setting of rules and policies and the words used to construct them, influences culture.

---

43 T Vrountas, 2018, "10 Common Phrases to Avoid with Dealing With Your Clients," *Marketing Agency Tips*, 6 April, https://instapage.com/blog/common-phrases-to-avoid, (accessed 23 June 2018).

Culture is further enhanced by the monitoring (or not) of how those rules and policies are used or not used. For instance, a policy with instructions on what 'not to do' and with little information on what 'to do', can end up being ineffective. Leaders can shape organisational behaviour through the policies they adopt and the information they seek about the effectiveness of policies in practice.

The table below shows the impact of policy statements. Two examples of rules and policies are provided. One uses language with a positive tone, the other uses language which is negative in tone (i.e. 'do not').

CSL—Company Values & Guiding Principles[44]	Wesfarmers—Code of Conduct[45]
CSL is committed to helping our employees and third parties to understand and abide by the principles and expectations contained within this Code. • Making Good Decisions • Raising Concerns An integral part of responsible business practice is making good decisions. When faced with a decision, you should consider the following: • **The Policy Test**—Is my proposed action consistent with this Code and other CSL policies?	"Wesfarmers is committed to making positive economic, social and environmental contributions to society, consistent with the principles of honesty, integrity, fairness and respect. The Wesfarmers Board has adopted this Code to provide a set of guiding principles which are to be observed by all Wesfarmers personnel, and against which we hold ourselves accountable. Wesfarmers personnel are expected at all times to act consistently with the principles set

44 CSL Limited, 2017, Our Code of Responsible Business Practice, July, p 7, https://www.cslbehring.com/-/media/csl/documents/crbp-languages/csl_crbp17i_english.pdf?la=en-us&hash=7A29BBF8C3434C334C630EEB8C1BB1 2A660C8E7C, (accessed 22 June 2018).

45 Wesfarmers website, http://www.wesfarmers.com.au/who-we-are/corporate-governance, (accessed 28 May 2018).

CSL—Company Values & Guiding Principles	Wesfarmers—Code of Conduct
• **The Legal Test**—Is my proposed action legal? Does it conflict with any applicable law or regulation? • **The Values Test**—Is my proposed action consistent with CSL's values? Is it ethical and honest? • **The Mirror Test**—What are the consequences of my proposed action? How will I feel about myself if I take the action? • **The Others Test**—What will others think about my proposed action? • **The Media Test**—Would I be concerned if there was a headline of my proposed action in the media?	out in this Code."[46] Wesfarmers personnel must observe the following at all times: • "do not offer or accept bribes, kick-backs and similar payments—Wesfarmers personnel must never offer or accept any irregular payment to win business or to influence a business decision in Wesfarmers' favour (such as bribes, 'kick-backs' and similar payments in any form). This restriction also applies to consultants and contractors. • do not accept gifts, entertainment or hospitality in breach of our policies—Wesfarmers recognises that accepting or offering gifts, entertainment or hospitality of moderate value is in accordance with usual business practice. • do not offer or accept gifts, entertainment or hospitality in circumstances which could be considered to give rise to undue influence—Gifts, entertainment and hospitality must be recorded in accordance with Wesfarmers' Anti-bribery Policy."[47]

Table 1: The impact of policy statements—CSL and Wesfarmers.

Note: These are excerpts taken from the organisations' policy statements on their company websites as referenced above.

---

46 ibid, p 1.
47 ibid, p 3.

Formal statements

In addition to rules and policies, leaders use a variety of formal state-ments to communicate their objectives and their values, from annual reports to media statements and interviews for public consumption. One of the most important formal documents for transmitting objec-tives and values inside the organisation is the mission statement.

A mission statement is a statement of purpose describing what the company is and what it does. It serves an important function for an organisation as part of strategic planning and gaining traction on stra-tegic objectives. While many companies have a mission statement, they do not always reflect the company's values and its purpose clearly enough. An effective mission statement transmitted to all employees during induction and well known by employees, influences employee behaviour. If the mission statement does not affect employee behaviour on a day-to-day basis it has little usefulness as a goal for understanding and sustaining the company's culture.

Costco is well known for its positive and ethical culture. Here is the way Barbara Farfan (writer for www.thebalance.com) describes the culture at Costco in an article entitled "Costco Mission Statement Has the Ethics and Compassion of Its Founders":

> *Customers know it when they feel it. There's something that's dif-ferent about the Costco Wholesale Warehouse experience. It's the physical space, the products, the services, the people, the exclusivity the … something more. The average customer can't identify it, but it's the compassionate culture, the ethical mission and the vision and values woven throughout the Costco culture that they sense with all their senses in every Costco Wholesale Warehouse experience.*[48]

---

48 B Farfan, 2017, "Costco mission statement has the ethics and compassion of its founders", *Small Business*, 28 April, https://www.thebalancesmb.com/costco-mission-statement-2891829, (accessed 31 May 2018).

And here is the Costco Mission Statement:

Costco's mission is to continually provide our members with quality goods and services at the lowest possible prices. To achieve our mission, we will conduct our business with the following Code of Ethics in mind:

- *Obey the law*
- *Take care of our members*
- *Take care of our employees*
- *Respect our vendors*

If we do these four things throughout our organization, then we will realize our ultimate goal, which is to reward our shareholders.[49]

And of course, the words used to express a company's mission, are critical. Enron is an often-cited example of 'a disconnect' between a company's mission statement and how the company actually operated. Their mission and values statement started with "As a partner in the communities in which we operate Enron believes it has a responsibility to conduct itself in accord with certain basic principles."[50] The Enron values statement included such statements as: "We do not tolerate abusive or disrespectful treatment. Ruthlessness, callousness and arrogance don't belong here."[51] How does this written statement compare with the words of the CEO quoted earlier? How does it compare with the

---

49 Costco Wholesale company, [website], 2018, https://www.costco.ca/about-us.html, (accessed 29 March 2018).

50 Enron Corporate Responsibility, 2016, (in text Csus.edu), *Statement of Human Rights Principles*, http://www.csus.edu/indiv/m/merlinos/enron.html, (accessed 19 June 2018)

51 J Kunen, 2002, "Enron's vision and values thing", *The New York Times*, 19 January, www.nytimes.com/2002/01/19/opinion/enron-s-vision-and-values-thing.html, (accessed 29 March 2018).

words in the Costco mission statement? Or the words of Shawn Talbot, CAE, Executive Director of the National Association of Insurance and Financial Advisors:

> *"I've found that it's the little things that make a difference. We celebrate staff birthdays by decorating their offices and hosting birthday lunches. We give several floating holidays for employees to use when they want. We also have a flexible schedule on Friday afternoons, so staff can take care of personal appointments or get a jump start on the weekend (if workload permits)."*

A mission statement that is taken seriously and widely communicated can provide insights into the corporate culture. Another positive example, The Mayo Clinic's mission statement reads: "The needs of the patient come first." This mission statement evolved from the founders who are quoted as saying: "The best interest of the patient is the only interest to be considered".[52] Mayo Clinics have a corporate culture that puts patients first. Unlike some other organisations, no incentives are given to doctors based on the number of patients they see. Because Mayo Clinic doctors are rewarded by annual salary and not by the number of patients seen, they have less interest in retaining a patient for themselves and more interest in referring the patient to other doctors when it is in the patient's best interest, not the doctor's.[53]

---

52 Mayo Clinic, 2016, "About Mayo Clinic", *Mayo Clinic College of Medicine & Science*, 1 June, https://www.mayo.edu/mayo-clinic-college-of-medicine-and-science/about/about-mayo-clinic, (accessed 22 June 2018).

53 A Underwood, 2009, "A New Way to Pay Physicians", *The New York Times*, 23 September, https://prescriptions.blogs.nytimes.com/2009/09/23/a-new-way-to-pay-physicians/, (accessed 22 June 2018).

Rituals

Rituals refer to repetitive activities within an organisation that have symbolic meaning.[54] Usually rituals have their roots in the history of a company's culture. They create camaraderie and a sense of belonging among employees. They also serve to teach employees corporate values and create identification with the organisation. For example, Australian hardware retailer Bunnings' sausage sizzles are enjoyed by thousands of their Australian customers every week. These 'ritual' events are used as fundraising opportunities for local community groups as a way of demonstrating Bunnings' commitment to the communities in which they operate (as an observation, Bunnings seem to have misread the local community culture in their expansion into the UK—'sausage sizzles' there have been seen as one of the negatives about shopping at Bunnings in the UK which illustrates a point made earlier about differences in national culture).

Physical space

Finally, the physical space where business is conducted—buildings, layout of offices, and other workspaces—communicates important messages about a company's culture. For example, the layout of office space can be an indicator of how interactions occur and the levels of status.

A company that has an open layout where senior executives interact with employees may have a culture of team orientation and egalitarianism, whereas a company where most senior executives have their own floor or a large corner office, may indicate more emphasis on hierarchy and status. Where employees tend to have offices with walls and a door there may be a culture of solitude, concentration and privacy.

---

54 R A Joyce, 2001, N Smelser and P B Baltes (eds), "Ritual and Symbolism, Archaeology of", *International Encyclopedia of the Social & Behavioral Sciences*, Oxford: Elsevier, Vol 1, p 13371.

In contrast, standard cubicles may reflect an egalitarian culture. The same values can be observed in avoidance of private and reserved parking spaces.[55]

Now that many companies have adopted flexible work practices, what, if any, are the rules about online engagement vs physical events? For example, are company backgrounds required to be used in online settings to indicate employees are at work versus at home? Not everyone has a home office space, some people have pets and small children who like to interrupt. The degree to which playfulness, humour, engagement and fun are part of a company culture may be indicated in the set-up of the office environment both online and in person. Leaders have influence over physical space and flexible work conditions. Both can be observed and standards of behaviour can be set which impact on tone and culture.

For example, Airbnb who are known for connecting people all over the world with unique places while travelling, have reflected their culture and how they will combine virtual working with physical spaces. Airbnb CEO, Brian Chesky sent an email to all staff to set the tone for Airbnb's approach to hybrid work:

"Airbnb is in the business of human connection above all else, and we believe that the most meaningful connections happen in person. Zoom is great for maintaining relationships, but it's not the best way to deepen them. Additionally, some creative work and collaboration is best done when you're in the same room. I'd like working at Airbnb to feel like you're working at one of the most creative places on Earth, and this will only happen with some in-person collaboration time.

The right solution should combine the best of the digital world and the best of the physical world. It should have the efficiency of

---

55   D Clark, 2007, "Why Silicon Valley is rethinking the cubicle office", *Wall Street Journal*, 15 October, www.wsj.com/articles/SB119240097861658633, (accessed 29 March 2018).

Zoom, while providing the meaningful human connection that only happens when people come together. We have a solution that we think combines the best of both worlds.

1. You can work from home or the office
2. You can move anywhere in the country you work in and your compensation won't change
3. You have the flexibility to travel and work around the world
4. We'll meet up regularly for gatherings
5. We'll continue to work in a highly coordinated way"[56]

The bottom line ...

Internal and external statements
Leaders, especially the CEO and senior executive team members, should examine the words being used in statements internally and externally. These statements influence the tone being set for the organisation's standards.

Behavioural and ethical standards
Leaders need to be aware of the behavioural and ethical standards the organisation is setting through its:
- rules and policies
- formal statements
- rituals
- physical space
- virtual settings

1.3 How the CEO sets the tone

Words are not things—they are representations and symbols we use to view, to think about and process our perceptions of reality and they are the means of sharing these perceptions with others. Yet few leaders understand how vital _conversation_ is to

---

56 Airbnb Newsroom, 2022, "Airbnb's design to live and work anywhere", 28 April, https://news.airbnb.com/en-au/airbnbs-design-to-live-and-work-anywhere/, (accessed 11 July 2022).

the health and productivity of their company culture.[57] Judith E Glaser (emphasis on 'conversation' is ours).

What does it mean to 'set the tone'—what is the meaning of the phrase? In the context of corporate governance, the origins of the phrase 'tone at the top' began with accounting firms. The concept was narrowly defined and referred mainly to the attitude of an organisation's senior leadership towards financial controls and the detection of fraud. Following a host of corporate scandals in 2002 such as Enron, it was popularised and applied more broadly to describe the general culture established by the leaders of an organisation, both management and the board.

'Tone at the top' is now described as the central element in building and sustaining a positive workplace culture. Leaders are not only responsible for creating standards for company conduct but living by those standards as well. And that's where the language that boards use, comes in—it's one thing to have policies in place, but it's how the CEO and senior management describe what is meant by these in day-to-day conversations, that sets the example for people throughout the organisation to follow.

"The tone at the top sets an organisation's guiding values and ethical climate" says Nicole Sandford, partner and national practice leader at Deloitte Enterprise Compliance Services. "Properly fed and nurtured, it is the foundation upon which the culture of an enterprise is built."[58]

Tone comes to life through words and words must be aligned with actions.

---

57 J Glaser, 2013, "Conversational intelligence: How great leaders build trust and get extraordinary results", Taylor & Francis Inc. Brookline, MA, 1 October, p 9.

58 2014, "Building tone at the top: The role of the board, CEO and CCO", *The Wall Street Journal, Risk & Compliance Journal*, 15 December, http://deloitte.wsj.com/riskandcompliance/2014/12/15/building-tone-at-the-top-the-role-of-the-ceo-board-and-coo/, (accessed 29 March 2018).

An example of a CEO found wanting is the story of Steve Wynn's demise as CEO of Wynn Resorts. Working for Steve Wynn has been described as a 'screaming, fist-banging and 'spit on my face' experience.[59] Fifteen casino dealers filed a complaint against Wynn with the National Labor Relations Board, saying he threatened to fire them if they unionized. They told a board judge that he made his point by throwing a tantrum, shouting, belittling them and slamming his fist on a table. At least twice, they said, he boasted of being "the most powerful man in Nevada."

He weathered that storm and other accusations of sexual harassment and misconduct over a period of years, but in the end a shareholder lawsuit about non-disclosure to regulators of an alleged pattern of sexual misconduct saw him step down as CEO and board chair. He paid $20 million to settle the lawsuit and the company's insurance carriers paid an additional $21 million.

Inappropriate words can affect careers—'word-smithing'

In the USA recently, we've seen further examples of how words can negatively impact a person's image and even their career. For example, in an article, "Senate hearings reveal importance of language for Donald Trump, Hillary Clinton and James Comey"[60] reporter Patrick Wood asks, "When is an FBI investigation not an 'investigation', and when does it become a 'matter'? And does the word 'hope' stir emotions of optimism, or is it a veiled threat and directive?"

At the time, Comey testified when discussing the investigation into Hillary Clinton's use of her email account that, "We were getting to a

---

59   A Franz, 2018, "Screaming, fist-banging and 'spit on my face': What it was like to work for Wynn", *CNN*, 11 February, https://www.cnn.com/2018/02/09/us/steve-wynn-employees-treatment/index.html, (accessed 11 July 2022).

60   P Wood, 2017, "Senate hearings reveal importance of language for Donald Trump, Hillary Clinton and James Comey", *ABC News Breakfast*, 14 June, http://www.abc.net.au/news/2017-06-14/trump,-clinton-and-comey-find-out-that-language-matters/8616024, (accessed 29 March 2018).

place where the Attorney-General, [Loretta Lynch], and I were both going to have to testify and talk publicly about it and I wanted to know was she going to authorize us to confirm that we had an investigation. And she said, 'Yes, but don't call it that. Call it a matter.' And I said, 'Why would I do that?' and she said, 'Just call it a matter.' Comey continued, "That concerned me because *that language* tracked the way the [Clinton] campaign was talking about the FBI's work, and that's concerning."[61] (Italics and parentheses are ours.)

This is a case of what is often referred to as 'word-smithing' which is a tactic used as a pejorative term, especially in relation to the recording of board minutes. Why do CEOs engage in 'word-smithing'? Because word choice matters, especially when it is recorded. There will be more on 'word-smithing' of the written word in a later chapter.

We've seen the downside that negative language can have on careers, organisations and even countries. Let's now turn to the language that CEOs and senior executives use, that positively impacts the organisation; the 'tone' that observers—employees, shareholders, media and the public—hear.

Positive tone supports openness and respect. What tone does the CEO set? Examining the behaviour and speech of CEOs gives insight into how tone supports success. When tone is positive, it is demonstrated in language that shows leadership, commitment to openness, honesty and ethical behaviour. Let's be clear. We are talking here about the actual speech and behaviour of CEOs, not documents produced by communications executives on behalf of CEOs—not 'spin doctoring' or 'word-smithing'.

We've emphasised the importance of setting the tone at the top, but establishing it and strengthening it over time requires a concerted effort from the CEO and senior team. To ensure this happens there

---

61   ibid.

are three elements of 'setting a positive tone at the top' that all leaders should consider, as illustrated in **Figure 4**:

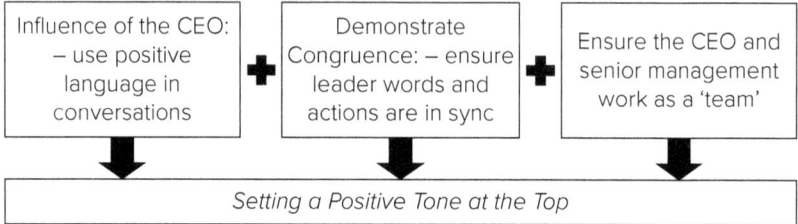

Influence of the CEO: – use positive language in conversations	+	Demonstrate Congruence: – ensure leader words and actions are in sync	+	Ensure the CEO and senior management work as a 'team'

Setting a Positive Tone at the Top

Figure 4: Three elements of setting a positive tone at the top.

The influence of the CEO through positive and affirmative conversation

Let's start with the foundations that foster a positive tone in management conversations. What words are used in senior team meetings? Is everyone's opinion listened to—really listened to? Do executives leave meetings feeling that they have contributed fully, or do they hold back fearing that they may be embarrassed? Or perhaps they have been accused of being 'too quiet' or 'too direct'?

The language the CEO and senior team use will have a major impact on the example they are setting for others in the organisation, and the relationships they develop with each other. Keep in mind that it's the CEO's role to implement not only the strategy, but also to demonstrate the desired tone in executing the strategy within the organisation. Consider the key tenet of this book that we mentioned earlier:

- **beneficial relationships** are built on **effective conversations**;
- **effective conversations** are built on **encouraging and affirmative language**; and
- **encouraging and affirmative language** is built on using **positive words**.

The CEO's ability to influence, not only happens through direct conversations with him or her, but also the conversations the CEO observes and is involved in with other levels of management and staff.

The CEO is the face of the organization and the person to whom employees ultimately look for vision and guidance. The CEO, more than any individual, sets the tone which affects integrity, ethics, and behaviour within the organisation.

Developing these beneficial relationships between executives requires language that demonstrates a shared attitude. But (and we use that word very rarely as will be explained later in the book), it's imperative that conversations around strategy, operations, policies and culture, are based on solid and ethical policies and values.

Developing a shared language—'we', 'us', 'our'

What does shared language that demonstrates an alignment among CEO and senior management sound like? In simplistic terms, people are likely to hear a lot of 'we', 'us' and 'our' in statements being made, particularly by the CEO when talking with other stakeholders such as management and staff.

However, it's interesting to note that people often hear language that sounds like shared language ('we', 'us' and 'our') when the CEO is addressing other stakeholders such as the media and shareholders. A word of caution; this could well be 'word-smithing' type language aimed at putting on a united front, when behind the scenes reality is quite different.

And again, shared language can demonstrate a poor attitude. For instance, Uber founder and former CEO, Travis Kalanick, demonstrated his attitude in his language in the documents leaked from his time as CEO which clearly demonstrate the tone he was setting from the top. For example, when dealing with the Paris taxi drivers' protest as Uber entered their market, not only did Kalanick show apparent indifference toward the possibility that Uber drivers might be hurt by taxi drivers, he appeared to welcome it. "I think it's worth it … Violence guarantee

[sic] success," he wrote in a text. And such violence wasn't just an abstract idea. It was no secret that the previous year, Uber drivers and their cars had been attacked in France.[62]

So, a strong point needs to be made here. The strategies, tactics, techniques and tips we are suggesting that leaders adopt throughout this book must be genuine and not merely 'a technique' for pushing one's point or getting one's way. People are very quick to spot the insincerity in whatever leaders are saying.

Demonstrate congruence between words and actions

Actions speak as loudly as words. Words will mean little if the actions of the CEO and senior management are not congruent with the language they use. Starting in the 1980s, and with each decade that passes, there has been more emphasis on company conduct. The result has been additional rules and a greater compliance burden placed on all organisations. Leaders are well aware of the increasing amount of regulatory and legal compliance for which they are responsible, and the level of liability associated with these measures. However, despite the increase in rules, examples of poor behaviour and unethical practices still continue to abound. We've already quoted many of these. So rather than creating more rules, it's interesting to consider how the language and behaviour used by the CEO (and board members) can impact whether senior management and the people they lead, comply with the rules.

As we asked at the start of this chapter, "does the CEO consider the language used in management meetings and in conversation with the senior team, demonstrate that the CEO means what they say?"

---

62 Harry Davies, Simon Goodley, Felicity Lawrence, Paul Lewis and Lisa O'Carroll, 2022, "Uber broke laws, duped police and secretly lobbied governments, leak reveals", *The Uber Files*, 12 July, https://www.theguardian.com/news/2022/jul/10/uber-files-leak-reveals-global-lobbying-campaign, (accessed 17 July 2022).

Ensure the CEO and senior management are working as a team

This can be quite challenging when we consider the limited number of meetings, and the amount of time the CEO and senior management interact with each other and others throughout the organisation. However, before we make some suggestions, here are two challenging questions:

- How well does the language used by the CEO reflect a positive approach to the role of CEO?
- How much does the language used by the CEO need to change in order to reflect a positive approach to leading the organisation?

These questions may lead to considerations about how CEOs use what has been termed the 'collective intelligence' of the senior executive team.

Collective intelligence—collaboration, collective efforts, competition

Collective intelligence (sometimes referred to as CI) is the shared or group intelligence that emerges from:

- collaboration;
- collective efforts; and
- the competition of many individuals.

In this early part of the book, we've already referred to the importance of 'collaboration' and 'collective efforts' of the senior team. However, this is the first mention of 'competition' among the individual executive team members. Often seen as a negative trait, competition, when managed positively can bring out the best in the executive team and lead to very effective decisions.

For example, it's been found that groups who use their collective intelligence cooperatively and positively:

- more often call on decision making experts within the group;

- call on those with new insights as well as the 'recognised authorities'; and
- continually learn from feedback from one another.

These actions produce 'just-in-time knowledge' for better decisions as opposed to groups that use the three elements of collaboration, collective efforts and competition, separately.[63]

Citing the work of Professor Anita Woolley at Carnegie Mellon, author and consultant Juliet Bourke points out the evidence supporting the view,[64] that the collective intelligence of a group is enhanced by:

- the interpersonal sensitivity of group members (their awareness of language);
- equal amounts of speaking up by each team member (using positive language); and
- a greater percentage of diverse team members (who provide different views).

With the exception of point three (diversity, which is a separate and important topic), the collective intelligence of an executive team can be improved by using language that is encouraging and affirmative—a 'we are in this together' approach—a point that we will return to a number of times in the remainder of this book.

The bottom line …

The CEO sets the tone by:

- **Demonstrating positive leadership** through the use of positive words.
- **Being aware of congruence between words and actions—acting as a role model** through setting rules and abiding by them
- **Ensuring that senior management are working as a team**—use language that is encouraging and affirmative—a 'we are in this together' approach.

---

63 A W Woolley et al, 2010, "Evidence for a collective intelligence factor in the performance of human groups", *Science*, Vol 330, No 6004, p 686–8.
64 J Bourke, 2016, "Which Two Heads Are Better Than One? How diverse teams create breakthrough ideas and make smarter decisions", *Australian Institute of Company Directors*, Sydney, p 38.

1.4 How leaders set the tone through the written word

Policies are critical; when properly managed, they trickle, with active oversight, *from the enterprise level to business units and departments, and then to individuals. In addition to articulating corporate culture, policies establish in writing the exact parameters of required individual business conduct—standards to which the corporation may be held legally liable.*[65]

Who reads the organisation's corporate policies? More importantly, who follows them?

It is interesting to note that in our research for this chapter, it has been difficult to find well-written and well-designed policies. We believe there are two reasons for this:

- Many policies are written in negative language, i.e. what people can't do rather than what the organisation would like and want them to do. This is quite limiting.
- Few policies have any visual or diagrammatic content. And yet, it's been proven that we think (and remember) visually better than we do with words.[66]

It is appreciated that most policies are not written by the CEO, nor in fact by senior management (although most will be initiated and approved by senior management). However, what goes into the policies is influenced by CEO and senior team discussions, strategy, performance goals and, above all (as mentioned in our opening quote

---

65 B Kerschberg, 2011, "Corporate Policy Management", *Forbes*, 28 June, https://www.forbes.com/sites/benkerschberg/2011/06/28/corporate-policy-management/#3f35fcfa7d3a, (accessed 29 March 2018).

66 M P Verdi, et al, 1997, "Organized spatial displays and texts: Effects of presentation order and display type on learning outcomes", *The Journal of Experimental Education*, Vol 65, No 4 Summer, p 306.

in this chapter) the corporate culture leaders wish to develop and maintain.

In the following chapters, we outline some ideas on how this can be achieved. We will focus on the language and the visuals that make policies vibrant rather than stagnant documents.

The impact of negatively worded policies

Researchers have found that high frequency negative words seem to attract additional cognitive resources:

> The overall pattern of results is consistent with a time line of word recognition in which semantic analysis, including the evaluation of emotional quality, occurs at an early, lexical stage of processing.[67]

In layperson's terms, that means that it takes far longer for people to read, absorb, comprehend and commit to policies written in a negative way than it does for policies written in positive terms.

There is another reason for wording policies in positive rather than negative language—empowerment. Over the last decade or so, 'empowerment' seems to have become the major buzz word used to engender commitment from employees. Yet few organisations know what it means. And fewer still, provide the wherewithal for employees to become 'empowered'. Our observations are that in many organisations it will be impossible for people to become empowered, as the organisation's policies are written in a way that stops employees from doing things rather than helping them to achieve the organisation's goals.

------

67   G Scott, et al, 2009, "Early emotion word processing: Evidence from event-related potentials", *Biological Psychology*, Vol 80, No 1, January, p 95, https://www.sciencedirect.com/science/article/pii/S0301051108000732, (accessed 19 June 2018).

For example, here are two illustrations of how companies word their social media policies quite differently.[68]

CNN's social media policy (the key point):
- UNLESS GIVEN PERMISSION BY CNN MANAGEMENT, CNN EMPLOYEES ARE TO AVOID TAKING PUBLIC POSITIONS ON THE ISSUES AND PEOPLE AND ORGANIZATIONS ON WHICH WE REPORT.

(Capitalisation is CNN's)

What would an employee of CNN be *allowed to do* on social media?

Intel's social media policy (the main points):
- Stick to your area of expertise and provide unique, individual perspectives on what's going on at Intel and in the world.
- Post meaningful, respectful comments—in other words, no spam and no remarks that are off-topic or offensive.
- Always pause and think before posting. That said, reply to comments in a timely manner, when a response is appropriate.
- Respect proprietary information and content, and confidentiality.
- When disagreeing with others' opinions, keep it appropriate and polite.
- Know and follow the Intel Code of Conduct and the Intel Privacy Policy.

---

68 L Dishman, 2010, "Corporate social media policies: The good, the mediocre, and the ugly", *Fast Company*, 9 July, https://www.fastcompany.com/1668368/corporate-social-media-policies-good-mediocre-and-ugly, (accessed 29 March 2018).

Notice that the CNN example tells people what they cannot do (quite explicitly), whilst the Intel policy is encouraging and affirmative. As Lynne D Johnson, Senior Vice President of Social Media for the US Advertising Research Foundation (and a former editor for *Fast Company*) points out: "You can tell Intel cares about its employees being brand ambassadors and that they've seriously thought about their guidelines. It's not just a step 1–10 guideline process, but a detailed, example-filled effort."[69]

The Intel social media policy statements:	How they enable people:
Stick to your area of expertise and provide unique, individual perspectives on what's going on at Intel and in the world.	*Work within your area of responsibility—it's yours. Be creative in your area/role. This reinforces the fact that employees have the freedom to make decisions within their roles.*
Post meaningful, respectful comments—in other words, no spam and no remarks that are off-topic or offensive.	*Although the second part of this statement is negative, it is used as an example. The key first part is very positive.*
Always pause and think before posting. That said, reply to comments in a timely manner, when a response is appropriate.	*Very clear instruction as to what to do (and great advice).*
Respect proprietary information and content, and confidentiality.	*This is an excellent example of using positive language (read the CNN example again to see the difference).*
When disagreeing with others' opinions, keep it appropriate and polite.	*What good advice! This is a clear indication of the culture Intel is developing.*
Know and follow the Intel Code of Conduct and the Intel Privacy Policy.	*Refers the employee to Intel's key culture policy.*

Table 2: The reasons why Intel's social media guidelines are enabling.

---

69   ibid.

'Word-smithed' messages and their impact

In addition to policies, the written language used in other communications emanating from the CEO and senior management, has either a positive or negative impact on employees (rarely neutral). We mentioned earlier, the downside of 'word-smithing' communication to stakeholders, particularly to external stakeholders. Similar sins can be committed by the CEO and senior management with word-smithing of internal communications.

When staff are impacted negatively by such word-smithed communications (which they see as false, or at best, misleading), they tend to get angry—in a word they feel 'conned'. Their response? They are dismissive of the message and in some cases, the messages are leaked to the media.

For example, a whistle-blower at a large bank is reported to have said an internal document containing the 'red ratings' showed the bank "never got its house in order when it comes to risk, risk culture and culture in general".[70]

The whistle-blower flagged concerns that serious issues within the bank are 'diluted' and 'word-smithed' as they are elevated up the chain of command. "I don't know whether it is plausible deniability but it has created a situation where a disaster is waiting".[71]

Plausible deniability, raised here by a whistle-blower, is where a person can safely and believably deny knowledge of any particular truth that may exist because the person is deliberately made unaware of the truth so as to benefit or shield the person from any responsibility associated through the knowledge of the truth. For example, a reporter

---

70 A Ferguson and R Williams, 2015, "Whistleblower's NAB leak reveals persistent bad behaviour in financial planning, fuels royal commission calls", *Sydney Morning Herald*, 21 February, https://www.smh.com.au/business/banking-and-finance/whistleblowers-nab-leak-reveals-persistent-bad-behaviour-in-financial-planning-fuels-royal-commission-calls-20150218-13hv1f.html, (accessed 19 June 2018).

71 ibid.

might ask, "Were you aware of this report?" and the CEO might say, "I see hundreds of reports a year I can't be expected to know whether I've seen this one". And as Alison Taylor points out:

> *When a corporate scandal occurs, it is common for leaders to deny personal knowledge. Sometimes these hollow-sounding explanations are literally true, if disingenuous. A leader does not need to personally sign off on a bribe payment to hold responsibility for how employees have been socialised into an organization and what behavior is sanctioned or rewarded.*[72]

In the bank example, one of the senior leaders said the bank is 'on track' to resolve the issues highlighted in the audit. As for the red ratings, "things have improved—and the ratings show the bank is not trying to cover up its problems."

"You wouldn't want to see a business blind to what's going on, rate everything green and move on," he was quoted as saying. "For us when we see a red, we see opportunities to improve."[73]

Note the words used by the whistle-blower vs the executive:

- Whistle-blower: 'diluted', 'word-smithed', 'plausible deniability'.
- Senior leader: 'on track', 'things have improved', 'not trying to cover up its problems'.

Would other employees be likely to believe the leader?

---

72 A Taylor, 2017, "5 signs your organization might be headed for an ethics Scandal", *Harvard Business Review*, 18 December, https://hbr.org/2017/12/5-signs-your-organization-might-be-headed-for-an-ethics-scandal, (accessed 22 May 2018).

73 A Ferguson and R Williams, 2015, "Whistleblower's NAB leak reveals persistent bad behaviour in financial planning, fuels royal commission calls", *Sydney Morning Herald*, 21 February, https://www.smh.com.au/business/banking-and-finance/whistleblowers-nab-leak-reveals-persistent-bad-behaviour-in-financial-planning-fuels-royal-commission-calls-20150218-13hv1f.html, (accessed 19 June 2018).

The message is clear—communications emanating from the CEO and senior management, either written or verbal, must be clear and unambiguous, so that 'plausible deniability' does not become an issue for the organisation.

One of the most serious aspects of plausible deniability is that it increases the level of distrust between senior management and employees. When trust is lost, the ability to lead is seriously compromised. While plausible deniability works some of the time, it doesn't fool everyone over the long run.

Words—"I'm sorry" versus "I apologise"

One of the most common written statements, is an apology when the organisation, or someone senior, 'stuffs up'. Often these are also word-smithed and as such, can be seen as insincere, leading to even more fuel to the fire for public detractors.

For example, Qatar Airways chief executive, Sheik Akbar Al Baker apologised 'unreservedly' for his unflattering description of US flight attendants as 'grandmothers' (he also called American air carriers 'crap'), a day after the remarks touched off a firestorm of criticism from US labour unions and American Airlines. Here's his apology:

I should like to apologise unreservedly to those offended by my recent remarks which compared Qatar Airways cabin crew with cabin crew on US carriers. The remarks were made informally at a private gala dinner, following comments about the Qatar Airways cabin service, and were in no way intended to cause offence. This is a time of strong rivalry between our airline and the US carriers, and we are of course immensely proud of our own cabin crew. However, cabin crew are the public face of all airlines, and I greatly respect their hard work and professionalism. They play a huge role in the safety and comfort of passengers, irrespective of their age or gender or familial status. I have worked for many years in the industry, and I have a high regard for the value that I see long-serving staff members bringing through their experience and dedication.[74]

Does this apology give the impression of being sincere? The words used in this statement appear to be word-smithing. Did people believe and accept his apology? It seems not. "Sheik Al Baker's apology was 'insincere', said Dan Carey, president of the US Allied Pilots Association. 'Sheik Al Baker is a well-educated man and I think it's corporate damage control."[75]

And on the website *One Mile At A Time*,[76] their reporter said:

Now I'm not sure Akbar's apology is much of an apology, but I suppose it's better than nothing. He starts by apologizing 'unreservedly,' but then the apology isn't really for what he said, but rather for those that it offended. He goes on to justify what he said, say he has respect for everyone in the profession, etc., but doesn't admit that what he said was wrong and in poor taste.

On the surface, Sheik Al Baker's statement seems like a reasonably well worded apology statement. So why was it seen as insincere? Which words resonate with insincerity? Are there any words that should be in the statement, but aren't?

74 2017, "Qatar Air boss Akbar Al Baker sorry for slighting US flight atten-dants", *Sydney Morning Herald*, 13 July, https://www.smh.com.au/business/companies/qatar-air-boss-akbar-al-baker-sorry-for-slighting-us-flight-attendants-20170713-gxa5mx.html, (accessed 29 March 2018).

75 ibid.

76 B Schlappig, 2017, "WOW: Qatar Airways CEO apologizes for 'grandma' comments", *One Mile At A Time*, 12 July, http://onemileatatime.boarding area.com/2017/07/12/qatar-airways-ceo-apology/, (accessed 29 March 2018).

The *One Mile At A Time* reporter perceived it well:

- "unreservedly"—which appears in virtually every apology statement that is issued—has lost its meaning, totally;
- "the apology isn't really for what he said, but rather for those that it offended"; and
- Sheik Al Baker "goes on to justify what he said".

In addition to the polished, yet poor wording of this apology statement, what's missing is the word 'sorry'—the word 'apologise' is used instead. The word 'apologise' should be used to admit a mistake (it relates to the speaker's reasoning for his/her error). The word 'sorry' should be used to show remorse for doing what he/she did and to demonstrate sincere regret for offending (or hurting) someone. We'll cover these two words in more detail in a later chapter and show how and when each should be used.

It's interesting to note, a news headline posted that day said:[77] "Qatar Air boss Akbar Al Baker sorry for slighting US flight attendants", when the impact of the statement had no such intention, nor did it mention the word 'sorry'.

The six stakeholder statements of intent and their influence on culture

How can the CEO and senior management start the process of using authentic, meaningful, and positive written language? The starting point is to develop a set of six statements of intent—one for each of the organisation's six stakeholders:

---

77 2017, "Qatar Air boss Akbar Al Baker sorry for slighting US flight attendants", *Sydney Morning Herald*, 13 July, https://www.smh.com.au/business/companies/qatar-air-boss-akbar-al-baker-sorry-for-slighting-us-flight-attendants-20170713-gxa5mx.html, (accessed 29 March 2018).

The Stakeholder Map

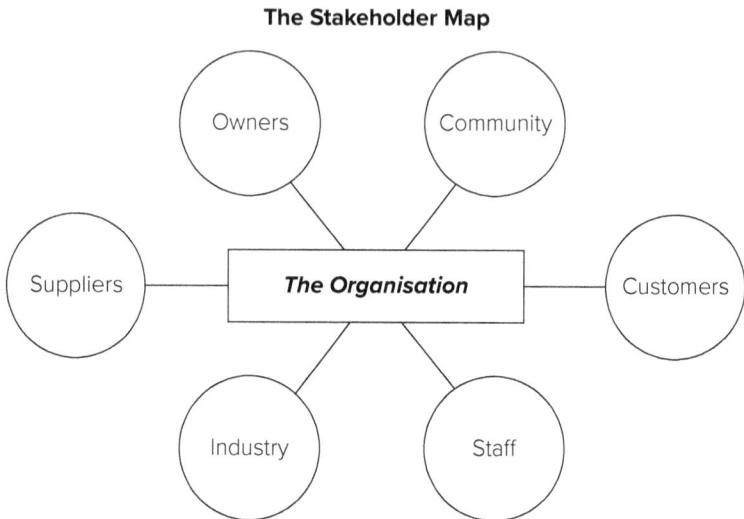

The organisation must answer the question
"How do we intend to be seen by each of these stakeholders?"

Figure 5: The stakeholder map.[78]

Firstly, the term 'stakeholder' needs to be clarified. 'Stakeholder' has made its way into the popular lexicon over the past few decades and is still misunderstood. Its original intention is based on the idea that a person or group of people may have a stake in how well something does what it is expected to do.

In the case of corporations, owners (shareholders) clearly have a stake in their corporation but, once it is set up and running, so too do several other groups of people. If a stake is defined as a two-way dependency, then in the same way that it depends on its owners and its owners depend on it, so too does a corporation have a stakeholder relationship with its customers and suppliers, its staff, the community in which it exists and the industry of which it forms a part. The corporation depends on all six stakeholders for its existence, and all

---

78 B Selden, 2011, "What To Do When You Become The Boss", Hachette, Sydney, p 35.

six stakeholders depend on the corporation to do the things they require it to do. The same set of stakeholders exist for government departments, NFP's—in fact all organisations—the one stakeholder that may need clarification in organisations other than corporates, is the "Owners" (e.g. in the case of government departments, it's the general community whose interests are represented by the government).

Stakeholder statements of intent

The basis for writing positive policies for any organisation is to have the CEO and senior management develop a statement of intent for each of the six stakeholder groups. This is often done as part of setting the strategic direction for the company and can be the first step in the process.

For example, a company in the financial services business might develop statements of intent such as:

Stakeholder	Statement of intent
Customers	We intend to be seen as a trusted source for advice on all our clients' financial needs, wants and concerns so that we build long-term relationships with them.
Suppliers	We intend to be seen as aspiring to develop a partner-relationship with our suppliers; to insist on the best quality and the most up-to-date services and products; to always pay on time, and to strive to provide our suppliers with the most accurate information available to enable them to provide us with the services/products we desire.
Owners	We intend to be seen as providing our shareholders with a premium rate of return on their investments, and to keep them advised in a timely manner, of developments that may affect the organisation's long-term performance.
Community	We intend to be seen as a responsible member of both the local, national and international community of which we are a part by contributing to the development of long-lasting, authentic relationships and where appropriate, partnerships with charitable and societal worthwhile causes.

Stakeholder	Statement of intent
Staff	We intend to be seen as one of the most successful 'Employers of Choice' in our industry by developing a culture whereby all employees can perform to their best, they see us as 'the ideal employer', and they recommend us to family, friends and acquaintances.
Industry	We intend to be seen as a strong and ethical competitor in the market place, admired and envied by our competitors, whose views are regularly sought by all the key industry groups, local, state and federal governments.

Table 3: Stakeholder statements of intent.

Once these statements of intent have been developed and agreed by the CEO and senior team, they form the basis for the drafting of all policy documents. They thus act as a very good checklist for senior management when signing off on newly written policies.

They also help in creating more effective external and internal communications in the following manner.

- External communications, particularly to the media and shareholders:
  - The CEO should ensure each message is in total sync with the stakeholder statement of intent for the stakeholders for whom it is aimed.
  - The CEO should ensure that the message complies with the organisation's social media policy and codes of conduct.
- Internal correspondence, such as emails:
  - must only include factual information;
  - should be read for their likely impact. If there is any hint of having an emotional impact, a face-to-face meeting should be used instead. The golden rule for emails is to include only facts and logic and avoid statements that may have an emotional impact on the receiver. (Paul Romer, The World Bank

Economist's email correspondence that we quoted in the Introduction, is an excellent example of what can go wrong).

Notice also, the importance of the words 'to be seen' in each of the six statements of intent, which leads to another important element of effective corporate policies—visuals.

Improve internal policies and external communication with visuals

Why are visuals so important in our communication? As humans, we started our development to eventually become the most intelligent species by adopting language-like symbols as a way to represent the world around us. For example, before a person says a word, their brain first has to have a symbolic representation of what it means. These mental symbols eventually led to language in all its complexity and the ability to process information which is the main reason we are the only hominin (human type species) still alive.

By taking advantage of what communication experts have discovered about the benefits of the visual medium and incorporating graphic elements into our largely text-driven communications, we can communicate more effectively. Pictures are not only easier to recognise and process than words, but also easier to recall. When words enter long-term memory, they do so with a single code. Pictures, on the other hand, contain two codes; one visual and the other verbal, each stored in different places in the brain. The dual-coding nature of images allows for two independent ways of accessing visual memories, increasing the odds of remembering at least one of them.

Adding illustrations to text aids comprehension and learning. Yet few of our corporate policies contain visuals. But there are some good exceptions. **Figures 6** and **7** below, available on the Campbell Page website, provide an example of how effective a combination of the written word and visuals can be in demonstrating mission, goals and values.

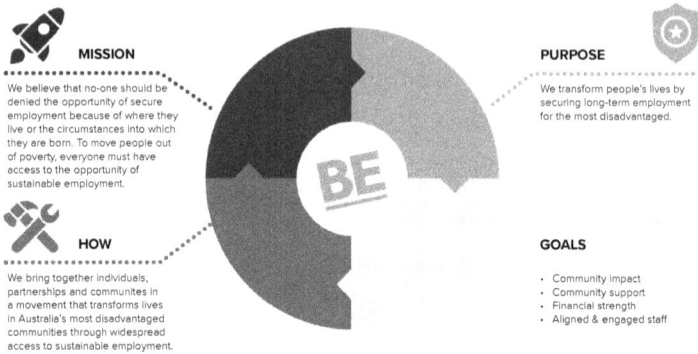

Figure 6: Demonstrating an effective combination of the written word and visuals—illustration on mission and goals from the Campbell Page 2017 Annual Report.[79]

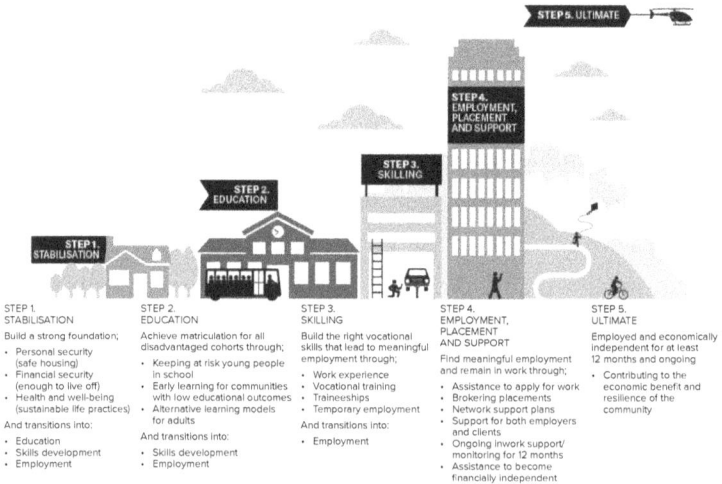

Figure 7: Demonstrating an effective combination of the written word and visuals—illustration on values from Campbell Page.[80]

79 "Campell Page Annual Report", 2017, *Campbell Page*, campbellpage.com.au/
    wp-content/uploads/2017/11/CP-2017-Annual-Report-Financials-Digitial-
    Size-Optimised.pdf, (accessed 28 June 2018).
80 Campbell Page, http://campbellpage.com.au/wp-content/uploads/2014/02/
    Our-Approach-1.pdf, (accessed 28 June 2018).

And one company has taken the use of visuals in their policies one step further. In May 2018, global engineering and infrastructure advisory company, Aurecon became one of the first companies in Australia to use a visual employment contract, eliminating more than 4,000 words from their employment contracts to create a succinct and meaningful visual contract that uses illustrations to complement the text. Developed in partnership with Law Professor, Camilla Andersen from the University of Western Australia, Aurecon's employment contracts are legally binding contracts in which Aurecon and its employees are represented by characters—free of legal jargon and similar to a comic strip format.

With workplace polls often indicating a lack of meaningful employee engagement and trust, according to Aurecon's Global Chief People Officer, Liam Hayes: "The issue of engaging our talent and building their trust is becoming one of the biggest competitive differentiators across many industries and companies."[81]

Obviously, the language used in the message is equally as important as the visual. As we progress through the remainder of this book, we trust you'll become more aware of which words to use and which to avoid, and we'll revisit this topic towards the conclusion of the book with some examples. For now, in keeping with our suggestion about using visuals, the key points to keep in mind with written communication are summarised in **Figure 8**. This summarises how the combination of positive words with visuals can improve the impact of policies by increasing understanding of the behaviour required by those policies.

---

81 Aurecon, 2018, "Australia's first visual employment contracts launched", 5 May, *Aurecon Australia Pty Ltd*, https://www.aurecongroup.com/about/latest-news/2018/may/visual-employment-contract, (accessed 8 May 2018).

Words used in policies *'Focus on what people can do'*	Visuals used in policies *'Enable people to remember'*	Impact of policies *'Increased understanding of behaviour required'*

Figure 8: Words with visuals improve the impact of policies.

The bottom line ...

Align intent and impact

While the CEO may not write policy documents, the CEO clearly can influence how written communication occurs both within the organisation and externally. To ensure intent and impact are aligned, the CEO and senior management need to make sure that:

- The organisation's policies are written in positive language, that is what employees can do, rather than what they can't do (Remember: this can have a significant impact on the development of a positive corporate culture).
- Wherever possible, policies contain visuals to ensure the policies are easily remembered and to assist with their accurate interpretation and implementation.
- All written communication emanating from the CEO and senior management are in line with the organisation's six stakeholder statements of intent.

1.5 Concluding comments on setting the tone at the top

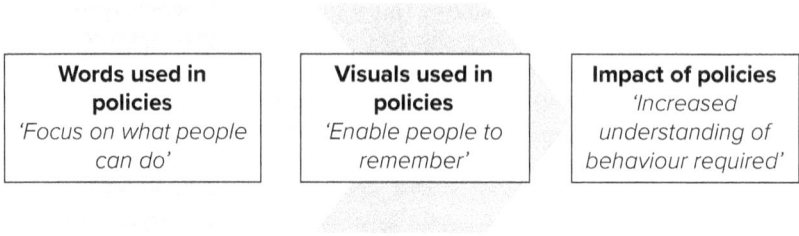

Words matter, especially what is said by the CEO and senior management. Whether it be verbally or in writing, what they say has the most impact on their ability to set tone and shape corporate culture, their words influence 'the way we do things around here'. The tone can be a positive one as with (Unilever) or a negative one (Enron).

There may be dire consequences where the tone is negative with negative language leading to a self-defeating culture (external locus of control). This was reinforced in a King & Wood Mallesons survey",[82] where an overwhelming majority (82.7%) of survey respondents considered that an organisation should be held accountable for an employee's misconduct and where such misconduct was directly attributed to the organisation's corporate culture. Survey respondents commented that:

- "it becomes an unwritten aspect of their employment contract to behave in certain ways";[83]
- "culture tells employees what is acceptable";[84] and
- the organisation should be responsible because it was "complicit in failure", and the conduct was "a monster of their creation" and "indicates systemic problems".[85]

If corporate culture is the mindset of an organisation, then it follows that the mindset of the CEO and senior management are critically important. The language the CEO and senior management, use to communicate gives everyone a window into their mindset. This book aims to help leaders to develop further their communication strategies, tactics and skills—that is the language—that will provide the CEO, senior executives and stakeholders with a clear view of their positive and ethical mindset.

Building positive relationships with all key stakeholders is a reflection of who a leader is as a person. The mirror he or she holds up to the world, is made much clearer through the words and language a leader uses in day-to-day conversations. The starting point for these positive relationships—commences with the words leaders use to develop a shared language such as 'we', 'us' and 'our' (and those to avoid, such

---

82 King & Wood Mallesons (KWM), 2016, "Directions 2016: Current issues and challenges facing Australian directors and boards", 3 March, http://www. kwm.com/en/au/knowledge/downloads/directions-2016-issues-challenges-australian-directors-boards-20160304, (accessed 4 June 2018).

83 ibid, p 25.

84 ibid, p 25.

85 ibid, p 25.

SETTING THE TONE FROM THE TOP

as 'don't' that was mentioned earlier). Remember also leaders need to be careful of 'word-smithing'; recall the FBI case of 'matter' versus 'investigation' and the furore that followed.

A leader's awareness of the impact of the language he or she is using and the impact it has on others (their level of sensitivity), and their ability and willingness to speak up and encourage others to speak up, can go a long way to improving the 'collective intelligence'.

At this early stage of the book, we've mentioned the word 'conversation' many times. And it will be mentioned many more times as we progress. The quality of conversations are critical to build and sustain culture—what employees say to one another in their breaks; and what they say to customers and suppliers and perhaps even friends and family members—reflects the culture in which they work and live. A series of studies using Glassdoor data demonstrates this point. Using analytical tools including AI and a large data set from Glassdoor to develop nuanced descriptions of specific elements of corporate culture based on words of employees, the studies demonstrate the impact of conversation on culture. The researchers found significant value for understanding and measuring culture in the way employees describe—in their own words—the pros and cons of working at a particular company[86] Wells Fargo is a case in point:

> *"Glassdoor data was used to predict a range of corporate outcomes, including future profitability, stock market returns, innovation, customer satisfaction, and financial fraud. In the years prior to the scandal, Wells Fargo employees were nearly twice as likely to discuss integrity in their reviews, and half as likely to discuss the bank's ethics in positive terms compared with other large banks."*

---

86 D Sull, C Sull and A Chamberlain, 2019, "Measuring Culture in Leading Companies, Introducing the MIT SMR/Glassdoor Culture 500", *MIT Sloan Management Review*, Reprint Number 61130.

The Wells Fargo scandal demonstrates the importance of conversations at all levels, especially at the top, conversations of the CEO and senior management, the board and other key stakeholders. It is conversation that *sets the tone at the top* and is critical to shaping culture.

Culture matters beyond its power to drive financial results. The average employee spends 40% of her waking hours at work. A vibrant culture can help people thrive professionally, enjoy their job, and find meaning in their work. A toxic culture, in contrast, can be soul destroying for people and for company performance. As we said in the introduction, 'it all starts with words' and now that we've explored some of the impact leaders' words have on others, Part 2 moves on to examine how words come together in those important conversations.

PART 2

SETTING THE TONE THROUGH CONVERSATION

2.1 How leaders harness collective intelligence

"Human cognition veered away from that of other primates when our ancestors developed *shared intentionality* … at some point our ancestors developed the ability to share mental representations of tasks that two or more of them were pursuing together."[87]
Jonathan Haidt

The 'use of knowledge' as opposed to the 'presence of knowledge'

Chimpanzees, our nearest animal relatives, have been found to be as good as humans at certain tasks. In some, they outperform us. Short-term memory is one such area where chimpanzees have been found to be superior.

---

87   J Haidt, 2013, "The Righteous Mind: why good people are divided by politics and religion", Random House, New York, p. 237

For example, at a science symposium in June 2016 on this subject,[88] Tetsuro Matsuzawa, a Kyoto primatologist, showed a video of a young chimp watching as numbers from 1 to 9 flashed on the computer screen at random positions. Then the numbers disappeared in no more than a second. White squares remained where the numbers had been. The chimp casually but swiftly pressed the squares, calling back the numbers in ascending order—1, 2, 3, etc.

The test was repeated several times, with the numbers and squares in different places. The chimp, which had months of training accompanied by promised food rewards, almost always remembered where the numbers had been. The video included scenes of a human failing the test, seldom recalling more than one or two numbers, if any.

"Humans can't do it," Dr Matsuzawa said. "Chimpanzees are superior to humans in this task".[89]

While chimps have been shown to outperform humans in tasks such as short-term memory and mathematical and spatial reasoning (in certain contexts), one key difference is our ability to access and share the knowledge we carry in our brains and use that knowledge in multiple, large complex groups and organisations, a trait that other species do not possess.

Our experience suggests that successful leaders employ this human ability to share knowledge to its full extent. It's the propensity for leaders (who often come from many different disciplines, cultures, and backgrounds, and who exhibit or display other differences), to share knowledge, that is the key to an organisation's success.

For example, we conducted a leadership development process for Mirvac, the highly successful Australian building and construction company founded in 1972. The process included 10 one-day

---

88   J Cohen, 2016, "Thinking like a chimpanzee", *Smithsonian Magazine*, September, https://www.smithsonianmag.com/science-nature/thinking-like-a-chimpanzee-55484749/, (accessed 4 June 2018).

89   ibid.

workshops conducted over a 12-month period, each workshop on a separate, yet related topic. There were approximately 30 of Mirvac's senior executives and managers attending. One workshop, specifically on leadership, entailed two of Mirvac's founding directors (who were about to retire), sitting with the group and discussing, "The mistakes we've made over the last 30 years and what we learned".

The conversation lasted an entire morning, and as you might expect, was enthralling. In fact, when we returned for the following month's workshop, the managers were still talking about last month's conversation. We would say that is a clear example of leadership in words and action.

How leaders employ the knowledge of individuals

The curse of knowledge is insidious, because it conceals not only the contents of our thoughts from us, but their very form. When we know something well, we don't realize how abstractly we think about it. And we forget that other people, who have lived their own lives, have not gone through our idiosyncratic histories of abstractification.[90]

Organisational knowledge is considered an asset that, although intangible, generates a competitive advantage for the organisation. Such knowledge resides in every employee of the organisation. What separates ordinary organisation performance from a high-performance one, is how this knowledge is shared and used. Knowledge is the organisational resource (that one won't find listed on any balance sheet) that enables the organisation to develop strategies, tactics and activities that generate improvement and innovation leading to a competitive advantage.

---

90   S Pinker, 2014, "The Sense of Style: The Thinking Person's Guide to Writing in the 21st Century", *Allen Lane*, Penguin Books, p 59.

The use and sharing of knowledge starts with meaningful conversation amongst and between the CEO and the senior leaders of the organisation.

How the CEO and senior executives use 'disclosure' to demonstrate leadership

There is a psychological term known as 'disclosure'. Disclosure is an important leadership trait because it relates directly to trust. The more open a person seems, the greater they are trusted. The trait of 'disclosure' has been well researched in the leadership literature and when used carefully and judiciously, can bring leaders much closer to the people with whom they are endeavouring to build relationships. As Lynn Offerman and Lisa Rosh point out in an *HBR* article, "Building trust through skillful self-disclosure",[91] "There is considerable evidence that leaders who disclose their authentic selves to followers can build not only trust, but generate greater cooperation and teamwork as well."

In Part 1, we referred to collective intelligence as the shared or group intelligence that emerges from:

- collaboration;
- collective efforts; and
- the competition of many individuals.

The key word in this description is 'shared'. How can the CEO and executive team employ the knowledge available throughout the organisation?

Wikipedia and YouTube are two of the most well-known examples of how collective intelligence is shared. In both cases, people freely volunteer their knowledge, expertise and time, to provide educative knowledge for others. As children we freely share knowledge and

---

91   L Offerman and L Rosh, 2012, "Building trust through skillful self-disclosure", *Harvard Business Review*, 13 June, https://hbr.org/2012/06/instantaneous-intimacy-skillfu, (accessed 22 June 2018).

resources, yet as we mature, we generally do so less often. Why is this so and how does it impact organisations? Our experience has been that in less successful organisations (and/or those where there is a poor culture), knowledge is held 'close to one's chest', so that managers who have the most knowledge, tend not to share to make themselves more powerful.

> *Antiquated beliefs about intelligence are holding us back. We need to break out of old habits, to realise that we don't need the stuff in our heads—it's our ability to know and find the people with the information we need.*[92]

Through our extensive observations of many organisations, we have seen how management can share knowledge to stay relevant. To harness employee expertise, what each knows individually, and connect it with what management knows, requires effort. Meaningful conversations are the key component. Here are three strategies that promote sharing—and they all involve meaningful conversations:

1. Leave ego at the door. Mohamed Bray, Engagement and Practice Manager at Saratoga (a consulting firm), strongly encourages people to make themselves dispensable, saying that "while seemingly counterintuitive, this practice demands that within teams, knowledge sharing and trust build stronger teams and produce far more solid outcomes."[93] By making themselves dispensable, leaders are opening up all of their knowledge and experience to the rest of the team. By leaving their ego at the

---

92 R Maserow, 2015, "People and the power of collective intelligence, the new corporate manifesto", *ITWeb*, 30 November 2015, https://www.itweb.co.za/content/3mYZRX79x2DvOgA8, (accessed 29 March 2018).

93 R Maserow, 2015, "Inter-view report 2015 ushers in new age for business analysis", *ITWeb*, 3 November 2015, https://www.itweb.co.za/content/XnWJadMbB4oMbjO1, (accessed 29 March 2018).

door, they are able to see the difference in the quality of their conversations.

2. Have regular 'Knowledge Sharing' sessions within the senior team, particularly when new executives join. New members of a group often have the most valuable insights. For example, leaders might pair up with each other before or after senior team meetings for a discussion of how things are going and what issues are being wrestled with.

Such regular knowledge sharing sessions, may develop into mentoring between leaders. Mentoring can be one of the most rewarding of shared experiences (our Mirvac experience is a wonderful example of sharing knowledge). A number of leading companies use this mentoring practice successfully.

3. Instigate 'Peer Reviews'.

Peer reviews that have as their basis, robust conversations, can be extremely rewarding. For example, we worked on the launch of a top team evaluation tool in Australia that used group responses, rather than individual answers. The tool allowed executives to visualise areas of agreement and disagreement. The data was then used to facilitate meaningful conversations of the underlying assumptions and differences in thinking among top team members.

How leaders develop trust through conversation

We were consulting to the HR Department of a large insurance company when something inspirational happened. During a scheduled meeting of the 12 company HR personnel (with us), an unexpected guest entered the meeting room. It was the CEO, who had been in the role for about 12 months. He asked if he could have 10 minutes with the team. The HR Director introduced us to the CEO (as consultants) and then, undeterred by our presence the CEO proceeded to converse with the HR team. He spoke about his experiences over the last 12 months, what he had learned and where he saw the organisation going. What gripped everyone's attention was his candour about the mistakes he had made since becoming CEO.

This was one of the most inspiring conversations involving a leader, we have seen. Many of the HR team asked questions, with some exchanging opinions (sometimes differing) with the CEO. Forty minutes (rather than the anticipated 10) later, the entire HR team were incredulous that someone so senior could be so open. We are certain the story of that conversation would have spread like wildfire throughout the company.

This is but one, albeit one of the best, illustrations of openness, an inclination to speak up, and an acceptance of other people's views as legitimate, that we have seen. As Jeffery A Sonnenfeld in an *HBR* article, points out:

> *Members develop mutual respect; because they respect one another, they develop trust; because they trust one another, they share difficult information; because they all have the same, reasonably complete information, they can challenge one another's conclusions coherently; because a spirited give-and-take becomes the norm, they learn to adjust their own interpretations in response to intelligent questions.*[94]

The bottom line ...

Impact of team collaboration on outcomes

Achieving results requires collaboration—sharing information and ideas, integrating perspectives, and coordinating tasks. Teams provide a structural mechanism through which this collaboration often occurs.

---

94 Jeffrey A Sonnenfeld, 2002, "What Makes Great Boards Great", September, *Harvard Business Review Magazine*, https://hbr.org/2002/09/what-makes-great-boards-great, (accessed 29 March 2018).

Collaborating to achieve a shared outcome starts at the top, so that a positive culture is role modelled throughout the organisation.

Leaders can work towards collaborative sharing of knowledge by:

- disclosing information and their own feelings in conversations to build trust; and
- encouraging peers to have conversations around 'ego' and its impact; knowledge sharing sessions; and the potential for peer reviews.
- responding productively when given feedback from others

2.2 How leaders manage the process a conversation follows

We have provided the rationale for sharing knowledge and suggested some strategies and tactics that all involve effective conversations, such as 'leave one's ego at the door', 'knowledge sharing sessions' and 'peer reviews'. The question now is, "how do leaders know their conversations are having the desired impact?" What follows is a description of the six phases through which all conversations progress—knowing about these phases, and how successful leaders manage their conversations through them, will provide an insight on the best way to manage their leadership conversations.

The six phases of a conversation and how they are managed productively

"Hello Alice, I'm Bob. Nice to meet you. (pause) So what do you do?" Bob asked as a conversation starter when meeting Alice at an event.

"I'm a banker, specialising in foreign exchange," she replied.

"Sounds interesting—do you enjoy it?"

Alice hesitated for a moment or two—she seemed somewhat uninspired by her profession. "It's pretty interesting, and I'll have a good lifestyle after I've been there a few years," she answered.

At this point Bob had two options: "I could continue the drudgery of the normal conversation and go on talking about her job (by which she seemed less than totally enthused), or I could reframe the conversation and try to build a deeper emotional connection. I decided on the latter."

"Sounds like a good plan. And what do you do that you're truly passionate about?"

Bob recounts, "At first Alice seemed a bit confused, and I wondered if she'd always considered herself enthusiastic about banking, but then she gathered herself and responded, 'You know, I actually love the idea of starting a corporate design business one day'."

So far in this book we've used the term 'communication' in a general sense to describe many interactions. However, 'conversation' becomes a far more specific form of communication. For example, you can communicate by sending an email or text, leaving a voice mail on someone's phone, writing a paper, or even accessing data from the internet. Conversation on the other hand requires interaction between at least two people, and that's where the challenges start.

Conversations can be funny things—we start out someplace and may end up at a totally different destination from the one we expected. For example, Bob's conversation with Alice went somewhere that he did not expect. "How was your day?" is another conversation starter used by millions of people around the world when they meet up again at the end of the day. What sort of responses do you get when you ask this question? Have you ever been surprised by the answers?

Conversation at its simplest takes place when participants perform these tasks which progress the conversation through the process outlined in **Figure 9: The six phases of a conversation**.

This diagram seems to depict conversations as very mechanistic. Yet, studies[95] have shown that's exactly the process that occurs in every conversation we have—whether it's chatting with a friend or

---

95 H Dubberly, 2009, "What is conversation? How can we design for effective conversation?" *Dubberly Design Office*, 1 May, http://www.dubberly.com/articles/what-is-conversation.html, (accessed 29 March 2018).

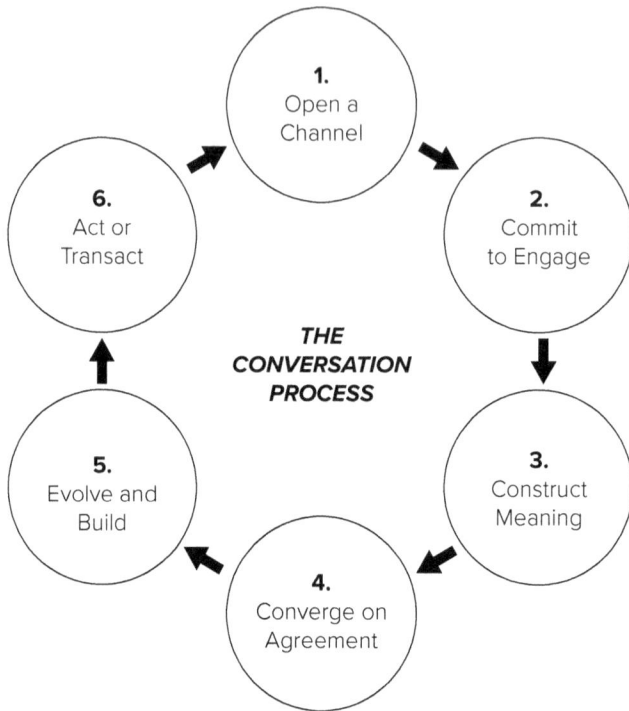

Figure 9: The six phases of a conversation.

in discussion with a fellow executive—we're just not consciously aware of following this six-step process.

With such knowledge, one can dramatically increase one's conversational effectiveness.

Notice here too, that we've used the word 'process' to describe what happens in a conversation—as mentioned earlier in the book, process management skills are vitally important in conversing.

Most often, we are so involved in the 'content', the subject of the conversation, that we're unaware of the six phases (process) through which the conversation is progressing.

A good way of becoming familiar with the six phases, and how a leader can actively manage each phase, is to recall a conversation that you have had recently with a team member—the conversation may have been constructive or otherwise. The point is to see how your recent conversation followed the six phases. To do so, please answer our questions and think about your recent conversation as you read through each of the six phases.

1. Open a channel

To start the conversation, the speaker says something that is comprehensible to the listener. This may seem basic but is essential. The situation must also seem comfortable, or at least non-threatening. For example, if the speaker says something in a language you don't understand or you can't hear what was said because of other noise, then a conversation does not start.

- In your recent conversation, why did it seem easy to continue?

2. Commit to engage

The listener must participate if only by continuing to listen. He/she is only likely to continue if they see value in the conversation. In your recent conversation:

- What value did you see in continuing the conversation, that is, why did you continue?
- What value do you think the other person saw in the conversation?
- Why did the conversation end? Was it too soon, too long, or about right?

3. Construct meaning

At this point the people are able to understand one another through previous conversations, shared knowledge, common language or social norms.

- What did the two of you share or have in common? How did you discover this shared meaning?

- Were there specific questions either you or your conversation partner asked that facilitated a shared understanding?

4. Converge on agreement

In an effective conversation, people share some understanding of the topic even if minimal, or a desire to understand it if the conversation is to continue (although they may totally disagree on one another's reasons, logic, philosophy and so on). Because of this shared understanding they will start to move toward an agreement, or at least an 'agreement to disagree'.

- What did the two of you agree on, or perhaps 'agree to disagree' on?

5. Evolve and build understanding

Either or both people are different after the conversation—this may be in their actions, beliefs or even a strengthening of their initial thoughts and ideas.

- What did the conversation identify, confirm or change for you?
- How did you feel following the conversation? Was this a different feeling from the one you had before?

6. Act or transact

Either or both people do something as a result of the conversation— this may range from undertaking some action, telling someone else, or continuing to think (consciously) about the topic.

- What have you done since the conversation (that was related)?
- Who have you told about the conversation? Why?

During a challenging conversation, it will be nigh on impossible to remember all six process tasks required to bring it to a satisfactory conclusion. After all, you will be totally immersed in the content, and rightly so. Remembering to complete these tasks will therefore be particularly challenging when your conversation is emotionally charged. So it will be useful to have some clear signposts to help manage the process and progress to a satisfactory destination. As a starting point, our diagram should be a useful map to follow. We encourage you to become familiar with it and observe how conversations with people around you—the CEO, the board, other colleagues—always progress through these six phases.

Here we've once again used the words 'content' and 'process'. In conversations these are important concepts to understand and manage. The content is what the discussion is all about—the problems, issues, challenges. People in all difficult or challenging conversations become heavily engrossed in the content.

The process on the other hand is how the conversation is managed—the questions, summaries, timing, format, etc. When difficult conversations end in an impasse, devolve into argument or just fail to reach any conclusions, it's almost always because the people are so focussed on the content and no-one is managing the process. It's by being a good process manager that leaders can dramatically improve the way they manage difficult conversations. We will cover the six phases of a conversation in more detail in Part 4 where it will be used to plan and manage those challenging conversations that all leaders have.

The bottom line ...

Conversations impact relationships and set tone

Setting the tone through conversation means managing conversations, particularly difficult ones, through the six phases:

1. **Open a channel**, so that others feel comfortable;
2. **Commit to engage**, by listening to the concerns, issues, challenges of others;
3. **Construct meaning**, by looking for common ground and shared understandings;
4. **Converge on agreement**, by indicating your understanding of the issues;
5. **Evolve and build** understanding, by identifying what the conversation changed or confirmed; and
6. **Act or transact**, by deciding on what action to take (or not) depending on the outcomes.

In the following chapter we continue our focus on process management in conversations which encourage the sharing of knowledge. We build on some of the suggestions already made with specific emphasis on individual leadership tactics, plus present suggestions on how leaders can use structured team processes in meetings to enhance effective decision making. We conclude the chapter with a diagram of many of the process management tactics, techniques and strategies—most of which you will be familiar with—that all successful teams use to manage the process of their conversations. We emphasise these here, because our experience suggests that successful leaders consistently and consciously use these to manage all their conversations.

2.3 How the CEO and senior team display leadership through conversation

There are two processes—individual and structural—that we'll provide examples of in this chapter. Each is a facet of demonstrating effective leadership through conversation, so that leaders will engage positively with one another. Two researchers, Boris Groysberg and Michael Slind[96] in fact describe leadership as 'a conversation'—an interesting description and we'll discuss their findings that led to this description of leadership shortly.

Setting the tone through personal leadership in conversations

Setting the tone by employing 'opening up' conversational tactics

We start with the individual process first. It may take some gumption to be a leader but setting an example for others to follow is what

---

96 B Groysberg and M Slind, 2012, "Leadership is a conversation", *Harvard Business Review*, June 2012.

leadership is all about. Suggestions for group conversations that an executive may lead or participate in appear below. Ordinarily, one would think that the following process management tactics and techniques would fall to the CEO. However, for the senior team to work effectively, we believe every team member needs to take a role in ensuring the conversational process is managed well. The following is not an exhaustive list, but it should serve as an example of what leaders can achieve through being aware of, and following, the six phases of the conversation process discussed earlier:

- **Leaders need to hone in on any silences in the conversation.** When people who are normally talkative clam up, it may mean they are afraid to give their opinion. In this case, executives can frame a question that explains why the topic is important and why they would like the other's input. For example, "This is an important issue for the organisation and I'd appreciate a wide range of differing views so that we can assess all the options". Note here the words "wide range", "differing views" and "all the options"—these frame the conversation to offer everyone 'permission to be different' (we'll discuss 'framing' in detail in a later section).

  Such questioning is particularly important in the opening phase of the conversation. It starts—to 'open a channel' (Phase 1) through which the conversation can progress—and gains the commitment of others to engage in the topic (Phase 2).

- **Leaders should encourage an atmosphere of 'open dissent'.** This is not disloyalty; it's encouraging others to share their opinions even if they differ from one another. Leaders need to make sure that their language separates the person from their view. For example use "What I'm hearing is" versus "You always say that". When a person becomes their view, often because they are the only person expressing dissent, then the dissent is attached to their personality rather than the point being made and the conversation shuts down. You will notice in this example, the positive use of 'I'm' versus the negative use of 'You'. We will cover such word phrasing in detail in Part 3.

When a meeting atmosphere is positive, and leaders are prepared to speak their mind, all conversations will quickly move through to 'construct meaning' (phase 3) where the best knowledge is shared, and issues are debated openly.

- **Leaders should be prepared to discuss the 'elephants in the room' or the 'sacred cows'**. These are topics that executives may not normally raise for one reason or another. For example, if a leader knows that the CEO has previously outlined his/her objection to a point, the leader may courageously raise it anyway. Once again, framing the statement is important, for example, "I know that this point has been raised previously *and* I believe it's important to visit this again as a number of things have changed".

  This is an example of a technique, 'framing', for managing the conversation through Phase 3—Construct Meaning. In Part 3 of the book, we'll discuss the use of 'framing' and using the word 'and' rather than 'but' to link ideas in a more positive manner.

- **Ask the opinion leaders for their input**. A good way of widening the topic is once the opinion leader has given his/her views is to ask "And what would be an alternative to that view?" This opens the door for others to contribute and helps team members to construct meaning for themselves on the topic (Phase 3). It also starts to move the conversation towards reaching agreement (Phase 4).

- **Leaders can create an ownership culture.** This is not just for the organisation as a whole but for people's particular views. One excellent way of doing this is for leaders to use three positive review questions when analysing a recent event, such as a project milestone or a board meeting:

- What went well?
- What did we learn?
- What should we do differently?

These questions are excellent examples of how leaders can manage the final phases of conversations—'Evolve and Build' and 'Act or Transact'. We encourage leaders to use these three review questions regularly to share the best learnings from current events, projects and company milestones. They are particularly useful for gaining knowledge on how the organisational culture is being maintained, developed or shaped.

- **Importantly, and where possible, leaders should give people advance warning on the topic**. Some people can readily 'think on their feet' whilst others need time to consider. A good way to 'Open a Channel' that will involve all leaders in the conversation, is to provide others with lead time to think on the topic.

Boris Groysberg and Michael Slind, whom we mentioned earlier in the context of 'leadership is a conversation', studied more than 150 leaders in over 100 organisations (large/small, FP/NFP),[97] and found that traditional corporate communication must give way to a process that is more dynamic and more sophisticated. Most importantly, that process must be conversational. They found that leaders who power their organisations through conversation, employ four strategies:

- creating a sense of intimacy;
- promoting interactivity at all levels;
- including employees in information sharing (for example, financials that they would not normally be privy to); and
- employing intentionality—have a defined purpose for conversations rather than letting conversations drift aimlessly.

---

97   ibid.

With the globalisation of many organisations, or at the very least, larger geographical spreads, we were particularly taken with Groysberg and Slind's inclusion of 'intimacy' which they sum up as: "Physical proximity between leaders and employees isn't always feasible. But mental or emotional proximity is essential."[98] This is especially important in today's hybrid working environments.

Setting the tone through open, trusting conversation

A significant example of the extent of openness and trust and the powerful impact these principles can have, occurred at the United Permanent Building Society (UP). The original premise behind Building Societies (we believe Building Societies were originally started in the UK in 1776 and spread to many Western countries—today, many have become banks) was that people became members, invested their savings (generally on a progressive weekly or monthly basis) and at some stage applied for a home loan. At that time (in the 1980's), Building Societies offered higher rates of interest than banks on invested funds, and under their constitutions members were only allowed to withdraw funds by cheque, not cash. These conditions; high interest rates and the inconvenience of withdrawals, proved to be real incentives to invest and to maintain one's savings. So over time they became more of a 'quasi-savings bank' where members saved for many different purposes other than just homes.

This was a time when the investment market was becoming highly competitive. The board and CEO of UP at the time found that the restriction on cash withdrawals was amendable in their constitution, so they decided to offer this service. They knew that no other Building Societies were contemplating such a move, as this would be revolutionary in the industry. In a series of conversations with all 800 employees, the CEO told staff about the organisation's plans, how revolutionary

---

98   ibid.

they were, and that it was to be kept secret in case any competitors found out about the strategy.

Over a period of about five months—when new IT systems were developed, branches (there were 80 at the time) physically altered (to allow for larger flows of cash), marketing concepts and materials developed, and staff trained—not a word got out. One Friday afternoon, the CEO told all staff that they were "changing the industry on Monday" and with saturation TV coverage over the weekend, UP opened on Monday with a totally new way of doing business. According to management and staff, the feeling on that Monday was 'euphoric'.[99] Setting the tone therefore occurred through trusting conversation.

Let us now turn to three further examples from our experience where we have seen how leaders worked effectively to improve their focus on the process management of conversations. Our first example, demonstrates how individuals, can employ a number of process management techniques in conversations that help motivate the senior executive team. The second example shows how a structured team exercise employs a process management strategy that has the senior team 'thinking and speaking as one'. And our third example introduces two key conversation tactics—labelling and priming—that are often potent pre-cursers to leader conversations and on which we will spend more time as we progress through *Setting the Tone from the Top*. Labelling and priming are particularly useful in handling those challenging conversations that we cover in detail in Part 4.

Setting the tone in meetings through group processes

Let's set the scene for this part of the chapter, where we discuss group process management strategies, by giving two personal examples of effective group conversational processes together with findings from Dr Catherine Bailey of Cranfield Business School. We believe using

---

99   B Selden, 2011, *What To Do When You Become The Boss*, Hachette, Sydney, p 35.

group processes such as those mentioned here, lead to more effective decision making.

We worked on a leadership development program in the early 2000s that was focused on helping senior executives understand how to lead teams capable of having genuine, open conversations. The company is a global player in the pharmaceutical industry, the executives were highly skilled, many with PhDs working on products that could seriously impact the health of many people. In this environment, the ability to form and reform project teams able to utilise all the knowledge available among team members to make effective decisions, was critical to success.

The CEO and the board agreed to fund and deliver a program for selected groups of senior executives. The program had no technical content in the scientific sense—only content relevant to group process. The format was mainly experiential and aimed at bringing the company values to life in a tangible way to ensure a shared meaning across departments, divisions and countries.

Each iteration of the program was an intense five days of process management activity with content topics such as:
- how we appear to others;
- bringing values to life;
- building trust; and
- networks and relationships.

The sessions were presented and facilitated in chunks to assist learning and practiced through an assignment to be completed in small groups. There were many challenges; language barriers, cultural differences and strong personalities.

Some of the insights about what prevents effective, productive discussion on difficult issues were:
- assuming the leaders need to know the answer;
- prejudging the answer; and
- lacking confidence in a productive outcome.

After working in the small groups for a week, sharing ideas and interacting with the senior leadership team, participants were able to say things such as "Now I understand how effective real life conversations work." One participant commented, "I feel honoured to work for a company that has a strong value system that is fully embraced by the board and the executive team"—a clear example of setting the tone from the top.

Our second example of effective group processes comes from Dr Catherine Bailey of Cranfield Business School, who says: "Never has it been more necessary for management teams to be able to work through the Zone of Uncomfortable Debate (ZOUD)—that unspoken process that prevents us from questioning too closely the things that are held dear in business."[100]

Several of the conversation management processes Bailey suggests are:

- Prepare people, process and place—give people the opportunity to prepare (i.e. high quality board papers), rotate the leader role, legitimise the responsibility for asking challenging questions by taking turns at playing devil's advocate. 'Taking turns' is especially important given that this is one of the elements that contribute to collective intelligence in groups.
- Ensure sufficient agenda time and choose different locations for difficult conversations (our best performing teams mentioned earlier were good at rotating venues and finding venues appropriate to the meeting).
- Find the right starting point and pace—take a stepwise approach by testing for agreement on the issue to be discussed, identify the decisions that need to be taken and what needs to be understood better to take those decisions. Identify the options along

---

100 C Bailey, 2011, "Working through the ZOUD", *Management Focus*, Issue 30, Spring 2011, p 14–15.

with the factors that should guide choices and the weight each factor should have (leaders who actively manage the six-phase conversation process mentioned earlier, do this very well).

- Act with emotional intelligence and political awareness— manage emotions, rather than leave others to guess a leader's worthy intentions. Ask questions to gain understanding and facilitate progress by asking "How can we move on, what would help us?"

In addition to the processes and skills leaders can develop to create open conversations, let's turn to our final example—a structural (group) process that can be used to encourage open conversations.

The 'Six Thinking Hats' process for managing meeting conversations

First, let us consider a historical story. It was the mid-1980s—the intranet was becoming popular in many large organisations, particularly banks (the internet was still in its infancy and hadn't hit the general populous yet).

We'd been called in by the IT Department of one of the major banks to help them with their strategic planning. Normally, they would have a 12-monthly update of their plan that had been developed some five years earlier. However, as they were becoming well aware, with the rapid changes that were occurring, their strategic plan was now truly out of date and a new approach was called for.

As consultants we knew very little about IT but had a few 'way-out' ideas on how to get the IT team thinking and conversing, a little differently. We introduced them to Edward de Bono's 'Six Thinking Hats'[101] which proved to be the catalyst for the development of strategies that would take the bank into the next decade and beyond.

---

101 E de Bono, 2016, *Six Thinking Hats*, Revised edition, Penguin Life Books, London.

In short, de Bono's Six Thinking Hats is a structured process to assist groups to be more creative, realistic and practical in their decision making. Note the words 'creative' and 'practical' which often seem to be diametrically opposed, used here in the same sentence. During a meeting, the team (in our case the IT Department) worked through a process of 'wearing' each of the six hats as they moved towards a decision or plan (with the IT Department, the hats were metaphorically worn, but on other occasions we have issued coloured hats).

White Hat	Red Hat	Black Hat
• Talk and think logic, data and information • Assess relevance of information • Assess accuracy of information • Separate fact from fiction	• Identify feelings and emotions • Name gut reactions • Anticipate how others might feel about this issue or decision	• Name the possible and existing negatives • Exercise caution • Make judgment and assessment of an issue or decision
Yellow Hat	**Green Hat**	**Blue Hat**
• Positive aspects of thinking • The benefits • Accept all suggestions/ thoughts, even if they seem way-out or not feasible	• Ask—What other alternatives are there? • Modify existing ideas • Provide new insights/directions • Think how this would work in the next century	• Manage the thinking process and the conversation progress • Get the best out of everyone • Focus and refocus, thinking • Keep an overview of what's happening

Table 4: Edward de Bono's 'Six Thinking Hats'.

How would this process work with an executive team? There are a number of advantages of using a process such as Six Thinking Hats:

- allows team members to say things without risk—it's merely a particular comment because of the mode of thinking generated by this hat he/she is wearing at this time;
- creates an awareness that there are multiple perspectives on the issue at hand;
- provides a convenient mechanism for 'switching gears';
- leads to more creative thinking;
- improves the quality of the conversation and ultimately, improves decision making; and
- provides executive teams with practice at managing the process of conversations.

Setting the tone through conversation tactics—framing and labelling

As we have emphasised, there are a number of conversation management processes executive teams can use—de Bono's Six Thinking Hats is but one. Senior teams should consider a group process that suits their purpose (for instance, 'one size does not always fit all' and despite our favourable experience with this model, it does have one shortcoming that may not suit a particular organisation's purpose. We'll discuss this potential limitation shortly).

However, whichever group process an organisation chooses to use, they all have one thing in common. They are a way of 'framing' a conversation, or 'labelling' certain behaviours that are easy to use and provide a way of legitimising various and different viewpoints around the table—a sharing of knowledge. Juliet Bourke refers to this as "a platform of acceptance that a group should discuss all six aspects of a problem to generate strong critical thinking".[102]

---

102 J Bourke, 2016, "Which Two Heads Are Better Than One", Australian Institute of Company Directors, Sydney, p 75.

As we move into Part 3 of the book, we describe further examples of conversational management tactics and strategies in addition to labelling and framing that can be extremely useful in team meetings.

Processes such as Six Thinking Hats can be used on an ongoing basis too. For example, the CEO who has used the Six Thinking Hats process at a recent strategy meeting (such as our bank IT Department example), during a subsequent meeting might say "Let's put our Green Hats on for a moment and see how we might develop a range of options on this issue". Or, when a particular team member is appearing to be overly negative on an issue, the CEO might say, "Pat, I wonder if I could ask you to take your Black Hat off for a moment. Try a White Hat approach for a few moments. If this were to work, what would be the logic behind it?"

Before we proceed, we should present an interesting side-bar to our experience with Six-Thinking Hats, and one potential limiting factor of this particular model. It comes from lawyer and consultant, Juliet Bourke. Through her many years of research and field study, Bourke and her colleagues found that whilst de Bono's thinking process is an extremely useful one for senior teams, he seemed to miss one import-ant point in this thinking process:

People seem to orient towards complex problems in one of six ways, and this gave us a starting framework to con-struct the six building blocks. In particular, even though they might have used slightly different words, we heard people talk about process, evidence, people, risks, objectives and options. (emphasis is ours)[103]

---

103 ibid.

> **Bourke's overlap with de Bono's Six Thinking Hats:**
> - Evidence = White
> - Risk = Black
> - Options = Yellow and Green
> - Process = Blue
> - Feelings = Red
>
> And a sixth, unrelated (to de Bono's) mental approach, "Outcomes".

Table 5: Bourke's six building blocks.

We believe Bourke's key finding is that people tend to have one, or at most two, dominant mental approaches to problem solving. And interestingly, Bourke found that leadership teams display a majority of 'options' and 'outcomes' (70%–75%) as their dominant mental approaches to problem solving.

If your senior team is already truly diverse in its makeup and consequently produces diversity in conversation around decision making, then a process such as the Thinking Hats, would seem suited. However, Bourke's finding now places an even greater emphasis on the need for leaders to employ conversation management processes that encourage, or should we say 'force', team members to be more expansive and critical in their thinking rather than always considering merely 'options' and 'outcomes'. After all, there is an old idiom that claims, "we do tend to recruit in our own likeness", and so we need to have ways of breaking that commonality or nexus of the senior team's thinking process and ensure a 'sharing of knowledge' at the top. Accordingly, it is essential to research and investigate a group process that will best suit your team's needs.

Conversation PROCESS (the 'how') versus conversation CONTENT (the 'what')

By now, we trust that our discussion on process and content manage-ment in conversations, and its importance in developing open and trusting conversations, has become clear. As a conclusion to this chapter, we thought it appropriate to summarise our learnings on conversation process management, particularly as it applies to executive teams.

We have combined experience of working with teams for over 60 years. Teams at all levels from the shop floor, through to middle and senior management, boards, government committees and even national sports teams. Indeed, the thousands of teams we have worked with come from all industries and many countries—some are local, some international and some 'virtual'. There are three observations we have made that are consistent across all these teams:

1. The best performing teams consistently focus on managing the process of their conversations (i.e. how they are working best together) as much and in some cases even more, than the content of their conversations (i.e. what they are aiming to achieve). With some teams, we have been amazed at what at first seems an inordinate focus on process at the expense of content, and then suddenly—everything comes together with lightning speed and they are outperforming all others.

2. Our second observation is that in the better performing teams (i.e. not the 'best' but better than average), there are at least one or two members who are good at managing the conversation process—and they are not always the leader or CEO.

3. Thirdly, those teams that consistently underperform or do not reach their full potential, place very little emphasis on process management.

Figure 10 illustrates the process management practices used by the best performing teams and decision-making groups. Proactive management of the process of communicating when working together—'the how'—improves conversation content—'the what' a group is talking about and ultimately trying to achieve.

PROCESS
the 'How' we will go about it

PLAN
- Set group objectives
- Agree how decisions will be made
- Set ground rules

PERFORM
- Involve all members
- Listen to the views of others
- Manage conflict effectively
- Keep to ground rules

MONITOR/COMMIT
- Summarise progress
- Manage individual performance
- Give one another feedback
- Commit to decisions of the group

EVALUATE
- Evaluate progress
- Review overall performance
- Manage failure
- Celebrate success

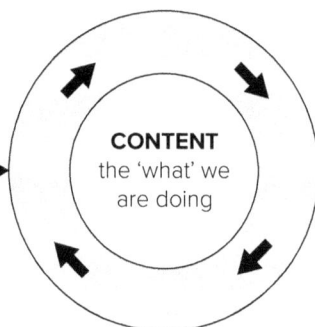

CONTENT
the 'what' we
are doing

Figure 10: Proactive process management practices improve the quality of conversation content.

The bottom line ...

Process skills impact the quality of task outcomes

- Leaders need to understand and manage 'process' issues in all their conversations—the 'how' impacts the quality of the 'what'.
- Some of the many process techniques leaders can employ include: encourage open dissent, hone in on silences, use opinion leaders to widen the debate, discuss the 'elephants in the room', generate multiple options, create an ownership culture, and give team members lead time to think on critical issues.
- Decide on and implement structured group processes (such as the Six Thinking Hats) to improve process management skills, and ultimately decision making.

2.4 Concluding comments on setting the tone through conversation

Remember when being in school and a substitute teacher would come into the room to teach? In just a few moments, students would decide whether this substitute teacher would be someone who would be strict, or if they were a person who could be walked over.

And then surprisingly (and unfortunately in our case, infrequently) this substitute teacher would set quite a different tone from either of the ones we expected—one that would set him or her up as a leader through the conversation they had with the class. In those early days, it was indeed setting the tone at the top through interesting and meaningful conversation.

It's just such an example that leaders need to set if the knowledge of all team members is to be shared and used to the organisation's advantage. One of the key principles (and often the hardest to admit and commit to) is to 'disclose', meaning to give of oneself so that others will follow the lead. In Part 2, where conversation is firmly in the spotlight, we believe the topic covered that will bring the fastest and longest lasting results is, disclosure. It's even been given a technical term by the psychologists—'reciprocity'—described as a 'social norm of responding to a positive action with another positive action'. In fact, studies have shown that reciprocity overpowers liking.'[104] Setting the tone through conversations that include disclosure is one of the most powerful tools a leader has in his or her toolbox (You may recall the example we gave earlier of the CEO who "disclosed" to the HR team).

Coming up in Part 3, we move to the specifics of conversation—the words we choose that help make the impact we intend. Most often in conversations, we use words either consciously or subconsciously that

---

104 D Regan, 1971, "Effects of a favor and liking on compliance", *Journal of Experimental Social Psychology*, Vol 6, p 627–39.

we have become comfortable with using over many years—they are 'front of mind'. In Part 3, we show how some commonly used words can alter both the tone and the outcome of conversations leaders have, either positively or negatively, and how using certain words and phrases can improve conversations leading to the development of beneficial relationships.

BENEFICIAL RELATIONSHIPS
are built on
EFFECTIVE CONVERSATIONS

EFFECTIVE CONVERSATIONS
are built on
*ENCOURAGING AND
AFFIRMATIVE LANGUAGE*

**ENCOURAGING AND
AFFIRMATIVE LANGUAGE**
is built on
USING POSITIVE WORDS

PART 3

SETTING THE TONE THROUGH WORD CHOICE

We start Part 3 by showing how many of the common everyday words we use, such as 'don't', 'but' and 'yes, but' have a negative impact on leader conversations. Part 3 also shows how a leader's personal language, the language they were born into and perhaps grew up with, can influence their thinking and behaviour. From there, we move to how leaders can apply commonly used conversation improvers such as 'metaphors' and perhaps less common or well-known strategies such as 'labelling', 'priming' and 'triangulating'. Part 3 concludes with a short chapter on how various types or categories of words impact the functioning of the brain, to demonstrate how positive word choice can help keep a leader mentally fit.

3.1 How words leaders use impact behaviour

The impact on behaviour of giving positive images of what you want a person to understand or do rather than using a negation such as the use of 'don't' in front of what you want them not to think about or do, was illustrated in the section on written communication with the

95

negative CNN versus the positive Intel examples of media policies: "Don't speak to the media without permission" (CNN) versus "When you speak to the media, do the following ..." (Intel).

Let's explain further the impact of words on behaviour with a simple example, which involves the impact of positive words used by a parent in a situation many readers may have encountered.

A mother enters a gift shop with two young children of about three or four years of age. At that age, the only thing children want to do is to touch and feel things—to explore. The store is stacked full of open shelves with many delicate and breakable items such as glass and chinaware. If you were the parent in this situation, what would be your natural instruction to your children?

Many of us would probably use the instruction "Don't touch anything". Those readers who are parents, will probably remember the many necessary corrective actions or commands which need to follow the instruction of "Don't touch anything". This instruction rarely works. Why?

By using an instruction such as "Don't touch anything" the only *visual image* the child receives is 'touch anything'. Although we put the word 'don't' in front of 'touch anything', the brain is unable to make a visual image for the word 'don't'. The child is left with the image of the act of touching anything and knowing children of that age, probably touching everything!

Not only is there no image for 'don't', it creates a further problem. The brain has to effectively double-process. This takes extra energy and effort and the human brain has evolved to conserve energy whenever possible. In our example, the child has to think "What does he/she NOT want me to do?" as well as "What does he/she want me TO DO instead?" This can be very confusing and difficult, especially if a person does not know or understand the 'to do' part of an instruction or has difficulty accessing it in memory.

Let's return to the mother and her children. Instead of saying

"Don't touch anything" surprisingly she said "Kids, keep your hands in your pockets until we get back outside this shop". Here the image is of 'putting hands in pockets'. There is no mention of touching anything. Not only has she given them a positive instruction of what to do, she has also put a finish-time on it, "until we get back outside this shop".

In a similar way, presentations and explanations can be confusing when leaders with different backgrounds and expertise may not have experience or understanding of the 'to do' part of an issue and no access to it in memory. For example, how does an engineer explain the risk in a bridge building project appropriately to a finance officer? How does the CIO explain cyber security risks to a CEO who is expert in many areas although has no background in computer science? Are the explanations weighted toward risks that should not be taken or toward what positive steps need to be taken?

Common everyday sayings used between the CEO and senior management, can impact the behaviour of others, for example:

- When a leader makes a suggestion, which seems appropriate, another executive may say "Why not?", meaning, "Why not do it." A more positive response would be, "Sounds good, how would that work?" When a leader hears "Why not?", although it's intended as an affirmation of the suggestion, the brain is subconsciously alerted to the potential negative consequences and this happens in a nanosecond. "Sounds good" on the other hand, in addition to being a positive response, can lead to a comment or further discussion on why the executive thinks the suggestion 'sounds good'.

- A negation that one hears almost every day is 'no problem' or 'no worries'. The words 'problem' and 'worries' immediately alert the brain to a potential difficulty and the 'fight or flight' response is activated. Instead, when a leader is asked to take some action to which he/she agrees, a more positive response could be "Definitely!"

- And when one executive asks another, "How is it going?" a response we often hear is "Can't complain". Once again, the brain is automatically alerted and past memories of complaining and complaints are subconsciously searched. A more positive response would be, "Fine", or "Everything's going well, thanks".

In addition to negations such as 'don't' being quite ineffective when given as an instruction, they can also be quite dangerous and even costly, as a government department found out recently in a lengthy compensation battle after a staff member's desk and chair heights were changed without the knowledge of the staff member.[105]

The ergonomic desk change led to a lengthy public service compensation case. The change to the employee's desk and chair height happened even though there was a sign on the employee's work station reading 'do not adjust or sit at this desk'. According to the press report, the initial compensation offered and the ensuing 18-month legal tussle. Through the Appeals Tribunal, demonstrated the potential liabilities of hot-desking where multiple workers use the same work station at different times. However, the real cause of the problem—the sign— read 'do not adjust or sit at this desk' and people 'hot-desking' at that desk, sub-consciously read the sign as 'adjust or sit at this desk'. What if the sign had read 'this seat is reserved for the use of 'x' only, or 'please advise 'x' if you must use this seat'?

Whilst this may seem a simple case of using inappropriate word signage at a local employee level, it has two important implications for leaders:

---

105 "'Do not adjust or sit at this desk': Tax office worker given compensation payments for TWO YEARS after 'hot-desk' colleague changed the height of her chair", *Daily Mail*, 18 February, http://www.dailymail.co.uk/news/article-2957692/Do-not-adjust-sit-desk-note-written-tax-office-worker-lead-two-YEARS-compensation-payments-colleague-ignored-changed-height-chair.html, (accessed 29 March 2018).

- Word choice in policies that say what employees can't do rather than what they can do (as was shown earlier in the CNN and Intel policy examples), filters down through the organisation. Such policies, written by managers reporting to the senior team, can be influenced by the stakeholder statements of intent set by the CEO and senior team, particularly those relating to frontline employees. The 'How we intend to be seen' statements set by the CEO and senior team for each of its six key stakeholders, are transformed into policies and procedures with appropriate goals and performance standards that demonstrate what is happening when each statement of intent is being satisfied, that is the positive behaviour expected.

- An organisation culture which has a negative tone, brought about through policies that tell employees what they can't do, can result in inappropriate behaviour and perhaps ultimately in unwanted public scrutiny.

And a final newsworthy example of the challenges presented by negative language is the 'ugly truth' story[106] about Facebook's goal of connecting people. An internal memo written by Facebook Senior Vice President, Andrew Bosworth, stated:

The ugly truth is that we believe in connecting people so deeply that anything that allows us to connect more people more often is 'de facto' good … I know a lot of people don't want to hear this. Most of us have the luxury of working in the warm glow of building products consumers love, but make no mistake, growth tactics are how we got here.[107]

---

106 R Cellan-Jones, 2018, "Facebook 'ugly truth' growth memo haunts firm", *BBC News*, 30 March 2018, https://www.bbc.com/news/technology/43594959, (accessed 31 March 2018).

107 ibid.

The story has been widely reported, many people read it, and the reputation of Facebook took another hit in the media. Bosworth followed up the posting of his memo to the press with a tweet that again used a negation:

'I *don't* agree with the post today and I *didn't* agree with it even when I wrote it.'[108]

What one's brain initially processes when reading Bosworth's original memo is a message about 'growth at all costs', followed by the message that 'Bosworth agreed with what he said'. Then the two messages have to be decoded to try to understand that growth at all costs was being put forth as a subject for debate. Mark Zuckerberg, Chairman and CEO of Facebook, is reported as saying "we never believed the end justifies the means."[109] This, of course, confuses the issue all over again.

By now we trust that the picture is becoming clear. Yes, words can certainly impact the behaviour of others and we can wield a great deal of influence by getting the words right.

How the words leaders hear affect their behaviour

We've shown that using certain words and phrases and eliminating the word 'don't' can be useful in helping to directly influence the behaviour of others. Over time, it can also vicariously help deliver a more positive

---

108 J B White, "Good even if 'someone dies in a terror attack'", *Independent*, 30 March 2018, https://www.independent.co.uk/life-style/gadgets-and-tech/news/facebook-vice-president-andrew-bosworth-leaked-memo-the-ugly-growth-a8280771.html, (accessed 20 June 2018).

109 L Segarra, 2018, "Mark Zuckerberg defends Facebook after a controversial memo called for growth at all costs", *Time*, 30 March 2018, http://time.com/5222179/mark-zuckerberg-defends-facebook-after-a-controversial-memo-called-for-growth-at-all-costs/, (accessed 31 March 2018).

personal outlook. However, it's not only the words leaders use, but also the words they hear that may impact their behaviour.

We'll start with providing some interesting research around commonly used every day words and their impact on behaviour, then show how this might apply to leaders.

For example, researchers at the universities of Neuchatel, Zurich and Heidelberg tested 83 male students between the ages of 20–27 in a high-end driving simulator.[110] As they 'drove' music and words were played as if they were listening to the car radio. Unbeknown to the subjects, the researchers were testing to see if certain words had any impact on their driving behaviour. Astonishing results: When the young male drivers heard masculine-sounding words such as 'muscle' or 'beard', they speeded up and the speed remained faster till the end of the driving session. Conversely, when they heard feminine-sounding words such as 'pink' and 'lipstick' they slowed down. There were no speed differences when the male subjects heard neutral words. These results were statistically significant. This study provides compelling evidence of the impact that hearing certain words can have on our behaviour.

The impact of gender sounding words

Not only do certain words, such as the 'gender sounding' words described in the 'driving' experiments affect a leader's own behaviour, the impact can also be felt by others around them. Recall the Domain (Fairfax Media) story mentioned earlier—hearing the regular use of words such as 'doll' and 'babe' was cited by a whistle-blower as evidence of lack of respect for women in a tough, hard-driving male environment.

---

110 M Schmidmast, et al, 2008, "Masculinity causes speeding in young men", *Accident Analysis & Prevention*, Vol 40, No 2, p 840–42.

Interestingly, Dr Judith Baxter, Lecturer in Applied Linguistics at the University of Reading, argues, that both male and female business leaders are equally able to switch between assertive 'masculine' styles and co-operative 'feminine' styles of speaking. However, while males are often praised for their use of co-operative speech, women are criticised for using direct or assertive speech. Terms like 'scary', 'bossy', 'aggressive' or 'hard' are used against them in negative or prejudicial ways—interestingly, both by male and female colleagues alike. This is particularly important for leaders to consider as organisations move toward more diverse workplaces. Baxter goes on to point out:

Women are involved in 'additional conversational work' to counter the effects of being typecast as 'irrational females'. While their developed linguistic skills can be very useful tools, the efforts required in exhibiting these skills is also potentially stressful, time-consuming, and undermining for the self.[111]

How a leader's word choice can positively impact both themselves and others

Keeping the above results in mind, i.e. the negative impact of words such as 'don't' and the many gender sounding words we use regularly, how can leaders work to create a positive climate in their organisations?

One technique for doing so, is to use 'priming', which we've mentioned previously. Technically, priming is described as a technique whereby being exposed to one stimulus influences a response to a subsequent influence. For instance, a simple example shows that someone who reads the word 'yellow' is subsequently faster to recognise the word 'banana'. So, leaders need to learn to consciously

---

111 J Baxter, 2017, "Resolving a gender and language problem in women's leadership: Consultancy research in workplace discourse", *Discourse and Communication*, Vol 11, No 2, p 141–59.

'prime' in a positive way rather than rely on people's subconscious. To consider how to achieve this, it is first necessary to explore a number of examples researchers have used previously in other contexts.

In 1996, researchers John Bargh, Peter Gollwitzer and their colleagues had subjects play a resource dilemma game.[112] The game involved subjects competing against others in a simulated fishing contest from a community pond with the aim of catching as many fish as possible, maximising profits (they were paid for the fish they caught) and winning the game. The challenge however, was that players could only take out so many fish before the pond became depleted; each player then had to decide whether to take a fish or put it back for the betterment of the community.

Unbeknown to the subjects they were primed in a number of different ways (Barch, Gollwitzer and colleagues actually carried out many variations of this experiment, as they were also interested in the effects of goal setting on behaviour, however, here we look at just three of their variations). Prior to the experiment the first group was given a series of random words from which they had to construct sentences. A second group was given a series of scrambled words that all stressed cooperation such as 'helpful', 'support', 'cooperative', 'fair', and 'share' from which they had to construct sentences. A third group was given no pre-reading nor sentence construction but were given explicit instructions that they must cooperate in the game if they were to be successful.

Bargh and Gollwitzer discovered that the simple act of reading and constructing sentences with cooperative words beforehand (priming) had a remarkably powerful effect on the subsequent behaviour of the participants. Specifically, the participants who used synonyms for

---

112 J Bargh, 2006, "What have we been priming all these years? On the development, mechanisms, and ecology of nonconscious social behaviour", *European Journal of Social Psychology*, Vol 36, p 147–68.

'cooperative' in their priming sentences returned 25 per cent more fish to the community pond than the people who were not exposed to these words.

Perhaps even more impressive was the fact that these cooperation-primed participants returned the exact same number of fish on average as participants who were explicitly primed in their instructions to act cooperatively.

The evidence is clear—the words we use not only influence others but can actually influence our own behaviour. What does that mean for leaders? How does it apply to setting the tone from the top? Does it mean that leaders have to be more careful with the words they use and when they use them? Potentially. Consider the discussion in the Introduction about locus of control. For leaders who want to become more internally focussed and take more responsibility for their own development, the answer is to start using positive words and sentences. For those who want to influence the senior leadership team, they should consider conversing with them using positive words and sentences on a regular basis.

However, as a starting point this requires some form of self-evaluation, which in essence is hard to do. How do you know or how can you tell if you are using more negative words than positive words or vice versa?

One way is to ask someone else for their opinion. However, this can be quite tedious and may be a little intimidating. In the meantime, it is useful to become aware of some of the more common negative and positive words that people use so that as a leader, you can make decisions about which words to use and which to avoid. A simple way to do this is to examine your emails, both sent and received over the past few months. What words are used most often?

For some time, people in certain occupations have been aware of the positive and negative impact of words when interacting with others. For instance, in the sales profession and amongst skilled negotiators, it's long been known that some sentences are written to convey an affirmative or negative connotation in order to influence or persuade a reader. Specific words are chosen to construct this affirmative or negative tone. The words purposely chosen to express a negative idea are sometimes referred to as a 'negation'. The following lists are common negative nouns, adverbs and verbs used to illustrate a negative idea.

Negative words:	Negative adverbs:	Negative verbs:
No	Hardly	Doesn't
Not	Scarcely	Isn't
None	Barely	Wasn't
No one		Shouldn't
Nobody		Wouldn't
Nothing		Couldn't
Neither		Won't
Nowhere		Can't
Never		Don't

Table 6: Examples of negations.

Research indicates that the overuse or regular use of a number of these negations not only influences our behaviour (as has been shown in the research) but can actually influence the way in which we perceive the world—in a positive or negative way. Mark Waldman and Andrew Newberg in *Words Can Change Your Brain*,[113] report that in addition to causing a negative perception of how we see the world, negative words have a damaging effect on our brain. For example, flashing the word 'NO' on a screen for less than one second produces a sudden release of dozens of stress-producing hormones and neuro-transmitters in the people watching the screen. These chemicals immediately interrupt the normal functioning of our brain, impairing

113 A Newberg, and M Waldman, 2012, *Words Can Change Your Brain*, Penguin Group, New York.

logic, reason, language processing, and communication. However, using positive words (for example flashing the word 'YES' on a screen) does not have the opposite and immediate positive affect on our brain. Similar studies have shown that because negative words are so harmful to the brain, we need to produce a minimum of five positive words to counterbalance the harmful impact of one negative word.[114]

This first chapter in Part 3 therefore, outlines some of the simple word choices leaders can make by eliminating many of the harmful negations from their conversations. As we progress through further chapters in Part 3, we'll outline alternative positive word choices available to leaders. Then in Part 4 (Managing Challenging Conversations) we will build on these findings of the impact of negations and provide further practical examples that show how using positive words, phrases and language, can also alter one's locus of control.

The bottom line ...

Language impacts relationships

In our relationships, negative language can add an unnecessary barrier. Sometimes negative language even causes conflict and confrontation where none is desired.

Leaders need to reflect on and practice phrasing sentences in the positive, to have maximum effect and impact:

- One way that leaders can display a more positive tone, is by eliminating common negations such as 'Don't'.
- Leaders should be aware of the impact gender sounding words such as 'scary', 'bossy', 'aggressive' or 'hard' have on conversations.
- Leaders should learn the technique of 'priming' to help make themselves more positive and promote positivity in conversations with senior management.

Eliminating negations also enhances a leader's Internal locus of control.

---

114 A Newberg and M Waldman, 2012, "The Most Dangerous Word in the World: This word can damage both the speaker's and listener's brain!", *Psychology Today*, 1 August, www.psychologytoday.com/blog/words-can-change-your-brain./201207/the-most-dangerous-word-in-the world, (accessed 23 June 2018).

3.2 The impact of a leader's 'personal' language

In the previous chapter, we discussed eliminating the word 'don't' and its impact on influencing others. We also saw how certain words can influence our own behaviour. Let's go one step further and see how our mother tongue (described by us as one's 'personal' language) might also influence a leader's behaviour.

M Keith Chen, Associate Professor of Economics at UCLA,[115] has found an association between the language people use (their native tongue) and their ability to save for their retirement, to resist obesity, and to stop smoking. Now if that's true, then this discovery is very powerful!

By the way they are structured, certain languages force us to express what we have done, are doing, or plan to do, in the past, present or future tenses (the delineation is particularly evident between present and future). Such languages are often referred to by linguists as hard future tense languages (FTL) and because of this people clearly separate present and future events, for example; "it rained yesterday" (past), "it is raining today" (present) and "it will rain tomorrow" (future). This tends to make the future seem far more distant to the speaker. English is one such hard FTL language, French is another.

Soft FTL languages (illustrated in Figure 11) such as Finnish, German, Dutch, Flemish and Chinese (both Mandarin and Cantonese) do not make such hard distinctions between today and the future: In **Figure 11** below it rained yesterday" (past), "it rains today" (present), "it rains tomorrow" (future).

As an economist, M Keith Chen was originally investigating people's savings habits in comparison with the language they spoke.

---

115 M K Chen, 2013, "The Effect of Language on Economic Behavior: Evidence from Savings Rates, Health Behaviors, and Retirement Assets", *American Economic Review 2013*, 103(2): 690–731, http://www.anderson.ucla.edu/faculty/keith.chen/papers/Final_AER13.pdf, (accessed 29 March 2018).

For example, in English – a Hard Future Language – someone might say:

"It rained yesterday"   "It is raining today"   "It will rain tomorrow"

Whereas, in German – a Soft Future Language – someone might say:

"Es regnete gestern"   "Es regnet heute"   "Es regnet morgen"
It rained yesterday   It rains today   It rains tomorrow

Figure 11: Example of Hard and Soft Future Tense Language.

Chen's hypothesis is that because people speaking hard future languages (such as French and English—he called these 'futured' languages) have to viscerally separate the present from the future with the words they use, find it harder to save money. That is every time they talk about the future, they disassociate the future from the present thus making it seem more different and more distant. For example, in expressing a desire to save more, futured language speakers might say "I will start saving tomorrow".

Soft future language (which Chen calls 'futureless') speakers however, because they do not instinctively separate the present from the future in the words they use, would find it easier to save. It's just a seamless process to them, as they would say "I'm saving" (they use exactly the same phrase whether they are talking about what they are doing now, or what they intend to do).

To illustrate how this might work in a business context, some years ago we developed a New Business Pack to help small businesses get started. When doing the research for the project, we found that one of the major reasons for failure amongst small businesses is the lack of planning. In addition to the lack of formal planning, this included the lack of taking a future oriented approach. Although many small business operators see the need for planning, they just tend to avoid it—and if they do make a plan, they often fail to follow it. So in the New Business Pack we studiously avoided using the words 'plan' or 'planning'. It may have been that we were subconsciously taking a 'soft futured' approach. If developing the pack today, we would now be far more conscious of the need to seamlessly mix the present with the future in the language used.

In Chen's studies,[116] he found that futureless language speakers, whose language construct allows them to express a future action as if it is already happening, save up to 30 per cent more per annum than their futured language counterparts. The figure for retirement savings was 25 per cent higher for futureless speakers. This difference held true even in countries where there was more than one language spoken in different parts of the country (e.g. French and Flemish in Belgium, French and German in Switzerland).

What seems to be happening with futureless language speakers is that the brain is being 'tricked' into thinking that something is already happening by the language being used.

How leaders can implement the futureless concept

Leaders can start implementing the futureless concept by simply rephrasing things they are planning to do or commence, by expressing

---

116 K Chen, "Could language affect your ability to save money?", *Ted Talk*, http://www.ted.com/talks/keith_chen_could_your_language_affect_your_ability_to_save_money?language=en#t-279198, (accessed 29 March 2018).

them as if they have already started. So, one can rephrase the way you describe the future as being similar to the present, for example:

- "We will start planning for the APRA inspection next week" now becomes "We are planning the APRA inspection."
- "I will start work on that analysis tomorrow" becomes "I'm working on that analysis."
- "We should start our strategic planning session much earlier this year" becomes "We are now planning the future."

The bottom line ...

Language impacts movement toward achievement of future goals

The futureless concept is quite easy to understand, yet a little more difficult to implement. After all, if as a leader you are a natural futured language speaker, it's something you've done almost since the time you learned to talk, so it may be quite a tall order. However, if you persist by using some of the techniques in this section, it will start to make a difference in the way you approach goal setting, problems, challenges and, dare we say, the future.

3.3 Metaphors and the use of 'and' as influencing tools for leaders

In meetings, one can often hear phrases like:

- "Let's look into that" (like a bucket you 'look into').
- "Moving forward" (as in fast-forwarding your future-life movie, in your mind).
- "Set up a company" (as in set up the dominoes).
- "It's a lot to take in?" (as in gathering things).
- "Let's call off the ..." (as in 'call off the meeting' or 'call off the dogs').
- "We are going to roll out the new strategy" (as in a carpet being laid across a new floor).

Yes, these are metaphors. Used constructively by leaders in conversations, they can be powerful tools for setting the tone from the top. Let's explore why.

Most leaders would use metaphors in every conversation they have. Some researchers suggest that we use about six metaphors every minute.[117] They are an excellent way of getting complicated messages across or merely speeding up the communication by saying in a few words what might otherwise take paragraphs. Notice too that a metaphor is nearly always visual. So not only does a metaphor shorten the communication process, it adds an image that triggers the visual part of the brain and enhances the prospect of the message being understood more clearly. Phrases such as metaphors that immediately access the visual part of the brain are particularly important for effective communication as most languages have words that have more than one meaning; for example, in English it's been estimated as high as 80 per cent of words have more than one meaning.[118] Accordingly, it is useful to understand their complexity.

In *The Cambridge Handbook of Metaphor and Thought*,[119] author Raymond W Gibbs quotes some of the compelling scientific evidence that demonstrates the power of metaphors in communication, summarised here as:

- Metaphors are conceptual mappings; they are part of the conceptual system (of the brain) and not merely linguistic expressions.
- There is a huge system of fixed metaphorical mappings, which means these are universally understood.
- This system exists physically in our brains so that when we hear a metaphor it is easily accessed in the system.
- Because certain metaphors are grounded via previous correlated experiences, they make immediate sense, for example 'more' is up (grounded via the correlation between quantity and verticality—you pour more water in the glass and the level goes up).

---

117 B Bowdle, and D Gentber, 2005, "The Career of Metaphor", *Psychological Review*, Vol 112, No 1.

118 S Gennari, et al, 2007, "Context-dependent interpretation of words: Evidence for interactive neural processes", *NeuroImage*, Vol 35, No 3, p 1278–86.

119 R Gibbs, 2008, "The Cambridge Handbook of Metaphor and Thought", Cambridge University Press, London.

Gibbs makes a very important point: "Much of our reasoning makes use of conceptual metaphors." So while it's easy to see how metaphors improve our communication processes, it's been found that they are even more important than that because we actually think metaphorically.

In 1980 two researchers George Lakoff and Martin Johnson published *Metaphors We Live By*[120] which examined how, when and why we use metaphors. For example, we understand *control* as being UP and *being subject to control* as being DOWN. We say, "I have control *over* him", "I am *on top of* the situation", "She's at the *height* of her power" and "He ranks *above* me in strength", "He is *under* my control" and "His power is on the *decline*". Similarly, we describe love as being a physical force: "I could feel the *electricity* between us", "there were *sparks*" and "they *gravitated* to each other immediately".

But there may be even more to metaphors than we realise. James Lawley and Penny Tomkins in *Metaphors in Mind*[121] contend that the metaphors we use, while simplifying our communication can also hide deeper feelings and thoughts. They suggest that if the issue is important to us, what's behind these metaphors needs to be understood.

And in a physiological sense, a team of researchers from Emory University reported in *Brain & Language*[122] that when subjects in their laboratory read a metaphor involving texture, the sensory cortex of the brain responsible for perceiving texture through touch, became active. Metaphors such as "the singer had a velvet voice" and "he had leathery hands" roused the sensory cortex.

---

120 G Lakoff and M Johnson, 1980, Metaphors We Live By, University of Chicago Press, Chicago.

121 J Lawley, and P Tompkins, 2000, Metaphors in Mind, Developing Company Press, London, p 13.

122 S Lacey, R Stilla and K Sathian, 2012, "Metaphorically feeling: Comprehending textural metaphors activates somatosensory cortex", *Brain & Language*, Vol 120, No 3, p 416–21.

Another example that demonstrates the power of metaphor is the story of a highly regarded CEO of a global office equipment supplier. He was speaking at the annual company Christmas gathering at the beginning of summer. Everyone received the gift of a red towel with the company logo in one corner. As the towels were being handed out, he acknowledged that everyone might well be wondering why he would give them a red towel. The reason for the towel, he told them, was that he hoped they would have plenty of good times at the beach with their friends and family over the holidays. And he wanted them to take the towel to the beach, and as they spread it out on the sand, to remember that it takes millions of grains of sand to make a beach, and every grain of sand on the beach counts. Just as every person in the company counted, and every single thing each of them did added up to what the company stood for, so too all of their good actions could be likened to a great summer day at the beach.

The executive who related this story to us also used a metaphor. She said working for this leader was like sailing on a ship led by a respected captain, one who made his crew feel capable of doing their jobs and arriving safely at their destination.

How leaders can use 'clean language' in conversations

So it seems that science is telling us that using metaphors can have an impact on our thoughts, feelings and even senses. And in terms of day-to-day communication with others, Lawley and Tomkins suggest a way that the listener can also better understand what the speaker actually means when using a metaphor by applying a technique called 'clean language' to clarify.

Clean language is a questioning technique that was first used in psychotherapy and coaching. It has the client discover and develop personal symbols and metaphors without contamination or distortion through the way the questions are put. It is now being used far more widely in areas such as training, facilitation, marketing, negotiating, management and even IT.

Clean language was first developed by David Grove[123] in the 1980s as a result of his work on clinical methods for resolving clients' traumatic memories. As authors Lawley and Tompkins describe it, "He realised many clients naturally described their symptoms in metaphor and he found that when he enquired about these using their exact words, their perception of the trauma began to change."[124]

Unlike other forms of communication, such as reflective listening where the listener reflects (and in so doing often interprets) what the other person might be feeling and thinking, clean language follows a series of questions that only use the other person's **exact** words to help them define their thoughts and feelings.

To ensure the questioner stays 'clean', every question starts with 'and'. This means that the questioner must follow the 'and' with the person's exact words. It's how the questioner uses the other's exact words that gives clean language its power. Here's an example of clean questioning used in a therapeutic context:

Client: "It seems that I'm stuck with no way out."
Clean language question: "And what kind of stuck with no way out is that stuck with no way out?" Note: This phrasing may seem clumsy to the non-professional, but has been found by therapists to be most effective when phrased this way because it places emphasis on the client explaining what "stuck with no way out" is like and how it is affecting him/her.

---

123 D Grove, 2015, "The principles of clean language", 22 November 2015, https://cleanlearning.co.uk/blog/.../principles-clean-language-coaches-online-course, (accessed 29 March 2018).
124 J Lawley and P Tomkins, 2000, "Metaphors in Mind", Developing Company Press, London, p 13.

As Lawley and Tomkins suggest:

This question works with the client's metaphor of 'stuck' and only assumes that for something to be stuck it has to be stuck somewhere. When the therapist is in rapport with the metaphoric information, questions like the above make perfect sense, and clients' responses have a quality of deep introspection and self-discovery. New awareness of their own process 'updates the system' and the original neural coding will automatically begin to transform; albeit in minute ways at first.[125]

Clean language questions are then asked of the client of each subsequent response. The process ultimately accesses conflicts, paradoxes, double-binds and other 'holding patterns' which previously kept the symptoms repeating over and over rather than delve into the root cause.

Lawley and Tomkins go so far as to suggest that, "… whatever a person says, sees, hears, feels or does, as well as what they imagine, can be used to comprehend and reason through metaphor".[126]

Now in a business context, one could also easily see how clean language (or an adaptation of it) could be readily used. For example, in a tense negotiation when the other person says, "We seem to be stuck here with no way out", a leader could easily ask "and what kind of stuck is that stuck with no way out?" The resulting conversation might very well describe exactly the sticking point and most importantly, what it means to the other person.

All 'and' questions pick up on the metaphor the other person is using and find out what's behind it, for example:
- "And that <u>bottleneck</u> is like what bottleneck?"
- "And that <u>roadblock</u> is like what roadblock?"

---

125 ibid, p 60.
126 ibid, p 6.

- "And that <u>treading water</u> is like what treading water?"
- "And that <u>impasse</u> is like what impasse?"
- "And that <u>mind-set</u> is like what mind-set?"

So too in day-to-day conversations we can see how metaphors can improve the communication process. There should be one note of caution though; metaphors can be culturally specific, so when purposely using a metaphor, choose your metaphor carefully when speaking with others from a different culture. There can also be cultural differences in the language used between English speaking countries, for example Australia and the US or the US and Great Britain.

To help you become familiar with metaphors here are some further examples:

- *We bought it off the shelf.*
- *It is tailor made for us.*
- *I need a new technique for my toolbox.*
- *We are being crushed by the weight of legislation.*
- *We must defend our market share.*
- *We're going through a stormy phase.*
- *We have to construct a new plan.*
- *I can't digest all these facts.*
- *We were sprouting new ideas all over the place.*
- *The senior management must move on if they don't want to be left behind.*
- *Our values are at the heart of this organisation.*
- *We have given birth to a new generation of products.*
- *We've buried our head in the sand about the competition.*
- *The books are looking pretty healthy.*

And here's a great example from a CEO who really understood how important metaphors can be when getting a message across. In terms of the importance of good communication in an organisation, he was asked; "Can you justify communication as a return on investment?" He responded; "Enormous! We can move faster, jump higher, dive deeper and come up drier than anybody else in the business. When we hang a left, everyone goes left. It gives us an enormous ability to work as a team. Other companies in our industry are yet to work that out".

Did you get a feeling of excitement and want to learn more about the communication process in his organisation? Hearing his colourful metaphorical explanation, we certainly did.

However, there can also be some limitations to the impact of metaphors if the metaphor has become dated or overused (where the meaning is understood, but the impact on a particular part of the brain is lessened). For instance, some scientists[127] have contended that figures of speech such as 'a rough day' are so familiar that they are treated simply as words and no more, that is while still metaphors they've lost the impact they may have had originally. So using a metaphor such as 'at the end of the day' to describe an ultimate outcome, no longer conjures up in our brain the picture of a beautiful sunset topping off a wonderful day—they're just words.

Yet there are also some very famous metaphors that stand the test of time and provide instant meaning, for example 'No man is an island'. Although originally from a poem by John Donne written in 1623, 'No man is an island' has come to be used as a metaphor for 'the need for cooperation; for connection (with people and places)'.

Metaphors, their impact and usage have been studied for many years now by various disciplines from linguists to neuro scientists. From all the research it's clear that they play an important part in our communication.

In addition to being useful in many difficult conversations, in a future section we'll be looking at how metaphors can also improve a leader's presentations and public speaking.

---

127 A Paul, 2012, "Your brain on fiction", *New York Times*, 17 March 2012, www.nytimes.com/2012/02/Sunday/the-neuroscience-of-your-brain-on-fiction.html, (accessed 29 March 2018).

And in terms of the clean language concept, since learning about it a few years back we've been using it very successfully in both personal and business situations. It certainly does provide a far greater depth of understanding in terms of what others are saying and particularly how they are feeling, so we'd encourage leaders to try it.

The bottom line ...

The power of using metaphors in communication

We all use metaphors every time we communicate, be it face-to-face or via some other means. Mostly we are not aware of using them as they seem to come from nowhere but are there when we need them. The aim of this chapter has been to raise the awareness of the importance of metaphors and how we can use them more knowingly to improve our communication intent and our understanding of the meaning or feeling behind what others are saying.

Words are powerful, and leaders harness this power when they use metaphors. The use of metaphors does three things:

- captures attention;
- creates connections with other people; and
- simplifies complex ideas.

Because metaphors 'seem to come from nowhere' leaders are encouraged to develop a store of metaphors they can use in different situations, for example around financial or forecasting discussions. It is also a good idea to now start listening consciously for the metaphors other CEOs and senior managers use, and their impact on the conversation and its outcomes.

Leaders are also encouraged to practice the skill of using clean language by putting 'and' in front of the metaphor another person is using to uncover the true meaning behind the metaphor.

3.4 How leaders use words, metaphors and actions to affect feelings

We've seen how words and phrases, and particularly metaphors, can impact our behaviour and thinking, but what about feelings? Does what we say also impact how we feel? Do feelings play a part in work conversations?

Consider the following example of an exchange between the CEO and Sales Director who has just reported the loss of a major sales contract at an executive team meeting (we've described the tone of voice expressed by each to enable you to gauge the emotions being displayed):

CEO (in a judging tone): Isn't it a case of having offered the wrong price?

Sales Director (in a firm tone): No, we did our homework on this very carefully, and the decision not to renew came as a complete surprise to us and we are reviewing it again.

CEO (in a critical tone): And you are sure that it's not a mis-calculation from their side?

Sales Director (in an irritated tone): We don't know at this stage; that's one of the difficulties in this matter. There is not a clear reason for their decision.

CEO (in a judging tone): Don't you think we should know? What will I tell the board?

Note here that the CEO started the conversation with a question that is not really a question, "Isn't it the case." In choosing words such as "Isn't it ...?" or "Sure it's not ...?' or "Don't you think ...?" leaders (and in our example it's the CEO) automatically develop a tone that is critical, accusatory, or perhaps condescending—and that tone immediately elicits a strong emotional response in the recipient. In our example, whilst the Sales Director may have expected a reasoned and logical discussion on the possible reasons for the loss, the CEO has immediately made his/her critical feelings about the matter felt.

The Sales Director trying to remain calm and professional, responds to this criticism in a firm manner with reason and logic "... we are reviewing it ..." and "... came as a complete surprise ..."

The CEO continues in an accusatory tone, "And you are sure …?" Which raises the Sales Director's level of emotion as he/she has just laid out all that is known about the situation, "… We don't know". It's likely that now that both the CEO and Sales Director are emotionally charged, little constructive dialogue will eventuate—at least not until both parties' emotional levels have subsided.

As Brundin and Nordqvist (whose research entailed listening to and analysing meeting conversations) suggest:

Being aware, and able to understand the subtle working of emotions in meeting processes are crucial for being an effective group member.[128]

How does a leader become aware of the emotions he/she is displaying, and most importantly, if these emotions are negatively impacting the conversation and its outcome, how does the leader mitigate such an impact?

Once again, it all has to do with the words a leader uses when he/she hears, sees and feels the emotional levels rising in the other's language, tone and perhaps facial expressions. To gauge an understanding of how this might be managed, with some simple word choice, we turn to a LinkedIn posting by Tony Robbins.[129] Robbins recounted a heated negotiation he and two partners had been engaged in with another group. Following the negotiation, one of Robbins' partners was furious about

---

128 E Brundin and M Nordqvist, 2008, "Beyond facts and figures: The role of emotions in boardroom dynamics", *Corporate Governance*, Vol 16, No 4, July, https://onlinelibrary.wiley.com/doi/pdf/10.1111/j.1467-8683.2008.00688.x, (accessed 4 June 2018).

129 T Robbins, 2012, "Change your words, change your life: The simplest tool I know for immediately transforming the quality of your life", *LinkedIn*, 26 October, https://www.linkedin.com/pulse/20121026164951-101706366-change-your-words-change-your-life-the-simplest-tool-i-know-for-immediately-transforming-the-quality-of-your-life, (accessed 24 May 2018).

how they had been treated and said so. Robbins too was frustrated and angry and said so. The third partner, while somewhat annoyed at the outcome, was relatively calm and merely described his feelings about their treatment as being "somewhat peeved". Robbins thought this was a bit weird and found the word 'peeved' rather amusing. So much so that he started to think about how using a word such as 'peeved' might change one's feelings from say anger, to bemusement. Over the next few weeks he decided to try this out.

An opportunity soon arose when he checked into a hotel one evening after midnight. Robbins had a speaking engagement next morning at 8am. The late (or early morning) check-in was not going smoothly and he was becoming annoyed—he just wanted to sleep. Instead of expressing his annoyance and perhaps mounting anger, he merely mentioned to the desk clerk he was feeling "a little bit peeved".[130] This immediately brought a smile to his face and that of the desk clerk. Robbins' annoyance subsided.

Priming to think, feel and behave differently

What's happening here? The technical term is 'embodied cognition', the idea that the mind is not only connected to the body but that the body influences the mind and is initiated by priming. We can prime ourselves (and others) to think, feel and consequently behave differently by giving instructions to the brain either consciously or subconsciously by the words we use and/or the actions we take. We've already seen an example in an earlier section where subjects were primed to act cooperatively in a fishing game, now let's look at how priming can also affect one's feelings.

Yale psychologist John Bargh is one of the foremost researchers in the area of embodied cognition. For instance one of his experiments[131]

---

130 ibid.
131 L Williams and J Bargh, 2008, "Experiencing physical warmth promotes interpersonal warmth", *Science*, Vol 322, No 5901, p 606–7.

showed that participants holding warm as opposed to cold cups of coffee were more likely to judge a confederate as more generous, caring and trustworthy after only a brief interaction. One question they were asked was how likely they would be to employ this person. Those who had held the warm cups said 'Yes' and those who held the cold cups said 'No' or 'Not sure'.

How powerful is priming—the use of words, metaphors and actions to direct our thinking and feeling? To illustrate, here are some examples of experiments that Bargh and others have carried out, all of which involved priming:

- Thinking about the future causes people to lean slightly forward while thinking about the past causes people to lean slightly backwards. *Future is Ahead.*
- Squeezing a soft ball influences people to perceive gender neutral faces as female while squeezing a hard ball influences people to perceive gender neutral faces as male. *Male is Hard, Female is Soft.*
- Those subjects who held heavier clipboards judged foreign currencies to be more valuable and their leaders to be more important. *Important is Heavy.*
- Subjects asked to think about a moral transgression like adultery or cheating on a test were more likely to request an antiseptic cloth after the experiment than those who had thought about good deeds. *Morality is Purity.*
- Subjects who read a passage about an interaction between two people were more likely to characterise it as adversarial if they had first handled rough jigsaw puzzle pieces, compared to smooth ones. *Rough is Harsh.*
- Subjects sitting in hard, cushion-less chairs during a negotiation were less willing to compromise on price than people who sat in soft, comfortable chairs. *Hard is Tough.*

In all these experiments (the subjects were not told of their purpose) while the subjects' conscious focus was on a very specific task, their subconscious was deciding on how they should feel toward everything around them. Lawrence Williams, who helped design the warm coffee cup experiment with John Bargh says: "It's no coincidence that we use the same word—warmth—to describe both a physical and an emotional experience. Somewhere in the brain, those two sensations are linked."[132]

Researchers such as Paul Ekman[133] have found too that the metaphor is based on the physiology of emotions. For example, 'happy' is up and 'sad' is down as in "I'm feeling up today" and "I'm feeling down in the dumps". It's no surprise that around the world people who are happy tend to smile and perk up while people who are sad tend to droop. If you happen to be a sports fan, take notice of a team that is losing badly—their shoulders and heads droop—their bodies are indicating how badly they feel about the situation.

Using the suffix 'ing'

In addition to using words that moderate or lessen intense and negative emotional feelings in a conversation, such as 'peeved' instead of 'furious' to reduce anger, there's another technique leaders can use to mitigate negative emotions or intensify positive ones. It's an interesting concept used in Neurolinguistics called 'Transderivational Morphology' which suggests that adding prefixes or suffixes to words results in an internal sense of movement. For example, adding 'ing' to nouns immediately increases our inner sense of movement as in 'hand → handing', 'flower → flowering', 'sleep → sleeping'. Joshua Cartright[134] suggests a simple

---

132 ibid.

133 P Ekman and R Davidson, 1994, "The nature of emotion: Fundamental questions", New York, NY, US: Oxford University Press, p 496.

134 J Cartwright, 2018, "The word is … 'unstucking': How changing your words can get your brain moving again", http://www.stevenaitchison.co.uk/blog/the-word-is%E2%80%A6-unstucking-how-changing-your-words-can-get-your-brain-moving-again%E2%80%A6/, (accessed 29 March 2018).

way of doing this—try it for yourself—that of adding the suffix 'ing' to each of the following words and saying each out loud:

- email   → emailing
- rock   → rocking
- smile   → smiling

Notice there is a real sense of movement when expressing words with 'ing', such as 'emailing', 'rocking' and 'smiling'. Adding 'ing' to some of the words we might use in general conversation when talking about our feelings, can change how we feel. For example, when you've had an interesting conversation with someone and you intend to take some positive action such as emailing them further information, instead of saying "I will email you about this" try saying "I'm emailing you about this".

Notice in this second statement "I'm emailing you about this" three things are happening:

- In your mind, the action of 'emailing' is already happening.
- Your brain experiences a sense of movement.
- Because this intention is expressed as if it's already happening (in the present tense), you feel good about it.

Recall our earlier discussion about phrasing statements concerning the future in the present tense as if they are already happening and how that has a positive impact on our actions such as saving, health activities and so on? Now there's a further reason to use this technique—it also positively impacts how we feel.

Replacing 'but' with 'and'

There's another very simple way of intensifying your feelings or making sure your positive feelings remain positive, and that's reducing the use of the word 'but' in our sentences, particularly when talking about our feelings. In a later section, we'll be discussing how the word 'but' can be a conversation buster. For the present, let's look at how eliminating 'but' from our thoughts and statements can help us feel more positive.

Day in and day out, we connect our thoughts with 'but'. In fact, it's so common we barely hear ourselves say it. That is, unless we are on the receiving end. Then the word 'but' seems to jump out at us. Consider the following statements that may be heard in a meeting and imagine how you would feel if it was aimed at you:

"I like your idea, but ..."
"That may work somewhere else, but ..."
"The CEO raises a good issue, but ..."
"I like the proposal, but what about ...?"
"You've done a good job on getting the report together, but I'd prefer to have the report a day or two earlier"
"I understand your point of view, but have you considered ...?"
"Your report is well written, but there are a few key points that need clarification"

Whenever we use the word 'but' in a sentence it tends to negate whatever has gone before it or it puts forward a counter argument/proposal. For example, a news report such as "The employment figures are good news, but only in the short-term" is typical of negating the good news on employment with the use of the word 'but'. In fact, 'but' shuts down the other person's thinking, and it becomes much harder to look at alternatives.

To test this, try saying each of these statements out loud:

"I feel great, but I've got so much to do"
"I feel great and I've got so much to do"

Feel the difference? It's highly likely that when you said the second sentence aloud, your tone went up at the end of the sentence, almost like a question, resulting in a completely different feeling to that experienced when saying the first sentence. 'And' can change one's mood.

Simply replacing 'but' with 'and' creates a striking change in connotation and can lead our conversations in an entirely different and often positive directions. That small change can make such a difference, especially in business communications.

Note the different feelings you experience when a colleague now delivers our earlier examples expressed with an 'and' rather than a 'but':

"I like your idea, and …"

"That may work somewhere else, and …"

"The CEO raises a good issue, and …"

"I like the proposal, and what about …?"

"You've done a good job on getting the report together, and I'd prefer to have the report a day or two earlier"

"I understand your point of view, and have you considered …?"

"Your report is well written, and there are a few key points that need clarification"

Not only does the recipient of the 'and' message feel more positive about the response, it forces the sender to think quite differently about their response. Indeed, they may start to think about and look for solutions (rather than problems) that will build on the original idea, and lead to more positive conversations.

We opened this book with the story of World Bank economist, Paul Romer, who was stripped of his management duties when researchers rebelled against his efforts to make them communicate more clearly, which included curbs on the use of the word 'and'. Romer admitted that it was possible he was focusing too much on precision and not enough on the feelings his messages would invoke. This is a clear example of how powerful the word 'and' can be in conversations with others; particularly in helping us understand how they are feeling. Now we have another use for 'and' in conversations with ourselves and in statements we make to others to help us feel more positive about what we are doing, saying and ultimately feeling. It also helps to promote positive feelings in the recipients of our 'and' messages.

Returning to the question posed at the start of this section; "Can what we say also impact how we feel?" The answer is a definite "Yes". It's been shown that words can make a big difference in terms of how we feel. To paraphrase Tony Robbins, he was probably on the right track to "grin and bear it".

The bottom line …

Managing emotions in communication—turning down the 'heat'

- When next you feel too emotional about a topic or the conversation in a meeting is not going the way you would like it, try replacing heavy emotional words (that are negative), such as anger, with lighter, more humorous words such as 'peeved'.
- Rephrase your commonly used statements from the future tense to the present by adding 'ing', such as "I'm emailing you on this" rather than "I will email you on this".
- Replace 'but' with 'and' when next you are refuting someone's point, or you are making a statement about two alternatives.

3.5 Eliminating words or phrases that make difficult conversations even more difficult

Think back to the last difficult, conflicting or angry conversation you observed or participated in when two people became quite emotional. What was the cause? Perhaps it was over a difference of opinion. However, while the difference of opinion may have led to the difficult conversation it was the words that were used by either or both parties that would have raised it to an emotional level.

Even if profanities were used, most probably, the word being thrown around more than any other and the one that caused the conversation to intensify into conflict was 'you' e.g. "You never do …",

"You always do/say that …", "Why don't you …?" Do any of these phrases ring any bells?

There's a problem with the word 'you' in conversations

Look at the following example given by a bank manager to a teller (this was written on a performance review, so it is a real example):

You are disorganised and as a result you don't get the work through on time. You don't seem to be really interested in getting the right results. You don't follow instructions at all well. You make too many silly mistakes in the balancing and I don't think you are really suited to the role of Teller.

How would the teller feel? Notice how many times the word 'you' is used: "You are disorganised and as a result you don't get the work through on time. You don't seem to be really interested in getting the right results. You don't follow instructions at all well. You make too many silly mistakes in the balancing and I don't think you are really suited to the role of teller."

What sort of response did this performance review assessment lead to? Well, here's the teller's reply:

I am not disorganised. I keep my desk clean for the benefit of the customers. Any mistakes I make are quickly corrected. As for my being suitable for the role, I am very customer oriented. Any uncertainty I show is not because of my skills but because of the way instructions are given. If instructions were given in a positive way by you and not as criticism, then I would be better at my job.

Why does a simple word such as 'you' cause such problems? Used in the past tense, it almost always infers blame or criticism (think

128

back to your difficult conversation—was there blame, criticism?). For example:

"You always say that."

"You never do anything I want."

"Why can't you do what I tell you?"

"You are always late."

"You always look for mistakes."

"You never give adequate information in the board papers."

"You should not push so hard. It's rude and it gets everyone upset."

"You are always so stuck on details, you need to think more strategically."

Have you heard about 'you' causing problems before? If not, it may seem a little strange; after all, we use 'you' practically every time we have a conversation, and not all conversations take a downward spiral.

Reading a LinkedIn posting recently by John Blakey (an experienced CEO and Group Chair for coaching organisation Vistage),[135] he too felt the same way. Blakey was attending a training program for CEOs which included a session on giving feedback when the facilitator listed a number of words to avoid. Blakey writes "It was the last two words that caught my eye. How can you possibly deliver feedback without using the words 'you' and 'your'? What purpose could there be in missing out these words? My colleagues in the group had similar reservations and a noisy debate struck up. Our facilitators brought the debate to a halt through a demonstration where they contrasted the following two pieces of feedback by saying:

---

135 J Blakey, 2014, "8 words to avoid when giving feedback", *LinkedIn*, 17 December, https://www.linkedin.com/pulse/8-words-avoid-when-giving-john-blakey, (accessed 29 March 2018).

- 'When the classroom has discussions, you are not really paying attention or asking questions; it seems like you are pretty detached.'
- 'In the classroom discussions, I have noticed not paying attention or asking questions; I wondered if this was detachment'."[136]

The second piece of feedback was given without the use of 'you'. Rather than 'you' as was used in the first example to confront the entire class, the focus is now very clearly on the behaviour being displayed, that of "not paying attention or asking questions". This results in the participants focusing on their behaviour rather than being affronted as they may have been with the first piece of feedback.

Getting rid of the problem word 'you' is difficult. It's very natural to say, "You are not paying attention". What do you replace it with? Look for the clue in the second example given by the facilitators above. It appears twice.

To see how an alternative to 'you' might work, let's return to the bank teller and hear how she gave feedback to the supervisor who had just roundly criticised her:

I am not disorganised. I keep my desk clean for the benefit of the customers. Any mistakes I make are quickly corrected. As for my being suitable for the role, I am very customer oriented. Any uncertainty I show is not because of my skills but because of the way instructions are given. If instructions were given in a positive way by you and not as criticism, then I would be better at my job.

This is a very good response. The teller replies in a confident, assertive manner and only uses 'you' once. Indeed, if the teller had

---

136 ibid.

deleted the words "by you", the response would have been perfect and would still make sense, without being confrontational.

What do you replace 'you' with, and how can it work in practice?

The 'I' message and how it changes the tone of a conversation

Notice that instead of using 'you' the teller has largely spoken from an 'I' perspective. Because the 'you' message implies criticism, when used as part of the feedback process it triggers the person's natural fight or flight defence mechanism. They either become quite angry and aggressive, or retreat into themselves. As a result, they tend not to accept the feedback.

Let's focus for a moment on what happens in the brain when it hears the word 'you' followed by a critical comment. All information coming into the brain passes through the thalamus which classifies information in a binary manner that is "Is this information, good or bad? Safe or dangerous?" If the thalamus decides it is 'safe' then it may get further processed elsewhere without causing any undue discomfort or stress. However, if the thalamus decides this information could be dangerous, then the brain automatically triggers the fight or flight defence mechanism and so it's easy to see why 'you' causes people to get upset so quickly. The brain is effectively telling us "this information could be harmful—be wary, fight back or get out of here!"

Returning to the teller and the manager—could the original message given by the manager to the teller have been given in a way that would have been accepted?

Yes. The answer is to avoid 'you' and use 'I' messages instead. Here's an approach the manager could have used:

Chris, thanks for taking a moment of your time to talk with me. I'm new to the role of supervisor, so I feel a bit uncomfortable with this. Please bear with me. I've noticed over the last two weeks that the batch work has not been getting through on time. This seems unusual to me, as it's normally OK. Has anything changed over the last two weeks that might have led to these delays?

Notice that as was the case with John Blakey's training facilitators, the emphasis in the manager's new message is now squarely on the issue, not the teller. In this way both participants in the discussion can focus quite rationally on solving the problem rather than debating and defending each other's words and actions.

Using 'I' messages is such an important rule, that below are some examples of how to change 'you' into 'I'. Next time you feel the need to tell someone they are annoying you, or that they've upset you, or perhaps that they've done something that concerns you, take a few moments to prepare your message. You can do this mentally or better still (if you have time) you can write out what you intend to say as an 'I' message before you have the conversation.

'you' message	'I' message
You broke your promise.	I felt let down.
You never do anything that I suggest.	I would like to see it done this way.
Why can't you do what I tell you?	I'd like my instructions followed please.
You always make that mistake.	It's disappointing to me that this mistake happens regularly.
You should not push so hard. It's rude and it gets everyone upset.	I get upset when I see people flinch sometimes during our conversations. My impressions are that they react negatively to the use of some words and phrases.
You made a mistake.	That's incorrect. I'd like to see it done this way.

'you' message	'I' message
You should have called earlier.	I'd like to get a call in plenty of time so that I can ...
Why didn't you call us when you found out about the changes?	I would like to hear about this sooner so that I can make the changes in plenty of time.
You shouldn't tell stories out of school.	I think telling stories that are not true about someone is unfair because others will believe the stories and dislike the person for the wrong reasons.
You have to file these forms on time.	I need to have these forms completed on time.
Your report was not handed in on time last week, which made me look very bad in the meeting.	I was disappointed that I did not get the report on time. This made it very hard for me during the meeting.
Your performance is not up to standard.	I'm disappointed that the performance standards we agreed to are not being met.
You have not met one of the key objectives we set at the start of the period.	I'm disappointed that all of the key objectives we set at the start of the period have been not been met.

Table 7: Examples of turning 'you' into 'I'.

The 'I' message—can 'you' ever be used in a difficult situation?

'I' messages are powerful, effective and positive, but is there any danger in using 'I' messages?

Yes, they can seem manipulative if they are inappropriately combined with 'you'. For example, "I feel unhappy that you are late" on the surface seems like a good 'I' message. While the words "I feel unhappy" are legitimate because they are expressing only your feelings, they become impotent and even blameful when the words "you are late" are added. In this case the person may now feel even more responsible for how you are feeling about their lateness. As a result, they are most likely to become defensive.

The manipulative use of 'I' messages becomes particularly unhelpful when there is a power or authority difference between the two people, for example when used by a CEO or a manager with an employee. We'll explore some of these with specific examples in Part 4.

The best way of ensuring that you get the 'I' message correct, is to follow four simple guidelines:

1. Describe the behaviour:

   e.g. *"When managers ignore me ..."*

   Make sure the word 'you' is omitted—use only 'I', 'me', 'my' or 'mine'.

2. Define the feeling it is causing:

   e.g. *"... I feel isolated ..."*

   Make sure it is only your feeling.

3. Define the effect the behaviour has on you:

   e.g. *"... because it starts to weaken my self-assurance."*

   Make sure it is only the impact it is having on you, not others (you can't speak for them).

4. Use 'you' only in the future sense:

   e.g. *"What can you do to help get managers to include me in the discussion?"*

   Note that 'you' is always used in a question about the future and is almost always a call for help.

The complete message, *"When managers ignore me, I feel isolated because it starts to weaken my self-assurance. What can you do to help get managers to include me in the discussion?"*, now shows that a constructive, non-blameful and supportive conversation is likely to follow.

The 'I' Message—are there any exceptions?

Can there be any exceptions to these guidelines? For example, is it possible to use 'you' in the present or past tense?

Using 'you' in the past tense as in "You've made that mistake a lot" is a definite no-no. Note here that we are talking about difficult conversations where our comment or opinion is likely to be negative or at the very least, something we or they will not like. In these cases, 'you' used in the past tense will infer criticism or blame. So 'you' should only be used in the future tense. And it's almost always as a request for help, guidance or assistance. For example, "What can you do to help get this report completed on time?" We've seen the logic that used in the past tense 'you' can infer criticism or blame, but the future hasn't happened. We can't change the past, but we can decide (together) on the future.

And while not quite as damaging as using 'you' in a critical way, using 'you' to give positive news can sometimes be problematic because it can cause embarrassment. For example, it's easier for a person to accept praise when we say, "I really like the way that project was completed—it was correct and on-time" rather than "You did a great job on that project".

However, there is one exception to our guidelines, and that's using 'you' in the present tense; but only in the present tense and only in some extenuating circumstances. For example, when we perceive that a good friend, or close colleague has a problem, the temptation is to say something like "What's wrong?" to which they will invariably respond "Nothing". One way of overcoming this barrier is to use an 'I' message as a question. For example, "I get the impression that you are unhappy. Am I right?" Although we have used a 'you', notice here that the emphasis is now on our "impression"–"Am I right?" It is now more likely that the other person will respond by opening up and talking about their unhappiness—or at the very least, they are likely to tell you why they are not unhappy—and so you move into a conversation rather than receiving a blunt "Nothing" in response. This is because we've used 'you' in the present tense and as a non-threatening 'I-question'. In such a way, 'you' becomes acceptable.

The 'I' Message—and what about 'we'—can leaders use 'we' instead of 'you'?

Often people suggest they can see the logic of not using 'you' and so they use 'we' instead, which they believe will soften the ensuing statements. Does this succeed?

For example, a person recalls a difficult conversation he was having with a colleague. "I can't recall the topic and only clearly remember his response after I said, 'I think we have a problem'. My colleague replied, 'We have a problem?' with great emphasis on the WE and it was definitely not used as a rhetorical question!" The target got the message straight away. His colleague was in fact saying, "WE don't have a problem, YOU do".

In this instance he had used 'we' illegitimately. It's easy to see why his colleague reacted so snappishly to the simple statement 'we' (as in the two of them) because they had not agreed on the problem or it's likely cause.

Can 'we' be used constructively?

Yes 'we' can be used but only when both parties have agreed on the cause or reasons for the issue/problem. That is both people understand very clearly what the problem is, and/or the reasons why it has arisen and the fact that they are both going to work hard at fixing it. So it is now a shared problem and both people can legitimately use 'we'.

For instance, a study at the University of California, Berkeley[137] has found that the use of 'we' more often than 'I' in conversations has

---

137 B Seider, et al, 2009, "We can work it out: age differences in relational pronouns, physiology, and behavior in marital conflict", *Psychology and Aging*, Vol 24, No 3, p 604–13.

been shown to indicate the strength of a relationship. "The use of 'we' language is a natural outgrowth of a sense of partnership, of being on the same team, and confidence in being able to face problems together,"[138] said study co-author Benjamin Seider. Keep in mind the caveat that the problem or likely cause must first be agreed upon.

In a difficult conversation, the order of using these three words, 'I', 'we' and 'you', becomes:

1. "**I** have a problem/issue/concern. This is how **I** see things …"
2. "How do **you** see it?" or "How can **you** help?" (Depending on the issue and situation).
3. "What can **we** do to work through this issue?" (This is once both people have agreed, and only when they've agreed that there is an issue or problem).

Often in a conversation if a leader jumps too quickly to the 'we', the other party will most likely contradict you, or they'll retreat into themselves as they know that the problem has yet to be defined and agreed by both people. In their mind, there is not yet any 'we'.

Reflective listening—inappropriate use of 'summary stems' in conversations

We're referring to some of the phrases that are often taught in reflective listening courses. In essence, there is nothing wrong with reflective listening. Used well and carefully it can be an effective communication skill. Although there are many times when the 'and …' technique of clean language, discussed earlier, can be far more effective.

The core principle on which reflective listening is built is that the person listening must be sincere. Some of the phrases that were originally developed many years ago as 'summary stems' to ensure the

---

138 Y Anwar, 2010, "Couples who say 'we' have a better shot at resolving conflicts", *Berkeley News*, 27 January, http://news.berkeley.edu/2010/01/27/couple-we-ness/, (accessed 20 June 2018).

listener summarised what was being heard, have now through overuse or inappropriate use, lost their effectiveness and can often be seen as insincere. For instance, one that has become quite hackneyed and turns many people off is, "I hear what you're saying" (often followed by "but"). For example, when one person says, "I hear what you're saying" they often mean, "I hear what you're saying but I disagree with it so totally that I am not even going to bother considering it. In fact, I have already forgotten it. Here's what I think ..."

Negative 'conversation busters'

Miles Kington[139] combined some of the common negative conversation busters (such as 'yes but') with ineffectual or overused reflective listening phrases to pen the following list of phrases to avoid (note that his article was written in 1996 and most, if not all, of the phrases are still being used inappropriately today):

"Yes but ..."
"That's all very well but ..."
"That may well be so but ..."
"Yes, I catch your drift, but ..."
"I can see where you're heading but ..."
"I take on board what you say."
"Even assuming that to be the case ..."
"You may well be right but ..."
"With respect ..."
"With the greatest respect ..."
"I see what you mean but ..."
"I see what you're getting at but ..."

---

139 M Kington, 1996, "I hear what you're saying but I'll ignore it", *The Independent*, 9 October, http://www.independent.co.uk/voices/i-hear-what-youre-saying-but-ill-ignore-it-1357551.html, (accessed 29 March 2018).

"I think I can see what you're driving at."

"Nevertheless …"

"Notwithstanding …"

"Still and all …"

"Other things being equal …"

"So what you're saying is …"

"I take your point, but …"

"The point, surely, is that …"

"We mustn't forget that …"

"What we have to remember is that …"

"What it all comes back to …"

"This doesn't alter the fact that …"

"We mustn't lose sight of the fact that …"

"When all is said and done …"

"At the end of the day …"

"When the chips are down …"

"What it's really all about …"

"In the real world …"

Often simply reflecting on such phrases is enough to prompt us to drop them. If you're using phrases such as these, we'd suggest making a note to change them to a more positive phrase. A simple 'yes, and' will probably cover most and will delete from your repertoire others that are superfluous.

The bottom line …

Techniques for managing difficult conversations
The rules for using 'I', 'you' and 'we' in difficult (or potentially difficult) conversations are:

- 'I' should be used at all times to express an opinion, feeling or describe feedback to another person. 'I' messages should replace 'you' messages. For example, "I have a problem/issue/concern. This is how I see things …"

- 'You' should only be used in the future tense. We can't change the past, we can influence the future, for example, "What can you do to help?"
- 'We' can only be used when both parties agree on the key issue or point of difference. For example, "What can we do to work through this issue?

And remember the 'yes, and' technique:

- Replace 'but' and 'yes, but' with 'yes, and'.

3.6 The importance of tone of voice for leaders

So far we've emphasised using certain words and avoiding others but is this enough to make a leader's communication effective? In order to communicate the meaning of the message we want to send and its intent, it's also important to match the tone of voice to the words. Our message can be quite easily misinterpreted when the tone doesn't match the words (and also of course when our facial expressions say something different again). For example, let's examine the following phrase:

I did not say he stole the money.

Please read it aloud (that will provide the tone of the message). Listening to your voice, what's the intent of this seemingly clear message?

Read aloud each of the following statements placing emphasis on the underlined words:

<u>I</u> did not say he stole the money.
I <u>did not</u> say he stole the money.
I did not <u>say</u> he stole the money.
I did not say <u>he</u> stole the money.
I did not say he <u>stole</u> the money.
I did not say he stole <u>the money</u>.

There are at least six different meanings for this simple sentence, depending on where you place the emphasis:

Sentence	Meaning or intent
I did not say he stole the money.	It wasn't I who said he stole the money.
I did not say he stole the money.	I definitely did not say he stole the money.
I did not say he stole the money.	I didn't "say" he stole the money. I may have inferred it. However, I didn't say so.
I did not say he stole the money.	It wasn't he who stole the money.
I did not say he stole the money.	He may have borrowed the money but did not steal it.
I did not say he stole the money.	He did not steal the money, however he may have taken something else.

Table 8: Changing tone of voice example.

Waldman and Newberg claim[140] that the tone of voice is equally as important as the words used, when it comes to understanding what a person is really trying to convey. Add facial expressions to that and the listener can be put in quite a quandary as to what is really being communicated. For instance, if when speaking a sentence the facial expression expresses one emotion, but the tone conveys a different one, neural or cognitive dissonance (the mental stress or discomfort experienced by an individual who holds two or more contradictory beliefs, ideas, or values at the same time) takes place in the brain of the listener, causing him/her some confusion. The result? Trust erodes, suspicion increases, and cooperation decreases.

To illustrate the importance of tone, here's an example of a conversation without any indication of how the words are expressed:

---

140 A Newberg and M Waldman, 2012, *Words Can Change Your Brain*, Penguin Group, New York.

COO: We need patience but there is a limit.

CEO: No, I feel that for every day that goes by, we need to make progress. We need to gain ground every single day. Any extra spare time we had is gone.

COO: Well, an awful lot has happened along the way here. Both regarding what we've taken into consideration and what we have not known about before now. But I think we are on track again ... unless there are more external things like this client that left us in a mess.

CEO: Is there anything else you want to say about your report?

Reading this dialogue, what impression does it give about the feelings being expressed by the CEO and COO?

Now here (*hear*) again is the dialogue with the tone expressed ...

COO: (in a resigned tone): We need patience but there is a limit.

CEO: (in a restless tone): No, I feel that for every day that goes by, we need to make progress. We need to gain ground every single day. Any extra spare time we had is gone.

COO: (with irritation): Well, an awful lot has happened along the way here. Both regarding what we've taken into consideration and that we have not known about before now. (In a calmer tone): But I think—or what do you say (turns to the Chair)—that we are on track again (goes back to irritation) unless there are more external things like this client that left us in a mess.

CEO: (in an avoiding tone): Is there anything else you want to say about your report?

Notice how the impact of sentences changes with the addition of tone.

It's not just <u>what a leader</u> says that matters, <u>how</u> it is said is equally important.

This is particularly relevant whenever your message is in any way emotional. Your message (the words) is what you're trying to communicate. Your tone of voice is how you communicate. Tone takes a statement and either breathes life into it (inspires others) or sucks the life out of it (makes others want to expire). Tone is also relevant when trying to interpret or understand someone else's underlying emotions which they may not be expressing in words.

Often because of the emotion or lack of emotion in the topic or issue, our tone changes subconsciously. That's human nature. It's always going to happen from time to time. However, we can and should become more aware of, and quite adept at, using tone to accurately convey the intent of our message.

Leaders can practice tone by undertaking exercises like those below where stressing certain words changes the feeling of what you're saying. Once again, please say these aloud as that's the only way you will be able to discern your tone.

Read aloud the following sentence, "What would you like me to do about it?" You'll see that it changes in feeling, meaning, and tone when you:

Say it defensively (by emphasising the words 'would you'),
"What <u>would you</u> like me to do about it?"
Say it with curiosity (by emphasising the words 'like me'),
"What would you <u>like me</u> to do about it?"
Say it with apathy (by not emphasising any of the words and merely speaking in a monotone),
"What would you like me to do about it?"

At this point some readers may be thinking, "Ah yes, that's all very well and good, but I've heard that most of the message in our communication is conveyed non-verbally by our facial expressions". For many decades, communication and management trainers have built their lessons on communication around the theory that:

- 55% of one's message is conveyed by facial expressions;
- 38% by tone of voice; and
- 7% by the actual words used.

However, those percentages are a myth. They are supposedly based on the research conducted and published by Professor Albert Mehrabian in 1967 and quoted out of context.[141] Mehrabian himself says: "Please note that this and other equations regarding relative importance of verbal and nonverbal messages were derived from experiments dealing with communications of feelings and attitudes (i.e., like-dislike). *Unless a communicator is talking about their feelings or attitudes, these equations are not applicable"* (italics are our emphasis).

So where does that leave us? How important are facial expressions, tone of voice and words?

As many writers have suggested:

- "If the figures of 55%, 38% and 7% are to be believed, I wouldn't need to buy headphones on a plane when watching movies."
- "If only 7% of the message can be attributable to the words, then it would be very easy to learn to communicate in a foreign language."
- "If you've ever played charades, you'll know that words and language are by far the most effective way of expressing complex and abstract ideas."

---

141 A Mehrabian, n.d., "'Silent messages'—A wealth of information about non-verbal communication (body language)", http://www.kaaj.com/psych/smorder.html, (accessed 29 March 2018).

- "How could a blind person communicate effectively if it were not for the words and tone of voice used?"[142]

Additionally, Dr C E Johnson points out just how important words are:

Words and language are probably the primary motivation factors for human beings and they can be enhanced by proper congruent tonality and body language. They can also be somewhat diminished by incongruencies which then often show up as confusion and bewilderment in relationship situations.[143]

Earlier we showed how important words are and how they impact certain areas of the brain. So yes, the words in any communication are very important—after all, sophisticated language is one of the key differences between humans and animals. But so too is tone, as tone can change the meaning of a word, phrase or sentence. When describing his research on tone, Dr Tobias Grossmann of the Centre for Brain and Cognitive Development at the University of London said:

Another important question addressed in this study was whether activity in infants' voice-sensitive brain regions is modulated by emotional prosody. Prosody, essentially the 'music' of speech, can reflect the feelings of the speaker, thereby helping to convey the context of language. In humans, sensitivity to emotional prosody is crucial for social communication. The researchers observed that a voice-sensitive region in the right temporal cortex showed

---

142 M Hall, 2010, "The 7%, 38%, 55% Myth: Blasting Away an Old NLP Myth", *Neuro-Semantics*, 9 February, http://www.neurosemantics.com/the-7-38-55-myth/, (accessed 20 June 2018).

143 C E Johnson, Coach Team, "The 7%, 38%, 55%, Myth", http://www.coachteam.no/Documents/MytenOmNonverbalKommunikasjon.pdf, (accessed 20 June 2018).

increased activity when 7-month-old infants listened to words spoken with emotional (angry or happy) prosody. Such a modulation of brain activity by emotional signals is thought to be a fundamental brain mechanism to prioritize the processing of significant stimuli in the environment.[144]

The bottom line ...

Tone of voice

- Whatever the words a leader is using to describe the issue or topic, it's the tone that communicates what they are feeling about it when they say them.
- We are often unaware of our tensions and attitudes (feelings) brewing underneath the surface of what we are saying. Check your tone and words to make sure they are both in sync. This is particularly important when you find yourself in a difficult or challenging conversation.

3.7 Phrases that promote cooperation and a positive approach to issues

Framing—seeing things through a different lens

In this chapter, we'll cover the techniques of 'framing' and 'triangulating'. Both are used to engender cooperation, especially when there is conflict (or potential conflict) or when commitment to an issue or decision is required. We'll suggest words that leaders can use with both techniques.

Framing is looking at one's perspective of an issue as if examining it through a lens, so reframing is to change that perspective; to 'look at it from another angle'. For example, you may be able to reframe yours or another's perspective by changing the words you use such as:

- expressing a **problem** as an **opportunity**;

---

144 EurekAlert, The Global Source for Science News, Cell Press, 2010, "Human brain becomes tuned to voices and emotional tone of voice during infancy", 24 March, https://www.eurekalert.org/pub_releases/2010-03/cp-hbb031910.php, (accessed 22 June 2018).

- expressing a **weakness** as a **strength**;
- expressing an **impossibility** as a **distant possibility**;
- expressing a **distant possibility** as a **near possibility**; and
- expressing **unkindness** as **lack of understanding**.

Although not specifically mentioned, we've used reframing extensively so far in this book. For instance, changing 'don't' to the positive is one example; turning negative 'self-talk' such as "What if I try and fail?" into "This is working for me" is another.

In many challenging conversations we are aiming to reframe another's perspective. The words we choose are important for example:

- "Yes, it does seem stupid (REFRAME) **and it may also be stupid not to look again and see what else can be done**."
- "It's not so much doing away with old ways as (REFRAME) **building a new and exciting future**."
- "We've shown we can argue well (REFRAME) **maybe this means we can also agree well**."
- "You say it can't be done in time (REFRAME) **what if we staged delivery or got in extra help? I'm sure we can produce an acceptable product in the timeframe**."

Framing is often used in day-to-day conversation as a metaphor to describe someone's attitude as their 'frame of mind'. Following, is an example of how a negatively framed message can be re-framed into a positive one:

Negative framing:

"I never seem to be able to fully grasp the subtleties of the consolidated budget reports."

Positive reframing:

"While the details of the consolidated budgets are challenging to comprehend, I do get the implications for the big picture of our financial situation."

As Henry Ford is reported to have said:

If you think you can do a thing or you think you can't do a thing, either way you're right.[145]

It's the words we use to frame our thoughts that propel us into action. As well as reframing our own words, a key objective is to influence others to reframe how they see things—to change 'their terms of reference' or 'their point of view'. This is the benefit of reframing.

Always keep in mind that a person's frame is valid (to them) and so it's important to start your conversation from that perspective, rather than saying "you're wrong" or merely thinking "they're wrong". And reframing has another benefit—it can help you manage your emotions and when used successfully with others, can also help manage their emotional level. Psychologist James J Gross has found that reframing (his term is 'cognitive reappraisal')[146] when someone is emotionally aroused, can lower their emotional level. For example, you may find yourself very annoyed that a colleague agreed to a meeting date and has changed the date for the second time. You can lower your level of annoyance by reframing such as "The delay may mean there will be more information available to consider when we do meet".

It is important for leaders to look for opportunities the company can exploit. Reframing negative statements such as the following, will focus them on what can be achieved, rather than what can't:

- "It could be worse." REFRAME: **"There are some opportunities for us here."**

---

145 J Foster, 2013, "Whether you think you can … or whether you think you can't … you're right!", *Wall Street Insanity*, 25 Feb, https://wallstreetinsanity.com/whether-you-think-you-can-or-whether-you-think-you-cant-youre-right/, (accessed 29 March 2018).

146 K Ochsner, and J Gross, 2008, "Cognitive emotion regulation: Insights from social cognitive and affective neuroscience", *Current Directions in Psychological Science*, Vol 17, No 2, p 153–8.

- "We seem to have a problem with …" REFRAME: **"This is a challenge we can learn from."**
- "This is a real stumbling block for the company" REFRAME: **"What's the best way of achieving our goals here?"**

The key to effective reframing is to focus on the action that you intend to take or the behaviour you intend to change (e.g., in our earlier example, 'number of changes' versus 'more information available', not the feeling, 'annoyed'). That's the key—focus on behaviour rather than feelings. The trick is timing. To lessen the emotional impact of a negative experience, you need to reframe it straight away. If not, the brain goes into action to alert various sensing parts of the body that there is something wrong and so your heart rate increases, your face may turn red, you sweat, tremble or whatever else your body has learned to do when aroused. As the saying goes, 'timing is everything'.

Many chapters in Part 4 will provide explicit suggestions as to how leaders can reframe their outlook and influence others to reframe their perspective in various challenging situations. In others we'll leave it to you to consider how you could reframe a particular situation. It's a great skill to learn.

Triangulating—from disagreement to cooperation

In geometry, 'triangulation is the process of determining the location of a point by measuring angles to it from known points at either end of a fixed baseline, rather than measuring distances to the point directly'.[147] In the social sciences, triangulation is often used to indicate that two (or more) methods are used in a study in order to check the results. So here we're going to borrow from both disciplines to present a tactic that can be very useful in challenging conversations.

---

147 Wikipedia, 2018, https://en.wikipedia.org/wiki/Triangulation (disambiguation), (accessed 20 June 2018).

One of the issues (that can be equally problematic or advantageous) in a challenging conversation is that the two people are standing facing one another. In a heated discussion this can be the 'stand up and fight' stance or perhaps the advice given to one as "You need to stand up to him". We are often in fight, not flight mode when having a challenging conversation.

We've mentioned previously the need to 'open a channel' at the start of a conversation. This can be achieved with such things as the words you use, your body language, where you have the conversation and the setting (e.g. comfortable chairs and even refreshments to make it easier for both people to have a productive dialogue). Triangulation is a further technique that can ease the situation when the conversation gets particularly challenging or even heated as it creates a feeling of partnership rather than competition. Triangulation can, in fact, re-open a channel that may have started to close up.

How do leaders triangulate?

In a tense negotiation where two people seem to be at an impasse, it can be useful for one to say, "Let's look at what we've each put forward and see if we can appreciate each perspective from a different angle". Notice the words "look at", "see", "each perspective", "different angle". They are all visual and invite each person to examine the situation through a different lens. This new lens is also likely to be more optimistic (in finding a solution) because the positive word "appreciate" was used as part of the invitation—an example of 'priming').

One person then steps up to a whiteboard or flip chart and asks the other to summarise both proposals (or points of difference). The situation although not resolved, is now moving through to reaching an agreement on what has been covered. Up to this point there has been total disagreement, now for the first time they are working together— one writing, the other providing the information. The person recording may then invite the other to stand and take the pen and as they discuss

THE ISSUE

New focus

New focus

TRIANGULATION

Person A ← — Original stance — → **Person B**

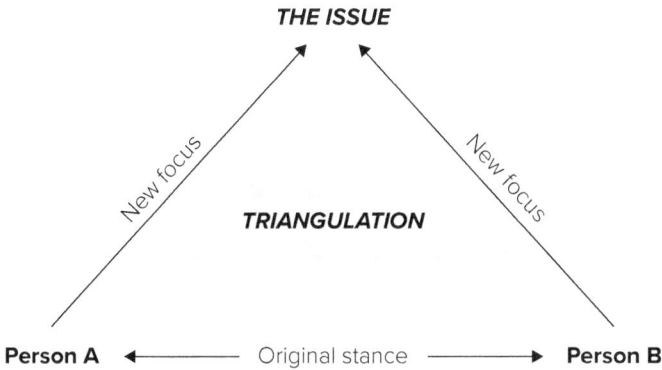

Figure 12: Triangulation—takes the focus away from the individuals and focuses on the issue.

each point, write a comment about how that could work (given certain circumstances). Both people although still standing are now looking at the board not at each other—the issue or problem has been triangulated.

Triangulating can be an extremely effective technique for leaders. For example, there may be an impasse over an important decision and members of the group have become polarised over two options. The conversation about the two options seems to be going in a circle (two executives at loggerheads repeating the same points) until one gets up from the table and makes a list on a whiteboard about each option so that the other team members can see all the points. All executives are now facing the board and not one another and discussing the points. The first executive then invites another colleague to come up and (perhaps through a rating schema) lead the discussion, while the first executive scribes the discussion points. Triangulating is now occurring, and the group is more likely to resolve the issue.

Triangulating can even be done when there are no physical things to help such as paper or whiteboard, by using one's hands. In this case the speaker looks down at both hands (held out in front of him/her), then while still looking down at his/her hands, moves both out to one side saying, "Let's look at this from another perspective". It's quite fascinating to watch the other person change their gaze from looking directly at the speaker's face to looking at the speaker's hands and then proceeding to come up with alternative suggestions. Triangulation has occurred.

Priming, framing, triangulating—used in combination with metaphors

Effective decision making is at the heart of good leadership. However, it isn't easy to manage the collective cognitive process that underpins effective decisions; qualities like an openness to alternatives and a willingness to question and challenge. When the going gets rough in a debate among senior team members as we have suggested, some practical ways to manage diverse points of view are priming, framing, and triangulating. These can be improved further by combining them with metaphors. Let's see how each might work.

John, the Chief Risk Officer (CRO), has just seen the finance and risk report from Chris, the CFO, to be tabled at the next Audit & Risk Committee meeting. He doesn't like what he sees. John immediately sends an email to the CEO and explains his concerns. The CEO shoots off a reply email to John, the CRO, copying the CFO, and saying the CRO "should stand his ground". The CFO wonders "What does this mean? Will there be conflict at the Audit & Risk Committee meeting? How should it be handled?"

To manage potential conflict and still have a meaningful discussion, 'priming' is a communication strategy the CFO can adopt. As mentioned previously, priming illustrates how we can prime ourselves (and others) to think, feel and consequently behave differently by giving instructions to the brain either consciously or subconsciously with the words we use.

Chris, the CFO, can 'prime' in two ways. Firstly, Chris might approach John, the CRO, prior to the committee meeting with the proposed report and say "John, we need to see a really sound, workable and effective report for the next meeting. Help me out here—shoot some holes in it so that we can get it right". Following this discussion Chris is more likely to have the CRO as a supporter rather than a person set to argue against the report (notice the powerful use of metaphor, 'shoot some holes in it').

Secondly, when presenting the report, Chris should prime John (CRO) and the committee members with positive words such as "We have a challenging road to navigate in the year ahead. Where is our compass? Where do we want to go? Do we sit still or do we move forward? I intend to present a road map that the Audit Committee believes will take us in the positive direction we need to go—forward." Notice the use of the metaphor of a journey: "navigate", "compass", "to go", "sit still", "move forward", "road map", "positive direction". Note also that Chris is using the first three metaphors as questions. This is an effective way to get her colleagues thinking about the topics raised in the report and potentially contributing to the discussion in a positive way.

Metaphors are often used in conversations as a way of framing or reframing a situation, and also in priming. We use them in every conversation we have. As was mentioned earlier in the book, researchers suggest that we use as many as six metaphors every minute. They're a fabulous way of getting complicated messages across or speeding up the communication by saying in a few words what might otherwise take paragraphs. As well as facilitating a better understanding of what's being said, they are also a good way of priming. Read again the case of CRO (John) and the CFO (Chris) and see the metaphors each used for the purposes of priming:

- "should stand his ground"
- "shoot some holes in it"
- "challenging road to navigate"
- "Where is our compass?"
- "Where do we want to go?"
- "Do we sit still or do we move forward?"

More than that, research has shown that we think in metaphors[148] (because they save us so much time and thinking effort) and so it's important to consciously develop the use of metaphors. Look at the example we gave earlier of a CEO using some great metaphors when he was asked: "Can you justify communication in terms of a return on investment?" He responded: "Enormous! We can move faster, jump higher, dive deeper and come up drier than anybody else in the business. When we hang a left, everyone goes left. It gives us an enormous ability to work as a team. Other companies in our industry are yet to work that out".

Taking an 'I' perspective—why it works in priming, framing, triangulating

We've covered the technique of using 'I' messages earlier in the book. As it's such an integral component of having a successful conversation—when using framing, priming and triangulating—it's also important to discuss the philosophy behind taking an 'I perspective', so that leaders can use it seamlessly with these conversation tactics.

At first glance it may seem that using 'I' is just another seed in the burgeoning 'me' society that has mushroomed over the last couple of decades. This 'me' society or as it goes by its pseudonym '*i*' seems to be all pervasive (for example the '*i* phone', '*i* pad', '*i* net' and so on) with its focus on the individual. All the marketing gurus have jumped on the band wagon (once Apple lost their court case to copyright '*i*'), so that now if a new product does not have a designation starting with '*i*' or as we've seen recently a double '*ii*', it's not worth promoting.

However, taking an 'I' perspective in conversations is not about 'me' it's about taking responsibility for our words and actions. Although

---

148 B Klein, 2013, "5 studies: the ubiquity of metaphor, 5 studies research and application", *The Psych Report*, 26 July, http://thepsychreport.com/research-application/5-studies-the-ubiquity-of-metaphor/, (accessed 22 June 2018).

described as a technique, it is both a conversational technique and a philosophy of approach. And there's also a sound scientific reason for taking an 'I' perspective. Studies[149] have shown that taking an 'I' perspective can lead to:

- greater valuing of others;
- greater helping of others; and
- a reduction in stereotyping of others and the groups to which they belong.

In fact, these studies also found that taking an 'I' perspective can lead to some overlap in self-concept between yourself and the other person, which means that when using 'I' the other person has an inclination to actually identify with you and you with them (as opposed to using 'you' which can lead to a widening of the gap between two people). Accordingly, it is a very powerful tool.

The bottom line ...

Techniques for increasing effectiveness of conversations

To have effective conversations where intent and impact tend to be in sync, leaders need to learn and develop the skills of:

- priming—providing others with positive words/phrases/pictures that will engender positive responses in a later conversation or presentation on the same topic;
- framing—rephrasing negative comments into the positive (both yours and others);
- triangulating—separating the problem or issue from the people by directing their attention to a third point—the apex of a triangle; and
- developing and using appropriate and exciting metaphors to use in combination with priming, framing and triangulating.

149 A Sharland, n.d., "Using 'I-statements", *Communication and Conflict* [website], https://www.communicationandconflict.com/i-statements.html, (accessed 29 March 2018).

3.8 How positive and negative words affect brain function

So far we have focussed on the impact that words and language have on behaviour, describing many strategies, techniques and tactics that leaders can use to build positive relationships. Doing so also pays off in another, perhaps unexpected way—using positive language can improve brain power.

"Sticks and stones may break your bones, but words can never hurt you", that's what the old nursery rhyme tells us. While we've always wanted to believe that words may not hurt us, can words make our brains healthier? It seems so.

Recent research by Andrew Newberg and Mark Robert Waldman[150] suggests that certain words have an impact on specific areas of the brain. As discussed earlier, we've seen that positive words can affect one's behaviour. This new research now shows why.

Positive words such as 'peace' and 'love' can alter what is known as 'the expression of genes'. Genes store information in our brain and act like a book, so the expression of genes occurs when the information in the book is accessed and communicated. When we use positive words they strengthen areas in our frontal lobes and promote the brain's cognitive functioning, making us more cognitively healthy. They propel the motivational centres of the brain into action, according to Newberg and Waldman, and build resiliency.

However, unlike the nursery rhyme premise, it seems that words can also hurt you. Newberg and Waldman's research points out five really important factors about how both positive and negative words affect our brain. This is particularly the case over extended periods. In summary:

---

150 A Newberg and Waldman, 2012, *Words can change your brain*, Penguin Group, New York.

1. By holding a positive and optimistic word in your mind, you stimulate frontal lobe activity. This area includes specific language centres that connect directly to the motor cortex responsible for moving you into action.
2. The longer you concentrate on positive words, the more you begin to affect other areas of the brain.
3. When using positive or negative words over an extended period, functions in the parietal lobe start to change, which alters your perception of yourself and the people you interact with.
4. A positive view of yourself will bias you toward seeing the good in others, whereas a negative self-image will lead you toward suspicion and doubt about others.
5. Finally over time, the structure of your thalamus will also change in response to your conscious words, thoughts, and feelings. These thalamic changes affect the way in which you perceive reality.

In terms of improved 'brain power' there's also more evidence from an unlikely source—fiction writers. It seems as though reading fiction (regularly) can also improve our self-image and indeed empathy for others.

Researchers Mar, Oatley and Peterson report that individuals who frequently read fiction seem to be better able to understand other people, empathise with them and see the world from their perspective.[151]

It seems that brain scans (through the use of functional Magnetic Resonance Imaging machines—fMRI) are revealing what happens in our brain when we read a detailed description, an evocative metaphor or an emotional exchange between characters. Stories stimulate the brain and even change how we act in life.

---

151 R Mar, J Oatley and J Peterson, 2009, "Exploring the link between reading fiction and empathy: Ruling out individual differences and examining outcomes", *Communications*, Vol 34, No 4, p 407–28.

Researchers have long known that the 'classical' language regions, like Broca's area and Wernicke's area, are involved in how the brain interprets written words. What scientists have now come to realise is that narratives activate many other parts of our brains as well, suggesting why the experience of reading can feel so alive. Words like 'lavender', 'cinnamon' and 'soap' for example, elicit a response not only from the language-processing areas of our brains, but also those devoted to dealing with smells.

Scientists now posit that our sensors (such as eyes, ears, nose, mouth) are merely devices that send messages to many parts of the brain, not as was once thought to specific areas such as the language areas (i.e., Broca and Wernicke). In his bestselling book *The Brain That Changes Itself* author Norman Doidge quotes neuroplasticity scientist Paul Bach-y-Rita as saying, "We see with our brains, not with our eyes".[152] The ability of injured or impaired people to learn to perceive senses such as sight, hearing, smell and touch through sensors other than those thought to be traditionally 'hardwired' to a particular sense is now further evidence that our brains can learn to change by the exercises we use to train them. Perhaps this knowledge may be additional motivation to try several of the ideas, suggestions and exercises in this book.

You can quickly test this theory for yourself. Place your hand horizontally, with your palm facing upwards in front of you and imagine holding a lemon. Look at the lemon. See the yellow and green tones. Feel the lemon resting in the palm of your hand. Smell the fragrant citrus aroma. Your mouth will salivate as a response to the thought. Your conscious mind knows no lemon is present, but it is sending signals to the parts of the brain that senses the sight, smell and taste of a lemon.

---

152 N Doidge, 2007, *The Brain that Changes Itself*, Penguin Group, London, p 15.

In addition to the many 'brain-changing' breakthrough training techniques that are now helping to cure the sick or injured, or people who have been born with disabilities, our growing understanding of how the brain can be trained to change the way we act, is useful for every one of us. For instance returning to the fiction example, Oatley notes:

Fiction is a particularly useful simulation because negotiating the social world effectively is extremely tricky, requiring us to weigh up myriad interacting instances of cause and effect. Just as computer simulations can help us get to grips with complex problems such as flying a plane or forecasting the weather, so novels, stories and dramas can help us understand the complexities of social life.[153]

Now this final chapter in Part 3 also provides conclusive evidence about what happens in our brain when we are using either positive or negative language. It shows the incredible power that words have on our thoughts, feelings and actions as they infiltrate various areas of our brain.

The bottom line ...

The impact of word choice

The types of words leaders choose to use can literally change the brain. A single word has enormous power to influence the expression of genes that regulate emotional and physical stress.

When leaders use positive words such as 'inspire', 'authentic', 'integrity', and 'ethically', they increase cognitive reasoning and strengthen areas around the frontal lobes. Therefore, utilising positive words more frequently than negative words can activate the motivation centres of the brain, prompting them into action.

---

153 A M Paul, 2012, "Your Brain on Fiction", *New York Times*, 17 March, https://www.nytimes.com/2012/03/18/opinion/sunday/the-neuroscience-of-your-brain-on-fiction.html, (accessed 20 June 2018).

Positive words are also known to engage the brain centre responsible for respect, active listening, empathy, problem-solving, and understanding the big picture, whereas negative words activate the fear centre. Accordingly, there are strong incentives for leaders to carefully consider the words that they use.

3.9 Concluding comments on setting the tone through word choice

Long before MRI machines were available to 'read our brains', psycho-linguists were aware of the differences in cognitive complexity between expressing something in the positive as opposed to the negative. For example, negation invariably leads to an increase in grammatical complexity which means it takes longer for the speaker to express and longer for the listener to interpret what is being said. Hear the difference between the following:

Affirmative	Negative
The report is here.	The report is not here.
The business has the money.	The business doesn't have the money.
One	None

Just as when we discussed the difficulty for the listener when interpreting a 'don't' statement or question (i.e. the lack of visual imagery and the need for double processing), the difficulty is also evident in virtually all negations. For example, when the listener has to process, "The business doesn't have any money" he or she has to conjure up the image of money; what it is, how much does the business "not have?", and perhaps start thinking about "Why doesn't the business have any?"

Intuitively too we know that negative phrasing and language often:
- tells the other person what cannot be done;
- has a subtle tone of blame;

- includes words like 'don't', 'can't', 'won't', 'unable to', that demonstrates to the other person what you or they cannot do; and
- does not stress positive actions that would be appropriate or positive consequences.

And we also know that positive phrasing and language:

- tells the other person what can be done;
- suggests alternatives and choices available to us and others;
- sounds helpful and encouraging; and
- stresses positive actions and positive consequences.

In Part 3, we've introduced many strategies, techniques and tactics for using words and phrases that should add to our 'intuitive' understanding of how conversations work, and most importantly how leaders can use these effectively in conversations. Before proceeding to Part 4, where we will discuss a number of specific challenging conversations leaders may face, it's worth summarising what's been covered here.

The 'don't' rule	Completely eliminate the word 'don't' from your vocabulary.	Think of what you would like (or want) people to do, and say so.
Eliminate negative words	Eliminate negative words from your conversation, emails, texts and other communication.	Replace these negative words with the positive alternative.
The 'futureless concept'	Express the future as if it's already happening.	For example, express things you are going to do as "I am" rather than "I will", "I must", or "I want to".
Practise using metaphors	Use metaphors, particularly in your written communication.	Also, try using 'and' (with an appropriate pause) to uncover the true meaning or feeling behind what someone else is expressing when they use a metaphor.

Practise changing the descriptions of your negative feelings into words that are 'quirky'	*Change negative feelings into words that are more positive.*	Better still, change negative words into metaphors that will enable you to lighten up the negativity you may feel in a challenging or difficult situation.
Use 'I' instead of 'You'	*Express concerns or problems with 'I statements'. Follow the 'I', 'you', 'we' process. Remember to replace 'but' with 'and'.*	1. I have a problem … this is how I see things 2. How do you see it? How can you help? 3. What can we do to work through the issue?
Prime, Frame, Triangulate	*Promote cooperation with positive words and phrases. Help others to see things through a different lens.*	Prepare yourself and others by priming with positive words relating to upcoming conversations. Reframe your negative thoughts and words of others into the positive. Encourage others to objectify a contentious issue through physically setting up a triangle in the conversation.

As you've seen, one of the key themes in this book is to be more positive by using positive words and language. The unfortunate news is that there are more negatively oriented words than positively oriented words in our language to choose from. Linguists Robert Schrauf and Julia Sanchez (quoted in *The Man Who Lied to His Laptop by Clifford Nass*)[154] have shown that in the two languages they studied, English and Spanish, 20 per cent of words have a neutral orientation,

154 C Nass with C Yen, 2012, "The man who lied to his laptop", Penguin Group, New York.

50 per cent have a negative orientation and the remaining 30 per cent have a positive orientation.

It comes as no surprise to us that as a society, we are inadvertently programming ourselves to be more negative by the amount of negative words we use and hear each day. And this starts at an early age. For instance it's been found that the average child hears 432 negative comments or words per day versus 32 positive ones.[155] If our maths is correct that's about 93% negative! From that starting point it is little wonder that so much of our language is negative.

Now with the evidence presented here, we can all start turning that figure around. A good place to start is with the senior leadership team.

---

155 K J Kvols, 1998, "Redirecting children's behavior", Parenting Press Inc, Chicago.

PART 4

MANAGING CHALLENGING CONVERSATIONS

4.1 The six phases of a conversation: How leaders manage each phase in challenging conversations

Challenging conversations are 'challenging' because we are often apprehensive about undertaking them, we may be concerned about the possible outcomes, or perhaps we expect the situation to become challenging if the conversation takes a different turn to what we planned. The aim of Part 4 is to provide leaders with the knowledge—strategies and tactics—to successfully navigate their way through the turbulent waters of the difficult conversation.

In Part 4, we'll highlight many of the points that we have covered in the earlier parts such as word choice and phrasing, and demonstrate how they can help guide leaders to set a positive tone, even when the topic or issue is quite challenging. Additionally, in certain chapters such as those on 'assertiveness' and 'giving constructive advice' we have included suggestions for applying these techniques in a variety of settings. Our reason for doing so is that many conversations occur outside formal meetings, and leaders may feel the need to develop these skills further before applying them in other settings.

Each chapter in Part 4 is stand-alone. You may care to read Part 4 in its entirety now, or refer to a particular section, when needed. We do recommend studying the following introduction to Part 4, as it covers in greater detail the six phases of a conversation—a process that leaders will find invaluable in all conversations and essential in challenging conversations.

> *Conversation presents a whole range of interface challenges. These include deciding when it is socially appropriate to speak, being ready to come in at just the right moment (on average we start speaking about 0.5 seconds before our partner finishes), planning what you are going to say while still listening to the other person, and, in multi-party conversations, deciding who to address. To do this you have to keep task-switching (one moment speaking, the next moment listening). Yet we know that in general multi-tasking and task switching are really challenging—try writing a letter while listening to someone talking to you.*[156]

Whilst this quote from Simon Garrod and Martin Pickering points out the challenges, there is also good news. In addition to being able to use the six-phase process map for conversations, there is a natural phenomenon that makes all conversations a little easier and it's known as 'interactive alignment'.[157] People can do this by making use of each other's choices of words, sounds, grammatical forms, and meanings. The scientific reason for this is that interactive alignment occurs because

---

156 S Garrod and M Pickering, 2004, "Why is conversation so easy?" *Trends in Cognitive Sciences*, Vol 8, No 1, p 8–11.
157 M Menenti, M Pickering and S Garrod, 2012, "Toward a neural basis of interactive alignment in conversation", *Frontiers in Human Neuroscience*, Vol 6, p 185.

the speaker activates linguistic representations in the listener's brain that are common to him/her. When responding, the listener (subconsciously) then speaks in ways that the other person will understand.

You will also recall from earlier chapters that using metaphors is a way of providing common meaning for people in conversation—these are a form of interactive alignment. As Raymond W Gibbs points out, "much of our reasoning makes use of conceptual metaphors".[158]

The function of interactive alignment is why it's so important to choose the most appropriate words for the content, context and for managing the process of a particularly difficult conversation. In doing so, the other participant or participants are more likely to 'follow the leader'.

It's also been found that not only do we align linguistically with the other person in a conversation we actually mirror their facial expressions, tone of voice and speed of talking. Commonly known as 'mirroring' the scientific term is 'emotional contagion', that is, we instinctively synchronise our facial expressions with those of others. Watch people who are in animated conversations and their mannerisms and even voice tone qualities will start to become similar. Note that this also occurs even when they are in disagreement about the context or content of the conversation, provided both are fully engaged in the conversation and not looking for 'a way out'. It has been found that some people with severely impaired vision or who may be clinically blind, also exhibit emotional contagion. It is a very powerful tool for leaders to be aware of, particularly in challenging situations.

With the knowledge of naturally occurring interactive alignment and mirroring, and armed with a good process map, difficult conversations can be more easily managed. Below appear some suggestions for how to use these conversational techniques.

---

158 R Gibbs, 2008, "The Cambridge Handbook of Metaphor and Thought", Cambridge University Press, London.

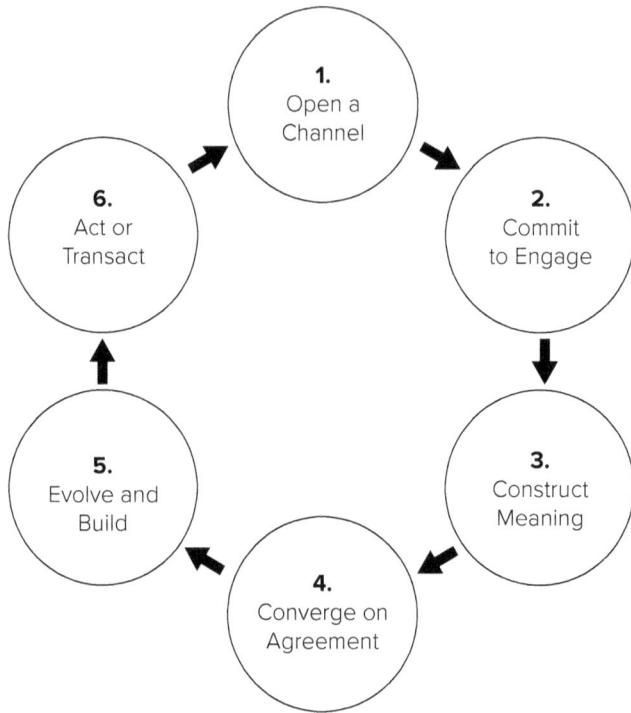

Figure 13: The conversation process map.

1. Open a channel

To commence, the speaker says something that is known to be comprehensible to the listener. Think of this as a discussion 'space' that opens up possibilities and helps both people make good decisions. In a challenging conversation it may take some time to get this space going but it's worth persevering (note the use of the word 'space' here as it should envisage an image in your mind).

This discussion space may be:

- an actual physical setting, such as a comfortable area with tea/coffee/water etc;
- the way you stand or sit (it's known, for instance, that it's easier for people to remain calm when they are sitting rather than

standing—a classic example is when executives sit next to each other on a sofa or at a table rather than facing each other across a desk); and

- in challenging conversations, such as when the CEO has to give some difficult feedback (the space selected is important, i.e., neutral territory and comfortable surroundings).

Most importantly, it's the manner in which a leader makes it easy for the other person to be open in terms of what they say and how they feel that sets the tone to open a channel for this challenging conversation. We recommend always holding challenging conversations face-to-face, or as a poor but necessary fallback, via phone and never online.

2. Commit to engage

The listener must commit to participate if only by continuing to listen. He/she is only likely to continue if there is value in the conversation. Demonstrating a commitment to listen impacts the other person's perception of the leader as being engaged (or people if there are more than one in the conversation) and builds the feeling of having something in common.

We'll make an assumption that you are familiar with the concept and skill of 'reflective listening'—perhaps you've even done some training in this technique. Reflective listening is a good communication tool. However, the overriding principle is that the listener must be sincere (you'll recall in an earlier chapter where the overuse or misuse of paraphrasing can mitigate effective dialogue). When listening reflectively, the listener wants to really hear what the other person is saying and most importantly, the feelings that are being consciously or subconsciously expressed. This type of listening should focus on what is being said without thinking about formulating a response.

If you consider yourself an effective reflective listener, then please continue using these techniques. If you'd like to take your listening skills to the next level then we suggest developing the clean language of 'and ...' and 'yes, and ...' that was mentioned earlier in the book.

Above all the one thing that will demonstrate a leader's willingness to engage in the conversation and that will help leaders navigate through any challenging conversation, is *the ability to listen to* both the facts and feelings being expressed, and to be able to distinguish between the two.

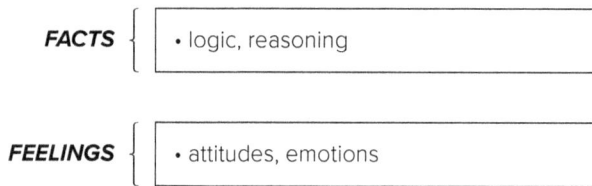

FACTS { | • logic, reasoning |

FEELINGS { | • attitudes, emotions |

Figure 14: The distinction between facts and feelings in conversations.

The important distinction between using the words 'feel' and 'fact' in conversations

Examining this distinction between facts and feelings is relevant before we cover the remaining four phases of the conversation process. All challenging conversations have an emotional undertone. For example, giving someone, say an executive, critical advice; an employee asking their manager for a raise; telling the senior team there will be no bonus this year; telling your teenager that he/she can't go out this evening, and so on. Although all of these examples are based on facts, that is giving feedback, asking for a raise, the lack of funds available for a bonus, and the directive to stop your teenager from going out, it's how both people feel about the facts that makes the conversation challenging. Both people will most likely have different feelings about the same facts.

This is a very important distinction.

There are some conversations where leaders will want to focus on feelings but there are other conversations where leaders will need to keep the conversation rational and fact based. This distinction and when to focus on each, will be discussed when we examine the challenging conversations further in Part 4.

Are there words that can help focus the conversation on either facts or feelings? Yes. Two of the most common are 'think' and 'feel':

- When asking someone "What do you think about ...?" they will invariably give you an explanation of *their reasoning or logic.*
- When you ask someone "How do you feel about ...?" they will most certainly *express their attitude, feeling, motivation or emotion* about the topic.

Note also that the first question started with 'What' and the second with 'How' which helped reinforce the fact or feeling response required.

To illustrate: we were asked to do some personal coaching with John, the General Manager of a heavy-duty manufacturing plant. Although the plant was successful and profitable, John's CEO was concerned about the high turnover rate amongst John's senior management team. Our first task was to get to know John and find out more about his role and his relationships at work. Following an initial discussion, we sat in on one of John's senior management team meetings and then early Monday morning went with him as he did a tour of the factory (which he did every Monday).

Listening to John talk with the management and staff, and during his team meeting, we were impressed with the regard in which John was held. So why was there such a high turnover in his senior team? Issues such as role structure, role clarification, conflict and so on were all ruled out as it was a well-run establishment and John was a very efficient manager. The thing that struck us most was that every discussion was about fact and logic. There was a total absence of discussion or mention of feelings, emotions and attitudes. As a result, the workplace was a very sombre environment.

During our subsequent discussion with John, we asked him to do one thing when he did his next rounds of the factory. "John, when you talk with each person next Monday, we'd like you to replace the word 'think' with 'feel'. For example, when you are asking about progress on the 'x' project, say 'How do you feel about the progress we're making?' rather than 'What do you think progress looks like on the 'x' Project?' You'll probably have to write out a number of these 'feeling' type questions before next Monday, so that they come naturally to you during the conversation."

At our next session with John after his Monday 'feeling' exercise, John had one word to say, "Wow!" He then went on to explain that he had learnt so much more in his rounds this Monday than ever before. People were still talking about some of the factual items, but now they were also expressing how they felt about things, for example their concerns and motivation. This then was the missing link in John's work place, emotion.

People need to know how others are feeling about things. They also want to feel that there is a safe place where they can express their emotions—both positive and negative. And it's the same in every good relationship—both people want to know they can express their feelings openly and honestly and get a 'sympathetic ear' when they need one. Earlier in the book, we explored the need to develop open and trusting relationships with techniques such as 'disclosure'.

In a difficult and emotionally charged conversation, many people are not really listening to what others say. Instead, they are often mentally 'reloading' their responses. This means they may fail to pick up important clues about the other's emotions and concerns, which also means missing opportunities to build trust and understanding. The most common mistake we all make at one time or another is that when emotions are running high, we tend to start speaking before the other person has finished (the 0.05 seconds overlap becomes far greater when emotions are high).

Listen, really listen; listen with the 'third ear' (the one that picks up the unspoken meaning or feeling—this is quite often your intuition or gut feeling), both to what is being said, and to what is not being said. It is important to note that you do not have to agree, but you do have to understand. The other person also needs to know that you understand their view. We often assume the other person knows we understand what they are saying, but if we don't demonstrate or *tell* them we understand, it can be a dangerous assumption to make.

With this distinction between 'facts' and 'feelings' in all conversations evident, let's now progress to examining in greater detail the remaining four conversation phases. Keep that 'third ear' listening for when a feeling or fact type response or an intervention may be more appropriate.

3. Construct meaning

Here, people are able to understand one another through previous conversations, shared knowledge, common language or social norms. This is achieved through skilled questioning which also enables leaders to bring to the surface and address people's underlying issues, needs and concerns. Questioning allows leaders to check assumptions—yours and theirs.

Leaders should be sure to ask lots of questions, both open and closed (e.g. who, what, when, how). The most powerful questions provoke the other person to think differently.

- Keep questions short. Ask one at a time (avoid compound questions) and pause for the reply. Use "Why?" sparingly, since "Why?" often evokes rationalisation and justification rather than reflection. Instead you can ask:
    - How might we work together to resolve this difficulty? (remembering to follow the rule about 'we' mentioned earlier)
    - What would we need to happen for things to be different?
    - What would it take for you to come along?
    - What else?
    - Tell me more?

These last two questions 'What else?' and 'Tell me more?' are in a way saying 'and' a little differently. People we've coached keep coming back with reports that their most powerful question has become "What else?"

And remember to listen for metaphors, as explained earlier. In a challenging conversation, metaphors are most likely to illustrate the feeling behind what the other person is saying.

4. Converge on agreement

In this phase, people share some understanding of the topic even if minimal, or a desire to understand it if the conversation is to continue (although they may totally disagree on one another's reasons, logic, philosophy and so on). Once again, questioning and listening are the keys elements here.

As the two of you start to reach agreement on the issue or problem and potential answers start being discussed, there's another form of questioning called 'constraints questions' that can be useful here. Constraints questions help to provide a clearer picture of what is happening and what can be done to improve the situation. For example:

- What stops you ...?
- What gets in the way ...?
- Do you have an example of ...?

And if you feel there is a need to look for further options, another useful tool is 'hypothetical questions'. For example:

- What if ...?
- If we could ...?
- If it were possible to do this, what would it look like?

These questions, together with effective listening (such as appropriate paraphrasing or preferably, clean language) are at the heart of reaching agreement.

Once you've completed Phases 1 to 4:

1—open a channel;

2—commit to engage;

3—construct meaning; and

4—converge on agreement.

Following this, phase 5—evolve and build, and 6—act or transact, should fall into place automatically.

5. Evolve and build

Either or both people are different after the conversation—this may be in their actions, beliefs or even a strengthening of their initial thoughts and ideas:

- What did the conversation identify, confirm or change for each person?
- How did each person feel following the conversation? Was this a different feeling from before?

6. Act or transact

Either or both people do something as a result of the conversation. This may range from undertaking some action, telling someone else, or continuing to think (consciously) about the topic:

- What has each person done since the conversation (that was related)?
- Who have they told (or will they tell/involve) about the conversation? Why?

If it's important for a leader to know what the other person is going to do following the conversation, she or he could ask the following questions (depending on the circumstances):

- "Who will you tell about our discussion?"
- "What are you going to tell them?"
- "What will you do if they disagree with what we've decided?" OR "What should we do if others disagree with our decision?"

It is also important to know *the words* a CEO or colleague has decided to use with their stakeholders or constituents. Remember, it's the words that will carry the impact of the decision that the two (or more) of you have decided on. Further useful questions to ask at this point are:

- "Now that we've agreed on the action that needs to be taken, it's also important that we agree on the words that each of us is going to use:
  - How will you describe this to your colleagues, the CEO, constituents, stakeholders, senior management, the media, etc.?
  - What words will be most appropriate? Are there any we should avoid using?
  - How will you phrase your statements?"

Using the six phases to navigate through challenging conversations

Earlier in the book we said that it would be "nigh on impossible to remember all six of these phases during a difficult or challenging conversation". As you've seen, it really is only the first four you need to remember and manage during the conversation, so hopefully this conversation process map will assist.

Below is a diagram of the six phases with relative tasks to complete as you progress through all challenging conversations:

There are growing bodies of experience, research, philosophies, principles, and practices that teach us about the power of conversations (where the right words are used) to create breakthroughs. Where conscious and constructive conversation happens, trust begins, cooperation starts and even violence disappears.

In Part 4, we cover many of the challenging conversations that leaders face. In a number of these we explicitly outline how the six tasks in the communication process are managed. In others, we leave it to you to discern when and how they are managed.

Ask for help:
- *"I'd be pleased if I could have this report by the next meeting"*

What action will each take?
- *What has each done?*
- *Who has each told?*

1.
Open a
Channel

Express feelings:
- *"I'd be pleased ..."*

6.
Act or
Transact

2.
Commit
to Engage

THE CONVERSATION PROCESS

5.
Evolve and
Build

3.
Construct
Meaning

4.
Converge on
Agreement

What's changed?
- *Actions*
- *Beliefs*
- *Ideas*

Find common ground:
- *"So that we can make a decision"*

Ask for specific help needed:
- *"Can that be achieved?"*

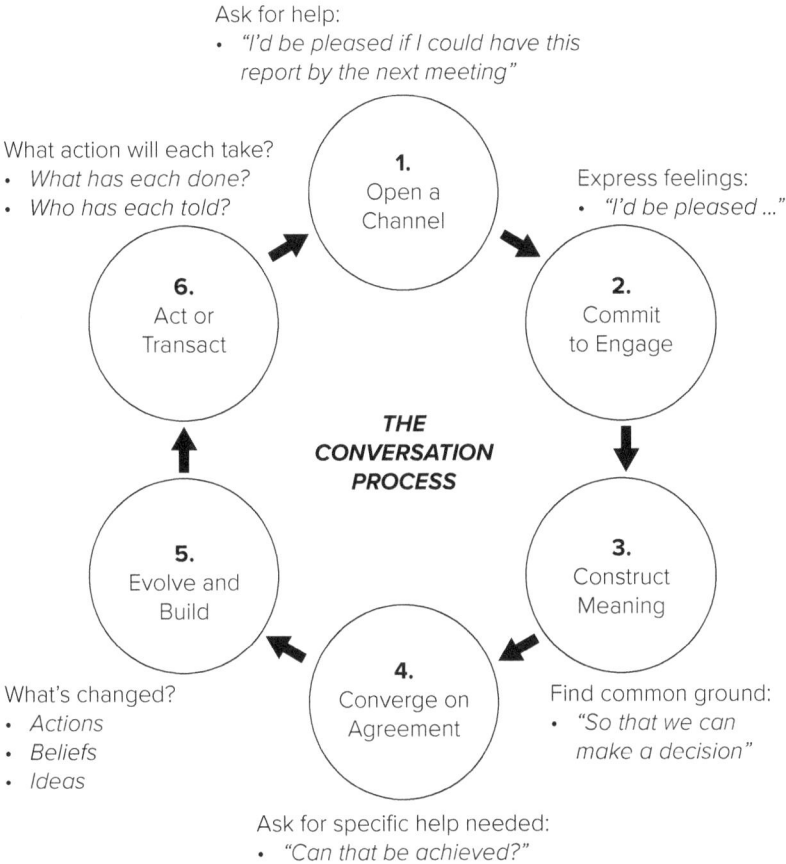

Figure 15: The conversation process map including the tasks to complete at each phase.

The bottom line ...

The value of asking good questions

The use of 'constraint' and 'hypothetical' questions are such an important guide when navigating challenging conversations, and particularly during the 'converge on agreement' phase, that we suggest practising them as much as possible. For reference, here are some examples again:

Constraint questions:
- What stops you ...?
- What gets in the way ...?
- Do you have an example of ...?

Hypothetical questions:
- What if ...?
- If we could ...?
- If it were possible to do this, what would it look like?

And excellent 'open' questions include:
- How might we work together to resolve this difficulty? (remembering to follow the rule about 'we')
- What would need to happen for things to be different?
- What else?
- Tell me more?

4.2 CEO, executive team and board

Fierce conversations do take time. The problem is, anything else takes longer.—Susan Scott.[159]

When we are faced with a difficult conversation, we have three options:
- avoid them;
- face and handle them poorly; and
- face and handle them well.

All too often, we tend to avoid the really difficult or fierce conversation, because we know that it will probably lead to conflict. Then, by the time we know that we must face it (we all have that 'inner voice' that tells us "I must have this conversation"), we're not in a good state of mind to do so, much less to handle it well. We are emotionally charged.

Challenging or difficult conversations and managing dissent is inevitable. But that doesn't mean that the outcomes have to be poor. When the emotions are high, and they generally will be in situations where

---

159 S Scott, 2013, "How people deal with difficult conversations", *Clearwater Consulting*, 24 October, http://www.clearwater-consulting.com/extraordinary-leadership-blog/bid/153745/How-People-Deal-with-Difficult-Conversations, (accessed 29 March 2018).

the stakes are also high, leaders need to keep the conversation constructive and avoid words that will lead to destructive, or at best, less than ideal outcomes.

The four types of communicators

How do we keep the conversation constructive? Are there words to avoid? Communication experts generally agree that in difficult conversations there are four types of communicators:[160]

- passive;
- aggressive;
- passive-aggressive; and
- assertive.

Passive

This person tends to clam up when faced with a difficult situation or they will try to avoid the discussion. Passive communicators will try to hide their emotions which can lead to stress, resentment and bitterness—thinking "Why doesn't he do something about it?", "Can't he/she see there's a problem?"

For example, when financial results are tight, a CEO in this mode may try to cover up the issue and fix it themselves without anyone else, leading to stress if they are found out. Such passive communicators can find themselves under even more stress when questions are asked because no one is comfortable with the answers or level of information they have given.

Passive communicators often have that inner voice in their heads, which unfortunately, rarely gets to speak out loud so that others can hear what's on their mind.

---

160 "The Four Basic Styles of Communication", 2018, *UK Violence Intervention and Prevention Centre*, https://www.uky.edu/hr/sites/www.uky.edu.hr/files/wellness/images/Conf14_FourCommStyles.pdf, (accessed 29 March 2018).

Aggressive

As the title suggests, this type of communicator tends to be loud and tries to control. They can also attack and provoke others with the words they use. They will often blame circumstances or other people for the problem (i.e. they will have an external locus of control).

For example, if there is a financial problem, the CEO might hear one of the executive members say, "Consumer spending dropped unexpectedly this quarter, no one could have predicted it. Our strategy is still on target. We would be short-sighted to pull back now."

Passive-aggressive

These communicators tend to express their feelings in an indirect manner. At first they seem pleasant and warm, giving compliments, which can, however, be taken two ways but may actually be cheap jibes. They will deal with the problem by making hints or subtle suggestions while acting as if nothing is wrong.

For example, one executive in passive-aggressive mode might say to another executive, "I thought you knew about the potential for a drop in revenue. We talked about it on the teleconference a few weeks ago. Must have put you on mute to keep you quiet! Sorry, just joking."

Assertive

This executive starts with a clear understanding of how they feel about the issue, what they think has led to it, and ways to approach finding a solution. While they are very clear about their feelings (and will express them), they are also willing to listen to others to clearly define the problem and identify options. They will state the responsibility they have in causing the problem and be prepared to work together to solve it (they often have an internal locus of control).

For example, the CEO speaking with members of the executive team, might say, "We've made some progress, but not as much as we wanted. So I agree. Let's take a step back and get some independent advice to look at where the value is and how we can do a better job."

From these four descriptions, it's obvious that the first three styles are somewhat negative and the fourth is more positive. Perhaps you may not see them as clear-cut as this and in your own case you can see a bit of yourself in more than one style. That's quite typical.

So, what is your natural style?

If you are aware of this and it's one of the first three, passive, passive-aggressive or aggressive, then the first step in managing a difficult conversation with others is to look at ways you can moderate your natural style. The best way of doing this is to be more aware of the style of language you are using and be more assertive with the words you use.

Before proceeding, it's important to understand what 'assertive behaviour' means. In common usage, the word 'assertive' may seem negative and is often confused with 'aggressive'. However, assertive-ness is the quality of being self-assured and confident without being aggressive. Assertive people tend to:

- feel free to express their thoughts, feelings and desires;
- are able to initiate and maintain comfortable relationships;
- have control over their anger;
- are willing to compromise with others rather than always wanting their own way; and
- have high self esteem.

In conversations, the three communication styles leaders use, are more likely to be:

Aggressive	Passive-aggressive	Assertive
"Could you make sure this report is presented to the executive team meeting?" Sounds like a question, but is really a command.	*"It would be good if we could have this report completed discussion at the next meeting."* Often said with a smile, although there is no humour intended and it is clearly heard as a veiled threat.	*"I'd be pleased if I could have a copy of this report by the next meeting so that we can make a decision. Can that be achieved?"* Notice here the use of "I" rather than "you" and the complimentary feeling expressed as "pleased".
Before continuing, we suggest doing a quick self-assessment of your natural style. If you were in this situation, which of the above most closely matches what you would say?		

Table 9: Three conversational styles.

Note: A further explanation of assertive/aggressive behaviour is covered in detail in Chapter 4.6 'The conversation you're having when you're not having a conversation'. 'I' statements were covered in Part 3. We recommend a brief review of Chapter 3.2 'The impact of a leader's personal language', then read Chapter 4.6 to ensure that you are familiar with the concepts and to provide a better understanding of your own natural style.

Look again at the assertiveness statement used above (in the third column). It follows the four-guidelines for using "I" statements that we outlined earlier in the book. And although we are only hearing one side of the conversation in this example, the words being used indicate that the conversation is likely to be well managed through the first four phases:

The 4 steps	Statement or question	Why each step works (process)
1. Ask for help	"... if I could have this report by the next meeting ..."	Opens the channel
2. Express feelings	"I'd be pleased"	Promotes interest for the other person to engage in the conversation
3. Say why you are feeling this way	"... so that we can make a decision."	Constructs meaning around the topic so that the other person understands why you are feeling this way
4. Ask for specific help needed	"Can that be achieved?"	This request for help, commences the process where the two executives can converge on agreement.

Table 10: Assertiveness style of conversation using the 4 Step 'I' statements guidelines.

Here's how and where these statements might occur in the conversation process:

Asks for help:
- *"I'd be pleased if I could have this report by the next meeting"*

What action will each take?
- *What will each do?*
- *Who will each tell?*

1.
Open a
Channel

Expresses feelings:
- *"I'd be pleased ..."*

6.
Act or
Transact

2.
Commit
to Engage

***AN ASSERTIVE STYLE
IN THE
CONVERSATION
PROCESS***

5.
Evolve and
Build

3.
Construct
Meaning

4.
Converge on
Agreement

What's likely to change?
- *Actions*
- *Beliefs*
- *Ideas*

Finds common ground:
- *"So that we can make a decision"*

Asks for specific help needed:
- *"Can that be achieved?"*

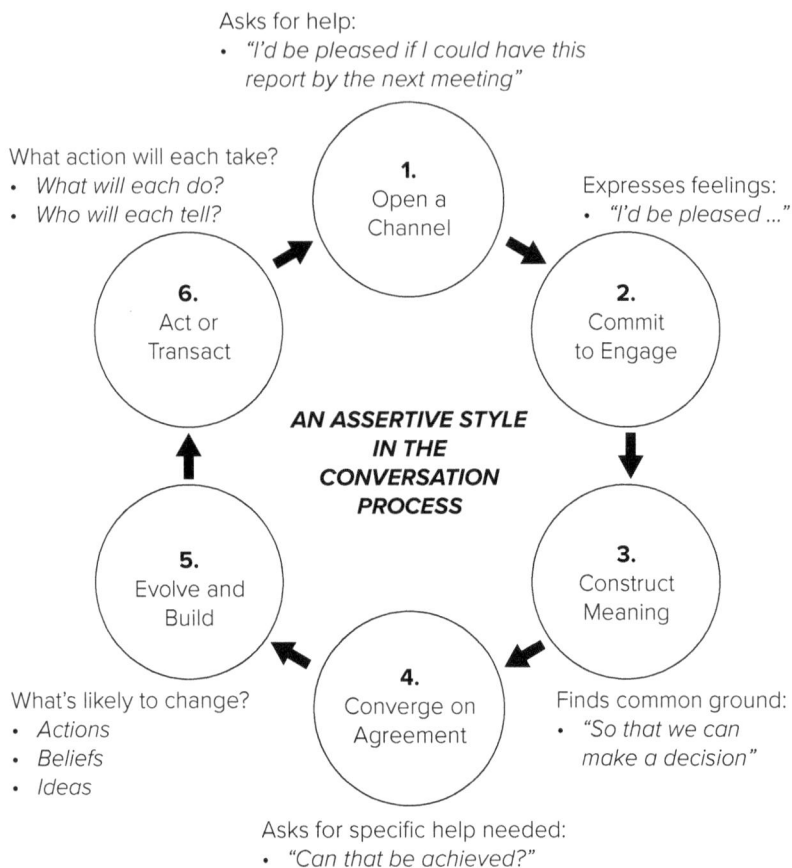

Figure 16: The conversation process map with examples.

Dealing with the aggressive or passive-aggressive executive or CEO

Through our research we have identified the two least developed skills in the workplace: the ability to have uncomfortable conversations and the ability to ask 'what if' questions. (italics are ours).[161]

---

161 J Glaser, 2013, "Conversational intelligence: How great leaders build trust and get extraordinary results", Taylor and Francis Inc. Brookline, MA, p 35.

Now that you have an idea of your own style and how to phrase requests in an assertive manner, it's time to look at how to manage the conversation when the CEO or another senior executive is displaying aggressive or passive-aggressive behaviour.

We've provided two typical examples of this type of communicator below. To become familiar with this type of communication, read the examples and identify the aggressive language used and consider ways to convert the less positive styles to assertive language. The concepts of 'framing' and 'triangulation' could both be used to improve the conversation and we have provided some examples following the situation descriptions.

Situation 1: CEO and senior team member—a clash over strategy

The scenario:

The company had been struggling for some time amid a consumer downturn and moves by some major retailers to ditch brand names in favour of private label products. The board hired a new CEO to replace one who had made controversial decisions to close a local factory and cut jobs to reduce costs. This is a new CEO, let's call him John. The board gave the new CEO five to six quarters to start turning poor company performance around.

The board signed off on John's five-year growth plan, which involved rebuilding customer relationships, leveraging the strength of key brands, expanding into new categories and distribution channels, and boosting investment in innovation.

Executive team meeting (one month ago):

At the end of the sixth quarter, there is still no change in the earnings trajectory. The CEO believes the board may be losing confidence in the strategy and calls an executive team meeting.

There is dissent at the ensuing meeting on whether to change course. This is how the meeting unfolds …

When presenting his performance report at the meeting, the Chief Marketing Officer (CMO) tells the CEO:

"Consumer confidence is weak, and the weather has been unseasonably warm, there is weakness across the sector, we can expect pre-tax earnings to be as much as 14 per cent below the previous forecast. Net debt levels may be higher in the short-term, but we will be able to make it up in the long-term."

The CEO responds, "I've heard this before. You may not have a long-term future if we don't start seeing a better short-term."

The CMO replies, "Is that a threat?"

The CEO: "Don't take it personally. You know what I mean. This is business, the board has given me a deadline. I'm talking about the whole company. We all know it's tough, and that you've been here a lot longer than me."

"You backed my strategy when I joined; a plan to create the sort of company that becomes known and respected by all for innovation and design. We want to be an inspiring and exciting company that makes things possible for people, for jobs in the community and for the market. We have to show we can make it happen."

The CMO: "You've only been here for 18 months. We've been struggling with this situation for a number of years. We've made progress but not as much as we wanted. It's a tough sector to operate in, but I think we are doing all right. Let's take a step back and get some external advice."

The CEO said: "And who is that going to be, I have to face the board you know?"

The current situation:

A month later the CEO accepted the CMO's resignation with regret saying he had led a "revitalisation" of the company's strategy, investment in future growth and was positioning it for better performance.

However, another source said that the "writing was on the wall" when the CMO wanted to get external advice, the CEO lost confidence.

Situation 1—Possible responses to some of the CEO's statements:

Comment from the CEO	Option for response from the CMO
"I've heard this before. You may not have a long-term future if we don't start seeing a better short-term."	*Triangulation* "I understand your concern about short-term results, may I ask others for their views?" This allows a third party to enter the conversation, a triangle is formed in the conversation which can relieve some of the pressure from the exchange between the CEO and CMO.
"Don't take it personally. You know what I mean. This is business, the board has given me a deadline. I'm talking about the company. We all know it's tough, and that you've been here longer than me."	*Framing* It's hard not to take it personally, I made a commitment to the new strategy when it was signed off, it's tough for all of us. The framing is 'we are in this together'

Situation 2: CEO's email to executive team members— an unintended impact

The scenario:

Following a clash between the CEO and the CFO at a regular team meeting over communication with staff (the CEO accused the CFO of "communicating too often with too much detail and holding too many meetings"), the following email was forwarded to other senior team members by the CEO:

I met with the CFO last week on one of my regular catch-ups and we discussed a variety of subjects, most of which you are all across through either committee structures or team meetings.

Overall, the communication senior management down through the organisation seems to be working adequately and this needs to continue with some minor adjustments made on how we interact with managers outside our senior team.

I would like to ask that everyone think about the following:

- *Communication of key initiatives is encouraged. However, we all need to use our judgment as to how often and what is discussed outside the executive team in the various interactions that we may have both formally and informally.*

- *If there are problems with the level of understanding of senior team decisions, please discuss them with me in the first instance so that I understand what is being asked, purely as courtesy and to ensure that we are not giving conflicting instructions to those outside the senior team.*

- *Please use as much as possible the established meeting structures to exchange and capture the necessary information and agreed actions without calling extra meetings.*

Another overall observation, please use email for key matters only, as I, like many of you, no doubt receive far too much email and anything to minimise this would be greatly appreciated.

I trust you all read this in the spirit of how it is intended and that is to keep the right relationships in place between the senior team and other levels of management and to be aware that unnecessary meetings take time that might be better spent elsewhere.

If there is any matter that may be concerning you at any time, please do not hesitate to call me.

If you have any suggestions on how we can improve in this area, I welcome this feedback.

I look forward to your continuing support and contribution in one of the most challenging periods of our history.

The CEO

Think about the CEO's communication style in this email, is it aggressive, passive aggressive or assertive?

We would call it passive-aggressive. The communicator is expressing feelings in an indirect manner by sending a message to the entire senior team. It may seem pleasant and warm, however, many of the comments can be taken two ways, for example, "communication is encouraged" and at the same time "we all need to use our judgment as to how often and what is discussed outside the executive team." The email attempts to deal with the problem by making hints and subtle suggestions while acting as if nothing is really wrong, when clearly something is wrong.

Do you think the email will have the desired effect of improving communication and eliminating unnecessary meetings?

We suggest it is unlikely that retreating to email can resolve the communication issues that arose in the clash between the CEO and CFO. Interpersonal conflict is best resolved face-to-face between or among people having difficulty with each other. The assistance of an external independent third party to support the conversation can be very helpful and is another use of triangulation.

Initiating a challenging conversation

When you are faced with the prospect of having to initiate a challenging conversation, say with the CEO or a colleague:

- Prepare some initial statements that follow the four-step process:
  - ask for their help;
  - express your feelings;

  – say why you are feeling this way; and
  – ask for the specific help needed.
- Consider your natural style. If it's closer to the aggressive end of the continuum, you may find the words in the four-step process challenging. Consider being more assertive. Also, give some thought to the natural style of the recipient. How might they respond to your approach?

Keep in mind the natural process through which the conversation will progress:

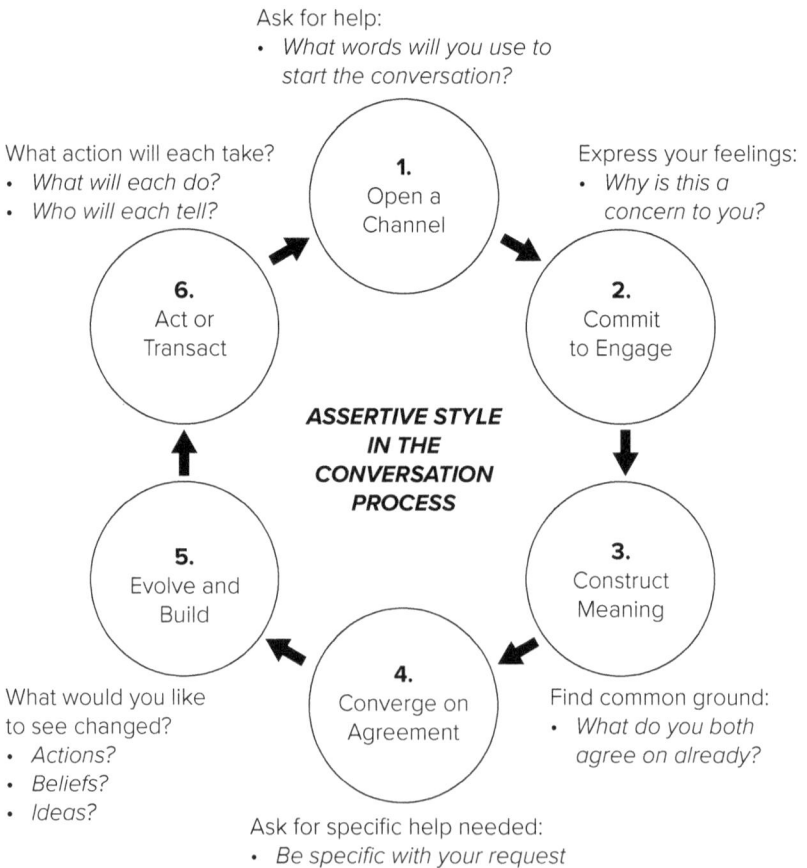

Ask for help:
• *What words will you use to start the conversation?*

What action will each take?
• *What will each do?*
• *Who will each tell?*

1.
Open a
Channel

Express your feelings:
• *Why is this a concern to you?*

6.
Act or
Transact

2.
Commit
to Engage

ASSERTIVE STYLE IN THE CONVERSATION PROCESS

5.
Evolve and
Build

3.
Construct
Meaning

What would you like to see changed?
• *Actions?*
• *Beliefs?*
• *Ideas?*

4.
Converge on
Agreement

Find common ground:
• *What do you both agree on already?*

Ask for specific help needed:
• *Be specific with your request*

Figure 17: The process map with actions to take during each phase.

4.3 Making a public apology

An obligatory apology is wanting to get someone off your back; a sincere apology is about wanting to be let off the hook; a heartfelt apology is about wanting to repair a relationship.—Pete Linnett[162]

On the 12th of May 2015 at around 9 pm, an Amtrak Northeast Regional Train No. 188 from Washington, D.C. bound for New York City derailed on the Northeast Corridor in the Port Richmond neighbourhood of Philadelphia, Pennsylvania. Of the 238 passengers and five crew on board, eight were killed and over 200 injured, 11 critically. The train was traveling at 164 km/h in an 80 km/h zone of curved tracks when it derailed.

A Message from President and CEO Joe Boardman on Train 188

The derailment of Northeast Regional Train 188 was a terrible tragedy that we are responding to with every resource we have available. The National Transportation Safety Board is leading the investigation to determine the cause of the incident, and Amtrak is providing full cooperation.

With truly heavy hearts, we mourn those who died. Their loss leaves holes in the lives of their families and communities. On behalf of the entire Amtrak family, I offer our sincere sympathies and prayers for them and their loved ones. Amtrak takes full responsibility and deeply apologizes for our role in this tragic event.

---

162 M Gouldston, 2012, "I'm sorry: Apologies ... The good, the bad and the heartfelt", 3 December, *Psychology Today*, https://www.psychologytoday.com/au/blog/just-listen/201212/im-sorry-apologies-the-good-the-bad-and-the-heartfelt, (accessed 29 March, 2018).

We recognize that for everyone onboard the train, including those who suffered injuries, the healing process may be long. Within 24 hours of the incident, Amtrak set up a Family Assistance Center in Philadelphia to work closely with the family of passengers and crew on the train. We are also working with the individuals and families affected by this event to help them with transportation, lodging, and of course, medical bills and funeral expenses.

Amtrak is ever grateful to the City of Philadelphia—its first responders who bravely worked in difficult conditions, including the dark of night, to rescue and provide aid to hundreds; its hospital personnel who went into full alert as patients arrived at emergency rooms; its officials who quickly implemented a response plan; and its citizens who opened their doors to offer assistance.

Although our current focus is on the passengers and employees affected by this incident and the resulting service disruption along the Northeast Corridor, we must also take time to learn from this event. Passenger railroading is at its core about people; the safety of our passengers and employees was, is and always will be our number one priority. Our goal is to fully understand what happened and how we can prevent a similar tragedy from occurring in the future. We will also continue to focus on completing Positive Train Control implementation in the Northeast Corridor by December of 2015.

Thank you for your support of America's Railroad during this difficult time.

Sincerely,

Joe Boardman

President and Chief Executive Officer[163]

---

163 J Boardman, 2015, A Message from President and CEO Joe Boardman on Train 188, n.d., *Amtrak News*, http://blog.amtrak.com/2015/05/message-president-ceo-joe-boardman-train-188/, (accessed 29 March 2018).

Sometimes the chair issues an apology for a corporate mistake; more often it's the CEO. Whoever issues the apology, verbal or written, it has an immediate impact on the reputation of the organisation, either positive or negative. Yes, that's right, an apology can enhance the reputation of the organisation despite the seriousness of the current situation.

How does the Amtrak apology compare with this example of Qatar Airways chief executive Sheik Akbar Al Baker?

I should like to apologise unreservedly to those offended by my recent remarks which compared Qatar Airways cabin crew with cabin crew on US carriers. The remarks were made informally at a private gala dinner, following comments about the Qatar Airways cabin service, and were in no way intended to cause offence. This is a time of strong rivalry between our airline and the US carriers, and we are of course immensely proud of our own cabin crew. However, cabin crew are the public face of all airlines, and I greatly respect their hard work and professionalism. They play a huge role in the safety and comfort of passengers, irrespective of their age or gender or familial status. I have worked for many years in the industry, and I have a high regard for the value that I see long-serving staff members bringing through their experience and dedication.[164]

Take the Amtrak example. What impression did you get when reading Joe Boardman's apology? The Qatar incident was to do with a loss of face. The Amtrak incident was to do with loss of life. Which apology was more positive?

---

164 A Baker, 2017, "Qatar Airways' Al Baker 'sorry' for sexist comments", *The National*, 13 July, https://www.thenational.ae/business/aviation/qatar-airways-al-baker-sorry-for-sexist-comments-1.548463?videoId=5620020761001, (accessed 29 March 2018).

Apologies can be an opportunity, although the circumstances may be severe, to improve the reputation of the organisation. We're sure that despite the tragedy, Amtrak's reputation was greatly enhanced by the quick and sincere apology of Joe Boardman, President and CEO (he also rushed to the scene of the crash immediately he heard the news).

The eight criteria for an effective apology

In addition to the wording of the apology (which we'll cover shortly), there are eight criteria that should be met when giving an apology:

	AMTRAK	QATAR
1. Give a detailed account of the situation	✓	?
2. Acknowledge the hurt or damage done	✓	✓
3. Take full responsibility	✓	?
4. Recognise your role or the company's in the situation	✓	?
5. Include a statement of regret	✓	✓
6. Ask for forgiveness	✓	?
7. Promise to ensure that it won't happen again	✓	?
8. Provide a form of restitution if possible	✓	?

Looking back at both the Amtrak and Qatar apologies to see how many of the criteria each met, the Amtrak apology meets all of the criteria while the Qatar example seems to be about an acknowledgement that hurt may have been caused, a statement of regret, and not much more.

And here's another apology that shines a favourable light on the organisation. At the Oscar Awards ceremony in 2017, the wrong envelope was given to the presenters, resulting in the incorrect picture being announced as the Oscar winner. PwC, the organisation responsible for the scoring of the awards, immediately gave this apology:

We sincerely apologize to Moonlight, La La Land, Warren Beatty, Faye Dunaway, and Oscar viewers for the error that was made during the award announcement for Best Picture. The presenters had mistakenly been given the wrong category envelope and when discovered, was immediately corrected. We are currently investigating how this could have happened, and deeply regret that this occurred.[165]

What separates a sincere apology from an unconvincing attempt at public contrition? It's the way in which it is worded and the intention of the organisation. In addition to following the eight criteria mentioned, here are some points to keep in mind with regard to your intention when giving an apology:

The apology should always be about the people that have been hurt or wronged by the mistake—it's never about you or your company. Avoid statements such as:

- "I (or we) didn't realise …"
- "I (or we) didn't mean to …"
- "I (or we) was trying to …"

which all hint of, or even imply, justification—people will see them as insincere.

Put yourself in the shoes of the people for whom the apology is intended. What words would you like to hear if this mistake affected you?

---

165 L Frykberg, 2017, Oscars 2017: Auditors PriceWaterhouseCoopers apologise for best picture boo-boo, *Straits Times*, 27 February, https://www.straits times.com/lifestyle/entertainment/oscars-2017-auditors-pricewaterhouse coopers-apologise-for-best-picture-boo, (accessed 22 June 2018).

Acknowledge their feelings and values. For example, from the Amtrak apology:

- "With truly heavy hearts, we mourn those who died."
- "We recognize that for everyone onboard the train, including those who suffered injuries, the healing process may be long."

Restore a sense of "us"—as a leader, these people are your customers, your employees, your suppliers, and members of your community. Once again, from the Amtrak apology:

- "Passenger railroading is at its core about people; the safety of our passengers and employees was, is and always will be our number one priority."

Should leaders use the words "I'm sorry" or "I apologise"?

It's an interesting conundrum, for the words, their meaning and their impact, are quite different.

	Sorry	Apology
Definition	• Refers to feeling sorrow, regret, or contrition	• Is a regretful acknowledgment of an offence or failure
Grammatical category	• Adjective	• Noun
Responsibility	• Doesn't necessarily imply that the speaker is taking the responsibility for the fault	• Implies that the speaker is taking the responsibility for the fault
Formality level	• More informal	• More formal than 'sorry' and is more often used in a professional context
Others' situation	• Is also used to express sympathy and regret about someone else's situation	• Cannot (in a sentence) be used to express sympathy about someone else's situation

Table 11: Comparison of the word 'sorry' with the word 'apology'.

Unfortunately, whilst the words 'apology', 'I apologise', or 'we apologise' are probably most appropriate (technically) for a corporate apology, they have possibly lost their true meaning and particularly their intended impact due to overuse and poor use. For example, "I would like to apologise unreservedly" is used in many formal apologies and is often followed by an attempt at justification. The intended recipients and the general public see right through such attempts.

The words 'apology' and 'sorry' have a different impact

- The word 'apology' is used to admit a mistake—it relates to the speaker's reasoning for his/her error.
- The word 'sorry' is used to show remorse for doing what he/she did and to demonstrate sincere regret for offending (or hurting) someone.

This is a very important distinction. 'Sorry' carries an emotional impact for both the person saying 'sorry' and the receiver. 'Sorry' elicits emotions, whereas 'apology' deals only with facts, reason and logic and does not elicit emotions, particularly in the receiver. Often people will say "I apologise unreservedly" and "I can honestly say ..."—the receivers hear these as insincere and so they question the sincerity of the person saying them.

In the ball-tampering issue of the Australian Cricket Team in South Africa in March 2018, the three people responsible for the transgression, Steve Smith (the Captain), David Warner (the Vice-Captain) and Cameron Bancroft (the cricketer who tampered with the ball), in their media interviews, all gave public apologies for their deeds.

Here is Steve Smith's apology:

Good evening, thanks for coming, appreciate it. To all of my teammates, to fans of cricket all over the world, and to all Australians who are disappointed and angry—I'm sorry. What happened in Cape Town has already been laid out by Cricket Australia.

Tonight, I want to make clear as captain of the Australian Cricket Team, I take full responsibility. I made a serious error of judgement, and I now understand the consequences. It was a failure of leadership—of my leadership. I'll do everything I can to make up for my mistake and the damage it's caused. If any good can come of this, it's that it can be a lesson to others, and I hope I can be a force for change.

I know I'll regret this for the rest of my life; I'm absolutely gutted. I hope in time I can earn back respect and forgiveness, I've been so privileged and honoured to represent my country and captain the Australian cricket team. Cricket is the greatest game in the world. It's been my life, and I hope it can be again. I'm sorry and I'm absolutely devastated. I'll take some questions.

And here is David Warner's apology:

First of all I'd like to thank you all for coming this morning. To the fans and the lovers of the game who have supported and inspired me on my journey as a cricketer, I want to sincerely apologise for betraying your trust in me. I have let you down badly. I hope in time I can find a way to repay you for all you've given me and possibly earn your respect again.

To my teammates and support staff, I apologise for my actions and I take full responsibility for my part in what happened on day three of the Newlands Test. To Cricket Australia, I apologise for my actions and the effect it has had on our game under your care and control. I want you to know that I fully support your review into the culture of the Australian cricket team. To South African players, administration and fans, I apologise unreservedly for my part in this and I am sorry. I brought the game into disrepute on your soil. South Africa is a fine cricketing nation and deserves better from its guests and deserves better from me.

To all Australians, whether you're a cricket fan or not, I apologise for my actions. I'm sorry for the impact those actions have had on our country's reputation. I can honestly say I have only ever wanted to bring glory to my country by playing cricket. In striving to do so, I have made a decision which has had an opposite effect and it's one that I'll regret for as long as I'll live. I do realise that I'm responsible for my own actions and the consequences that that brings. It's heartbreaking to know that I won't be taking to the field with my teammates that I love and have let down. Right now it is hard to know what comes next but first and foremost, is the wellbeing of my family.

In the back of my mind, I suppose there is a tiny ray of hope that I may one day be given the privilege of playing for my country again but I'm resigned to the fact that that may never happen again. In the coming weeks and months, I'm going to look at how this has happened and who I am as a man. I will seek out advice and expertise to help me make serious changes. I want to apologise to my family. To my wife and daughters. Your love means more than anything to me, I know I would not be anything without you. I'm very sorry for putting you through this and I promise I'll never put you through this again.

Before I take questions, I want to again say thank you, I take full responsibility for my part in what happened and I am deeply sorry for the consequences of what I was involved in. I failed in my responsibilities as vice-captain of the Australian cricket team.

I will now answer your questions.

In the apology of Steve Smith, he only used the word 'sorry' whereas David Warner used 'apology' more often (although he did use 'sorry' twice—however, it immediately followed 'apologise' and so had very little impact). At the end of Steve Smith's interview, many of the press were sympathising with him, saying things like "Good luck, Steve",

"All the best, Steve", whereas as Warner left the room, reporters were still asking questions.[166]

Every organisation will at some stage have a crisis that requires an apology whether that be a loss of a major client (or perhaps market share); a natural disaster that has affected the company, the people, the community; a self-made disaster (such as the BP oil spill in the Gulf of Mexico); or even loss of life (such as the Dreamworld theme park tragedy in Australia, 2016). In all of these, it is normally the CEO who makes the initial apology. It's imperative that the CEO and all of senior management, are well versed and trained in how to make an apology that is sincere, when the eventual crisis occurs.

As an example, here (in part) is an apology from Apple using the word 'sorry' appropriately:

At Apple, we strive to make world-class products that deliver the best experience possible to our customers. With the launch of our new Maps last week, we fell short on this commitment. We are extremely sorry for the frustration this has caused our customers and we are doing everything we can to make Maps better.[167]

And you'll recall that whilst Amtrak used the word 'apologizes' rather than 'sorry', in this instance because it was sincere, we believe it had a similar impact to 'sorry': "On behalf of the entire Amtrak family, I offer our sincere sympathies and prayers for them and their loved ones. Amtrak takes full responsibility and deeply apologizes for our role in this tragic event."

---

166 D Warner, S Smith and C Bancroft, 2018, "Transcripts: Warner, Smith, Bancroft", *CRICKET.com.au*, 31 March, https://www.cricket.com.au/news/david-warner-press-conference-transcript-steve-smith-cameron-bancroft-ball-tampering/2018-03-31, (accessed 31 March 2018).

167 Cited in D Thier, 2012, "Tim Cook apologizes for Apple Maps", *Forbes*, 28 September, https://www.forbes.com/sites/davidthier/2012/09/28/tim-cook-apologizes-for-apple-maps/, (accessed 29 March 2018).

The bottom line ...

Guidelines for communicating apologies

Whether you are the CEO or a senior executive, when you have the responsibility for issuing an apology for something your organisation has done that is incorrect or hurt various constituents, keep in mind the following points:

* adhere to the eight criteria for formulating an apology;
* the apology should always be about the people who have been hurt or wronged, not about the organisation;
* put yourself in the place of your constituents and use the words that immediately come to mind as if the apology was directed at you;
* acknowledge the feelings and values of your intended audience;
* aim to restore a sense of 'us' with your constituents; and
* decide on when it's appropriate to use the words 'sorry' and/or 'apology' to be sincere.

4.4 Managing that media interview

Leaders are expected to know about the issues that may impact their organisation and what may be brewing deep within their organisations. And they are expected to act upon that knowledge. Plausible deniability is not acceptable. The public, shareholders, and media are holding CEO and senior executives accountable as never before, and therefore they must consider the way they speak, especially to the media.

Consider the case of Ardent Leisure's response to four deaths at its Australian Dreamworld theme park in October 2016. The CEO of Dreamworld was appointed spokesperson for the company, and two days after the tragedy, the board went ahead with the annual general meeting and voted then CEO, Deborah Thomas, a long and medium-term incentive package potentially worth $860,000. The resulting public criticism was immense.

Following public and media outcry, Ardent chairman Neil Balnaves took some responsibility for the company's response.[168] However, he defended the board's actions and told the press the board had made the best decisions it could under difficult circumstances, although in hindsight he wished the board had deferred voting about CEO pay. His explanation was that the company had legal advice stating it was not allowed to postpone the annual general meeting within 48 hours of the starting time. The meeting went ahead with the agreed agenda, which included the CEO pay item. To all outside Ardent, it looked like the company was awarding the CEO a big pay package after four lives had been lost.

"If I had known that motion could have been deferred I would [have] deferred it," Mr Balnaves said. "It was obviously misconstrued." He went on to praise the performance of the CEO. "Deborah has handled it superbly given the complexity and the advice coming from every corner making it difficult to do as you instinctively want to do," he said."

The 'golden rule' for managing media interviews

Having seen both poor and excellent media conversations with CEOs and senior executives over many years, and having advised them on how to manage the media, we have developed a strategy that we call 'the golden rule for media interviews:

- go into every interview with a **theme** you are promoting;
- **three key points** that underpin your theme; and
- **practical examples** of the three key points.

This 'rule' holds true whether the interview is a planned media release, an impromptu call from a journalist asking for comment on a current issue, a response to or initiation of an issue/topic on social media, or a more serious corporate catastrophe.

---

168 M Smith, 2016, "Ardent Leisure's lesson in crisis mismanagement", *Australian Financial Review*, 27 October, http://www.afr.com/brand/chanticleer/ardent-leisures-lesson-in-crisis-mismanagement-20161027-gscciq, (accessed 23 June 2018).

Following the tragedy at Dreamworld, the Ardent Leisure CEO had an opportunity to focus on the theme of compassion. Three key points that could have been used to underpin that theme were acknowledgement of hurt, acceptance of responsibility and support for the families of those who died and the witnesses who experienced trauma. As a practical example of these three points, think about what might have happened if Ardent Leisure/Dreamworld had used a version of the Amtrak apology mentioned earlier.

1. Acknowledgement of hurt:
   With truly heavy hearts, we mourn those who died. Their loss leaves holes in the lives of their families and communities. On behalf of the entire Dreamworld family, we offer our sincere sympathies and prayers for them and their loved ones.
2. Acceptance of responsibility:
   Dreamworld takes full responsibility and deeply apologises for our role in this tragic event.
3. Support for those who have experienced loss and trauma:
   We recognise that for the families who have lost loved ones and everyone who witnessed the tragedy, the healing process may be long. Within 24 hours we will set up a counselling centre to work closely with them. We are also working with the individuals and families affected by this event to help them with transportation, lodging, and of course, medical bills and funeral expenses.

As we progress through this chapter, the following diagram provides a visual road map of how we intend to apply the 'golden rule' to all media interviews in which leaders may be involved—either by participating in the interview, deciding what the media strategy will be, or in coaching the CEO on how to conduct the interview effectively.

5. Use positive language:
- Practice your language beforehand
- Listen carefully to the question
- Take your time
- Reframe the question
- Make it count – less is more
- The buck stops with you

1. Prepare for your interview:
- Identify major points
- Demonstrate empathy
- Use simple language
- Stick to the facts
- Highlight benefits
- Prepare 15 questions

GOLDEN RULE

2. Use techniques to get your message across
- Answer 'plus one'
- Answer in your own time
- Use silence to your advantage
- Avoid 'no comment'
- Avoid jargon
- Use customer testimonials
- Have fun!

4. Learn how to deal with difficult questions:
- Overcome the 'I don't know' syndrome
- Avoid speculation
- Stick with the facts

3. How to answer questions:
- Think about how questions might be framed
- Get behind the question
- Question the questioner

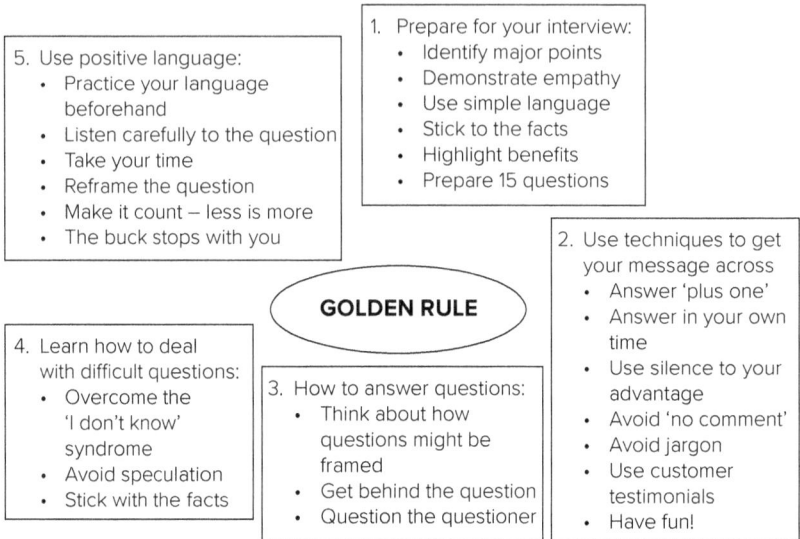

Go into every interview with a theme you are promoting
PLUS three key points that underpin your theme
PLUS practical examples of the three key points

Figure 18: The 'golden rule' for managing media interviews.

How leaders prepare for the media interview

Putting the 'golden rule' into practice requires preparation—which is vital prior to any media interview. So, to develop the **theme**, your **three key points** that underpin your theme, and the **practical examples** of your key points, use the following suggestions:

- Write down all the major points relating to the issue. In doing so, include information all stakeholders and the public want to know.
- Prioritise points from most important to least important. Ensure the first few points clearly explain the basics of the story and give context to the answers.
- Remember the heart; demonstrate empathy. This will make your response more acceptable to the media and the public. Write down some words that you feel others will feel when they hear your message.

- Use clear, simple and economical language. This means avoiding jargon and phrases that may not mean anything to those outside your organisation. The same with acronyms—unless you are talking about something that's well known.
- Stick to the facts. Avoid claims that can't be backed up. Keep your answers simple, clear and short. If you think of something 'on the spot' during the interview to add, it's probably best to avoid it as it has been unplanned.
- Highlight the benefits/achievements/positives. If it is relevant, offer positives.
- Finally, prepare 15 questions that you are likely to be asked. Then have someone else in your organisation do the same. Combine the two lists and develop answers to the potential questions (there will be more on the type of questions most likely asked, shortly).

Seven practical techniques leaders use to get their message across

The following seven points are adapted from the advice given by Australian media communications expert Catriona Pollard in her blog *Women Sharing Business Ideas*.[169] Catriona is also one of the top 100 PR people followed worldwide on Twitter, so her advice is well founded.

Answer 'plus one'

Always maintain control of the interview—keep in mind, as a leader of the company, you are in charge, not the interviewer. When asked a question, always restate your key theme and give one of your examples. Use the interviewer's questions as an opportunity to make your points. This is called 'answer plus one'. Answer the question then add one of your key points.

---

169 C Pollard, 2018, "Women sharing business ideas", http://www.womensnet-work.com.au/blog/author/catriona-pollard, (accessed 29 March 2018).

Answer in your own time

The journalist is interested in what you have to say. If you can't think of an answer immediately, take your time, collect your thoughts and take a deep breath before you answer.

Use silence to your advantage

Some journalists use silence as a technique in the hope you will fill the silence with unplanned information. Silence can be powerful and there is no need to fill it. Allow the silence to sit—let the interviewer 'break' first. This is a technique that needs to be practised, as it is very tempting to 'jump in' to break the silence.

The "no comment" rule

Unfortunately, "no comment" implies confirmation of the question. The audience will interpret it as guilt or a cover up. The rule of thumb for responding is to explain why you can't respond and use one of your key points. For example, "I can't respond directly to that for legal reasons, however, what I can tell you is … In this context, and we have to be conscious that this is a matter before the courts, so there is a limit to the response I can give …"[170]

However, never allow wrongful allegations to stand. If the journalist says something that is wrong, correct them immediately. Do not repeat the incorrect information or question. If you do, it will only reinforce it in the listener's mind. Remember from our 'don't' discussion earlier—if you repeat the incorrect information, it will provide the audience with the potential to think 'he or she has repeated it, so that is really the issue', even though you may be denying it.

---

170 B Mitchell, 2017, Transcript of CBA Catherine Livingstone press conference, *Financial Review*, 14 August, https://www.afr.com/business/banking-and-finance/transcript-of-cba-catherine-livingstone-press-conference-20170814-gxvme9, (accessed 29 March 2018).

Avoid jargon

Every industry has its own jargon. Remember who your target audience is and communicate in language they will understand. Also, the journalist may not understand your jargon.

Use your customers as testimonials

Depending on the topic of the interview, it may be effective to use one of your valued customers to validate your key messages. You would have to ensure that they are comfortable speaking to the media or that you can use them as an example. Often this is an effective way of illustrating your point and helps your audiences understand and identify with you, plus it provides instant credibility.

Most importantly—stay positive

The interview is a wonderful opportunity to promote your business, product or yourself. Take control, prepare and enjoy every moment.

How leaders answer questions that show them in a good light

Despite diligent preparation, a leader can never know exactly how an interview will go so it is important to remember—actively listen and keep the following guidelines in mind when responding to questions (and by the way, these guidelines can apply to difficult meeting discussions as well):

- **Think about how questions might be framed**—remember that it is the job of a journalist to be sceptical, get answers and write a story that people want to read. A good story has drama and it usually has good guys and bad guys. It pays to anticipate how you might be framed—will you be 'the hero' or 'the villain'? All too often, executives are cast as the villains which means you can anticipate facing questions about ulterior motives, the validity of your claims and who is to blame.

- **Get behind the question**—often you need to interpret the question rather than take it at face value. If you simply answer the question asked, you may end up stuck on the journalist's side of the bridge. This can be dangerous if the journalist has you in the negative frame. This is where the answer 'plus one' technique mentioned earlier will assist.
- **Question the questioner**—sometimes you will be asked a question that is vague or open to interpretation. Be sure you understand what is being asked, for example, "I'm not sure I understand the question, could you please rephrase it." This is also a useful technique for finding out what's behind the journalist's question. Jumping in too quickly when you do not fully understand the question, can lead to an incorrect answer or one that could paint you or the organisation in a bad light.

How leaders deal with difficult questions

As we've said earlier, it's the journalist's job to get answers. Remember when they ask difficult questions, they are on the outside of your organisation and may not understand or appreciate the internal sensitivities of your situation. There are three types of questions that all good reporters try to ask—after all, they are after a story that will make news:

- questions the reporter thinks you may not know the answer to—the "I don't know" response;
- questions that call for speculation—the hypothetical—"What would/could happen if?"; and
- questions that ask for your personal opinion—the "Yes, but— what do you personally think (should happen etc.)?"

- **Overcoming the "I don't know" syndrome**—what if you are asked a tough question and you don't know the answer? It is easy to get stumped during a live interview when you don't know the answer. You have two choices:

- Say, "I don't know."
- Tell the journalist what you do know related to the topic of the question.

There's nothing inherently wrong with choice one, and it's often a better option for adversarial interviews. However, it does often give the audience the impression that you are not knowledgeable in this area. A nice way of overcoming the "I don't know" situation, is to bridge from the question you've been asked to an area that you do know about. For example, you could respond with "Well that's unclear, but what I do know is …"

- **Avoid speculation**—imagine you're a CEO in the midst of a takeover bid. You're being interviewed when the reporter suddenly asks, "So, what's the bottom line? Is this acquisition going ahead?"
  - Stick with the facts. Answer by saying something such as, "Well, support from shareholders is building and we are more hopeful than ever that we can get this across the line."
  - If pressed again, you can follow up with, "Well, although I can't speculate, I can tell you that …"
- **Avoid giving personal opinions**—remember that when a leader is identified as a spokesperson for a company, group, or organisation, there's no such thing as a personal opinion. The media will identify the leader as a representative of your organisation. Therefore, keep your personal opinion to yourself. Instead, say, "Well, I'm speaking for the organisation, not myself, and what we believe is …"

Former Whole Foods Chairman and CEO John Mackey found this out the hard way when he sparked a customer rebellion after writing an opinion piece for the Wall Street Journal opposing President Obama's health care reform proposal. He defended himself days later, by writing, "I was asked to write an op-ed piece and I gave my personal opinions. Whole Foods as a company has no official position on the issue". But the damage had been done and he stepped down.[171]

- **Questions that ask for your personal opinion**—"Just on a personal note, how concerned are you that …?" This is typical of a question from an experienced journalist who is seeking your personal opinion. It's an excellent question (from the journalist's perspective) for the following reasons:
  - It generally comes later in the interview and after some rapport has been built between the two of you.
  - It's conversational, starting with "Just" and adds "personal note" making it seem a natural part of an ordinary conversation, not an interview.
  - It assumes that "you are concerned" and is only asking "to what extent?"
  - It contains the feeling-type word "concerned" which psychologically is more likely to elicit a response (we respond to people's feelings more so than facts).[172]

In summary, if you don't know the answer and you make a guess that is wrong or give a personal opinion that journalists will be able to use as a quote forever, your credibility is at risk.

Many people still remember the statement made by Tony Hayward, CEO of BP at the time of the Deepwater Horizon oil spill in April 2010. After one of his many apologies, he said, "There's no one who wants this over more than I do. I would like my life back." He got his wish because he was out of his job at BP just six months later.

---

171 H Horn, 2009, "The whole foods controversy in 15 minutes", 17 August, *The Atlantic*, https://www.theatlantic.com/politics/archive/2009/08/the-whole-foods-controversy-in-15-minutes/348385/, (accessed 29 March 2018).

172 J McCroskey, 1969, "A summary of experimental research on the effects of evidence in persuasive communication", *Quarterly Journal of Speech*, Vol 55, No 2, p 169–76, https://www.tandfonline.com/doi/abs/10.1080/00335636909382942?src=recsys, (accessed 29 March 2018).

And then there was the famous use of the word 'don't' by Mike Jeffries, the controversial former CEO of US fashion chain Abercrombie & Fitch. He made no secret of how he only wanted thin, attractive people in his stores, famously saying in one 2006 interview: "A lot of people *don't* belong [in our clothes], and they can't belong. Are we exclusionary? Absolutely." In 2013, as the company went through a very tough patch, his comments resurfaced and, a year later, he retired.

One of the main themes of this book is using positive language and avoiding negative language. When it comes to managing the media, positive language is what works. According to Jane Jordan Meier, "Do whatever you can to avoid negative language. Quite simply negative language is toxic."

We have used a number of examples throughout to demonstrate the brain's response to negative words, particularly the word 'don't'. The brain translates 'don't do that as 'do that' so when a spokesperson for the board or the organisation says something such as "that's not how we do things", the immediate response from a reporter is "why not?" which is a negative question. Leaders are likely to struggle to find a positive response to a negative question and end up off track. When it comes to the media and portraying one's organisation in a positive light, best to say what is rather than talk about what isn't.

How leaders stay positive during a media interview

- **Leaders should practice their language before hand**—we have mentioned this before; regular practice, such as reframing negative language into positive language, builds your positive capacity. Start practising before you have a situation which involves the media and practise your responses before a media interview.
- **Listen very carefully to the question**—think about how you, the leader, will be framed. Remember, that it is the journalist's job to be sceptical and get answers. A nice way to ensure you

remain positive is to write the journalists' potential headline for the story before the interview—this will be how you want the organisation and yourself to be portrayed.

- **Take your time**—pause for a second or two and breathe before saying anything; use that moment to think rather than to respond immediately.
- **Reframe**—the negative loaded question can be turned into a positive.
- **Make it count**—less is more, stay focused on saying what is and resist the urge to ramble about what isn't. Make sure your tone is appropriate and authentic; demonstrate both head and heart in a positive way.
- **Know that the 'buck stops' with the person at the top**— public perceptions matter more than ever before, responsibility for a proper response is placed on the shoulders of the board as well as management. And remember, the other key stakeholders who will be interested in these interviews are the employees.

The bottom line ...

Media interviews

Media interviews are such an important part of the role of CEO and senior executive, and that they need attention, yet generally they occur infrequently. And yet their impact can be quite dramatic—either very positive and enhancing your reputation and the organisation's reputation—or quite the opposite. Our final three thoughts are worth your consideration:

1. Media training

    First, we suggest undertaking media training. After all, leaders spend a lot of time developing expertise in their various technical and professional disciplines, and ensuring they are proficient in governance requirements, so it's equally important in the area of media performance. And yes, it is a performance—so practice is required. We've seen fantastic results from leaders (previously unsure or nervous during media interviews) who have turned in stunning performances following expert media training.

2. Practice

   When you know that you are to be interviewed, take some time to practice. Have someone from your organisation, perhaps a colleague or a good friend, who is prepared to play the role of the interviewer. Get them to ask you a selection of questions from the list of 15 that you have developed during your preparation time. If you happen to be called for an impromptu comment, tell the reporter you will call them back in 25 minutes. This gives you the opportunity to do some brief preparation. Remember our golden rule: major Theme, three points to illustrate and three practical examples to demonstrate.

3. Relationship with reputable journalist

   If it's likely that you will be called on regularly, you may like to consider developing a relationship with a recognised and reputable journalist. For example, from time to time you could offer to make comment on an industry/ profession issue that's current. Developing such a relationship will make you feel more comfortable when being interviewed by him/her and they are likely to treat you more favorably when the situation is difficult (for you or your organisation) if you have built up this relationship by being helpful and available in the past.

4.5 Managing the communication in a crisis

After 168 years of publication, the British newspaper *News of the World* published its final edition on 10 July 2011. At the time, the newspaper was profitable. News Group Newspapers Ltd, the unit within News International responsible for the *News of the World* and *The Sun*, reported an operating profit of 18.2 million pounds in the year ended 27 June 2010. So what led to the demise of this historic newspaper?

As the press reported at the time, the closure was not about profits or profitability (although advertisers were reported as departing rapidly). The closure was about reputation—in particular, the reputation of one of the world's richest men, Rupert Murdoch, Chairman, CEO and founding director of News Corp.

It's been said that leaders emerge in tough times. 'Tough times' can describe natural disasters such as flood, fire or earthquakes.

These can also be man-made such as war, riots, environmental or economic disasters. And of course companies can experience disasters due to mistakes, malpractice or just poor decision making.

In such times, we've seen leaders such as Churchill, Gandhi, and Mandela handle crises in ways that have set them apart as people who could be trusted in very trying circumstances. What is it about these leaders that imbues confidence? What do these leaders do and say that others do not?

As Jane Jordan-Meier points out: "Nowhere is an organisation more vulnerable than when a crisis strikes. Crises are defining moments for organisations and their leaders. They are 'make it or break it moments'."[173]

Where was the leadership at News Corp in the phone hacking scandal unfolding in the UK in 2010? Rupert Murdoch had his 'make it or break it moment' when he appeared before the UK Parliament Committee hearing. As Bloomberg reported:

Rupert Murdoch's refusal to take responsibility for the hacking scandal that has slashed $5.89 billion from the market value of News Corp, may undermine his credibility as chief executive officer. Governance experts who heard Murdoch's performance before the UK Parliament yesterday said that by blaming under-lings and saying he wasn't responsible he didn't do enough as Chairman and CEO to acknowledge his accountability.[174]

---

173 J Jordan-Meier, 2011, "Showing Leadership in a Crisis", *International Leadership Association*, 7 December, http://ila-net.org/Webinars/archive/201112, (accessed 23 June 2018).

174 C Hymowitz and A Fixmer, 2011, "Murdoch's refusal to take responsibility may dent credibility", *Bloomberg*, 19 July, https://www.bloomberg.com/news/articles/2011-07-20/murdoch-s-refusal-to-take-responsibility-may-undermine-credibility-as-ceo, (accessed 29 March 2018).

Despite describing this as "the most humble day of my life"[175] Murdoch insisted that wrongdoing at the newspaper and efforts to clear it up were far below his level. Is this the behaviour and words we expect from a leader during a crisis? What type of tone is this setting?

Are you prepared to communicate when your crisis occurs?

What should a leader do and say during a crisis?

When interviewed for this chapter, Jane Jordan-Meier said:

Put simply, the readers and the storytellers themselves, perhaps unknowingly, expect to hear, see and read about stories of courage, death defying events, people surviving against odds, and that someone, somewhere can be held accountable for their losses. There has to be an explanation for why the government took so long to respond, or why there was in-fighting in the company, or why it was yet another tale of bad boys behaving badly. We want to know that someone cares and has the determination, conviction and compassion to do something to make sure that the 'worst' can never happen again. We heard very little, if anything, of this in the phone hacking scandal.

---

175 K Kissane, 2011, "Most humble day of my life", *Sydney Morning Herald*, 20 July 2011, https://www.smh.com.au/world/most-humble-day-of-my-life-20110719-1hndl.html, (accessed 29 March 2018).

Jordan-Meier's research shows that crises go through four distinct stages[176]

STAGE ONE: The spotlight is beaming squarely on the incident.	This is the 'breaking news' stage. "What happened?" is the key question. And the news travels very fast in Stage One to Stage Two—it doesn't take long for the story to jump the 'fire line', quite often via social media.
STAGE TWO: Is characterised by the focus on the 'victims' and the response from the organisation.	The light now moves quickly from the incident itself (although new facts will continue to emerge) to the 'drama'. How could this have happened? How many people are hurt, missing and/or dead? How is the organisation responding? How quickly did the responders get to the scene? The light will shine brightly on the perpetrator or who we think the perpetrator might be. This stage is key. This is the 'make it or break it' stage, the reputation forming stage, the stage where the rallying on social media sites, both negative and positive, becomes a focal point.
STAGE THREE: This is the one best avoided, although inevitably we all want to go there— yes, the blame, finger pointing stage.	Think back to the devastating oil spill in the Gulf of Mexico when the executives of the three companies at the heart of the massive oil spill were severely chastised over attempts to shift the blame to each other. In this finger pointing stage—everyone has an opinion about you, your product, your organisation, your industry, even your country—lots of "woulda, coulda, shoulda." Stage Three is all about blame with the key question focused on "Why?" The spotlight is more like a floodlight. The crisis is beamed everywhere.

---

176 J Jordan-Meier, 2011, "The Four Stages of Highly Effective Crisis Management", CRC Press, Taylor and Francis Group, Boca Raton, p 44–78.

STAGE FOUR: The light begins to dim in Stage Four which is the fallout/ resolution stage.	The spotlight now dims but can easily be turned to full glare again if there is a slip up, or something similar happens in the industry. The crisis is perpetually in print, on Google, in Wikipedia—searchable and discoverable. Your 'sin' will be for everyone to see forever—you can't take it back—your words may come back to either haunt you or enhance your reputation. Typically, this stage marks the end of the crisis; there is some resolution. There might be a funeral, a government inquiry, or a government hearing. Your product goes back on the shelf, workers go back to the plant, victims return to their homes.

Table 12: The four stages of a crisis.

As Jordan-Meier points out, these stages are very clear:

"If you take a close look at any crisis you will see distinct, predictable patterns in how the media behave … That's the good news. The bad news is that, now, the reporting of a crisis happens at a blistering speed thanks to the advent of social media."[177]

Jordan-Meier also points out there is a need for a recognised and credible spokesperson to handle each stage. Communicating in a crisis is not for the faint-hearted or the un-trained. In a crisis, speed, decisiveness, authority and often significant courage are needed. The choice of spokesperson is a critical component for effective crisis management. Crises have the potential to destroy entire industries, bring down governments, and adversely affect large regions of the globe.[178]

How did Murdoch handle these stages in his crisis? When the story started to break in early July, News Corp hired two public relations

---

177 ibid, p 43.
178 ibid, p 85-89.

advisers to assist the company during its phone hacking scandal. "Sard Verbinnen & Co in New York and Glover Park Group in Washington will work with the company's communications, investor relations and government teams", Julie Henderson, a News Corp spokeswoman, said in an interview.[179] This is the 'breaking news', the 'what happened?' stage. Julie Henderson is Senior Vice President, Communications and Corporate Strategy at News Corp and despite the impressive title, sits below the senior management team level.

Was this an appropriate response to Stage One, the 'breaking news' stage? Was Julie Henderson the appropriate spokesperson? And what of the delegated responsibility given to the PR firms? Would this enhance News Corp's reputation?

Then the phone hacking story quickly moved to Stage Two. As Jordan-Meier points out, the second stage is where the focus shifts to the victims and the response from the government or organisation.[180] In this case, the incident that really triggered the huge public outcry in the UK was the phone hacking of murdered school girl Milly Dowler. The News Corp response? The first was to close the newspaper, *News of the World*. Would this make the crisis go away? Then, in short succession there were resignations from key News Corp executives. Notable amongst these was Rebekah Brooks, CEO of News International, the company responsible for the UK operations. The scandal had now also caused the resignation of two of the UK's top police. Where was the key crisis management spokesperson in Stage Two?

Finally, Murdoch appeared and provided a personal apology to the family of Milly Dowler. Remember, Stage Two is key. This is the make

---

179 B Selden, 2011, "Are you ready for your Murdoch moment?", *Management Issues*, 22 July, http://www.mangement-issues.com/opinion/6246/are-you-ready-for-our-murdoch-moment, (accessed 29 March 2018).

180 J Jordan-Meier, 2011, "The Four Stages of Highly Effective Crisis Management", CRC Press, Taylor and Francis Group, Boca Raton, p 60.

it or break it stage, the reputation forming stage, the stage where the rallying on social media sites, both negative and positive, becomes a focal point—How did Murdoch score?

In this example, we've now moved very clearly into Stage Three, the 'blame', 'finger pointing' stage. Rupert Murdoch and his son James, CEO of BSkyB, the UK television arm of News International, appeared before a UK parliament investigating committee. Whilst it appears that James' reputation may have been enhanced, Rupert fared less well.

"The *News of the World* is less than 1 per cent of our company," Rupert Murdoch told Parliament's Culture, Media and Sport Committee. He said he may have "lost sight" of the paper because it was "so small in the general frame of the company."[181] Is this an appropriate response from the chair and CEO to capably manage Stage Three?

Stage Four probably started with the punch thrown by Rupert's then wife Wendi in the parliamentary enquiry[182] (Stage Four includes 'fallout'—an appropriate nomenclature). From a leadership perspective, the important thing for us to consider is 'Could this happen to me?' We may think we are immune to crises, yet who can predict the future? Remember, crises can occur for any number of reasons, some of which are outside a leader's control.

The one thing leaders can do, however, is to be prepared. Does your organisation have a crisis communication management plan in place? Are there designated spokespeople to handle each of the stages? Has everyone been trained? Are you ready to handle your crisis?

---

181 B Fenton and S Davoudi, 2012, "Murdoch 'not fit' to run a global company", *Financial Times*, 2 May, https://www.ft.com/content/5bf423a0-937a-11e1-8ca8-00144fe-ab49a, (accessed 29 March 2018).

182 G Levy, 2011, "Rupert's tiger wife who clawed her way up … and caught her billionaire", *Daily Mail Australia*, 21 July, http://www.dailymail.co.uk/news/article-2017066/Wendi-Deng-Murdoch-Ruperts-tiger-wife-clawed-way-up.html, (accessed 20 June 2018).

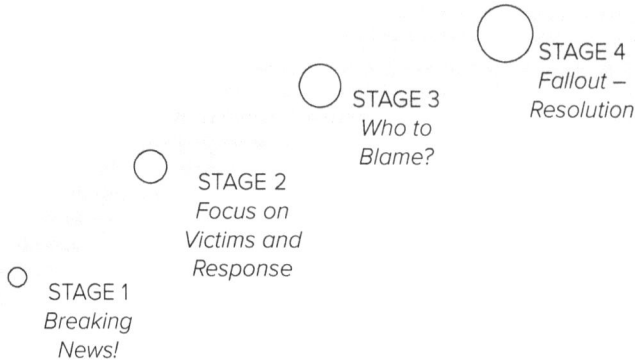

STAGE 4
Fallout –
Resolution

STAGE 3
Who to
Blame?

STAGE 2
Focus on
Victims and
Response

STAGE 1
Breaking
News!

The bottom line ...

Have a crisis communication plan in place

It is critical that organisations have a crisis communication management plan in place that specifically includes:

- designated spokesperson (or persons) to manage each of the four stages of the crisis;
- the CEO, the Chair and specific others, trained in presenting the corporate message;
- protocols for handling all potential crises; and
- how to apologise should the organisation have erred or hurt people (we gave an explanation of how to manage this communication earlier in the book).

4.6 Giving critical feedback

Research has shown that those who explicitly seek critical feedback (that is, who are not just fishing for praise) tend to get higher performance ratings. Why? Mainly, we think, because someone who is asking for coaching is more likely to take what is said to heart and genuinely improve. But also because when you ask for feedback, you not only find out how others see you, you also influence *how they see you. Soliciting constructive criticism communicates humility, respect, passion for excellence, and confidence, all in one go.*[183]

We see something that a colleague is doing or perhaps we hear about something they are going to do and we think "Oh, oh, that's probably not right", or "That doesn't sound like a good idea", or "That's going to cause (or has caused) a bit of a problem". Why do we so often avoid saying something to help them out? Are we seeing something they can't? Then why not tell them?

Often we are concerned about the other person's reaction:

- "What if the person gets angry?"
- "What if they take it the wrong way?"
- "What if they tell me I'm an idiot?"
- "What if they get defensive and starts blaming *me*?"
- "What if they are actually right and I make a fool of myself?"

Another thing that makes it hard, is not knowing what to say. "How can I tell another person that most other people see it differently?"; "What words can I use that will not cause offense?"; "How can I tell a person such bad news and still expect them to respect me?" These are hard questions to deal with—in fact it's estimated that 53 per cent of us dodge such challenging conversations and 80 per cent worry about causing an angry response.[184]

And according to a survey by UK mediation firm Globis, 97 per cent of respondents were anxious about stress levels, 94 per cent were

---

183 S Heen and D Stone, 2014, "Find the Coaching in Criticism", *Harvard Business Review*, January–February, https://hbr.org/2014/01/find-the-coaching-in-criticism, (accessed 29 March 2018).

184 K Jones, 2015, "Nailing difficult conversations", *Sydney Morning Herald*, 13 May, https://www.smh.com.au/business/small-business/nailing-difficult-conversations-20150511-ggyxa0.html, (accessed 29 March 2018).

worried about damaging self-esteem and 80 per cent of people were afraid of an angry response when asked about giving feedback to a colleague.[185] So it's no wonder we are somewhat reluctant when it comes to speaking with a colleague about a difficult topic that may affect them, and perhaps our relationship.

We may also subconsciously be thinking or remembering when we received some critical comments. Consider for a moment the last time you received some critical feedback from a colleague. How did you feel? We'll wager that it wasn't an 'over the moon' feeling. No matter how right or well-intended the criticism may be, we do not like to hear about our flaws, shortcomings, or wrongdoings.

Here's an example of what happened when Bud Hennekes, blog owner of *A Boundless World* received some feedback from a friend:

> The other day I was toying with the idea of starting a flower business by creating a website where you could buy flowers for a random person in need. I'd work with the flower companies to make it affordable. People could buy flowers for individuals in need of love. And I'd be helping bring smiles to hundreds of individuals. Greatest idea ever.
>
> While doing my research I sent an email over to my friend Sean Platt who worked in the flower industry for many years. I just knew he would love my idea and all would be merry. Eh … not so fast. Long story short, Sean gave me some honest feedback. The jury had decided: My idea sucked.
>
> Whether or not I could have made the business model work is beside the point. What struck me was at how honest Sean

---

185 L Solomons, 2016, "Two-thirds of managers are uncomfortable communicating with employees", *Harvard Business Review*, 9 March 2016, https://hbr.org/2016/03/two-thirds-of-managers-are-uncomfortable-communicating-with-employees, (accessed 20 June 2018).

was. Instead of lying to me and saying that it would all work out, he was frank and up front.

His reaction to my idea most certainly bruised my ego, but in the end he saved me hundreds of hours of hard work. [For the record I love Sean, and he wasn't overly harsh.]

In today's society honest feedback is frowned upon. Criticism is almost always countered with the 'haters gonna hate' mantra. And while I too admit there are plenty of negative Nancy's of the world, I sincerely believe criticism has its place.

Criticism helps us grow. Coddling does not.

Bud[186]

You can see two things from Bud's response—his ego was bruised and he appreciated the honest feedback.

Let's start with ego—everyone has one—and it's a very important part of our makeup. Unfortunately, the word that's often associated with ego is 'big' as in " 'x' has got a big ego". However, ego or as it's sometimes referred to 'ego-drive', is a personal need for achievement in every endeavour; sports, education, career, life. People with a strong ego-drive are always trying to better themselves. They are motivated by challenges, opportunities, and the high standards they create, so it's no wonder that when something they do or say gets a knock-back or criticism from a colleague, their ego becomes dented.

As someone who is reading this book, our intuition (or our 'third-ear') tells us that you have a very healthy and strong ego (and our experience suggests that many directors and executives have strong ego-drives). Do you feel like Bud when your ego is knocked or dented? When was the last time you received some critical feedback from a colleague or someone else? How did you feel? Keep this feeling in mind

---

186 B Hennekes, 2015, "How To Give Honest Feedback", *A boundless world*, 1 August, http://www.aboundlessworld.com/honest-feedback/, (accessed 21 May 2018).

as we progress through the remainder of this chapter as one of the keys to giving constructive feedback is to minimise the damage done to the other person's ego.

We're not privy to the words Bud's friend used. However, our best guess is that they were supportive, critical and honest. Let's see how that might work and why Bud appreciated his friend's honesty.

Unfortunately, the words 'feedback', 'critical', and 'bad-news' seem now to be synonymous. So when we hear someone say "Let me give you some feedback" or "I have some feedback for you" we know that it's most likely going to be critical, not favourable and our brain automatically goes into fight or flight mode. Therefore, we're reframing the word 'critical' to 'favourable'. We'll go one step further: we suggest dropping the word 'feedback' altogether and depending on the situation replace it with 'advice', 'pointers', 'counsel' or 'guidance'. This is another example of reframing and while this may seem like a play-on-words or a little bit of a stretch, we have some very good reasons for suggesting we reframe 'feedback' and use a positive, future oriented word instead:

- Feedback, although starting out as neutral (it was originally an engineering term referring to the conveyance of information fed back from an output, or measurement to an input, or as an engineer might say, something that affects the system) has now become synonymous with bad-news.
- Feedback tends to focus on the past and what has happened whereas words such as advice, pointers, guidance and so on, all refer to future actions.
- Future oriented words force us to talk about 'what might be' rather than 'what is' or 'what has been'.
- Future oriented words lead to statements that we own such as "I'd suggest that it be handled this way" rather than inferring criticism such as "I think you should have …" or "Why don't you do it this way …?" or "Why did you do that?"

According to executive coach Marshall Goldsmith, the fundamental problem with all types of feedback is that it focuses on the past, on what has already occurred—not on the opportunities that can happen in the future. Instead of rehashing a past that cannot be changed, Jon Katzenbach, (*The Wisdom of Teams*), and Marshall Goldsmith coined the term 'feedforward' to encourage spending time creating a future.[187]

Successful people (with strong egos) like generating ideas that are aimed at helping them achieve their goals. They tend to resist negative judgment. We all tend to accept feedback that is consistent with the way we see ourselves and to reject or deny feedback that is inconsistent with the way we see ourselves. Successful directors and executives are more likely to respond to (and may even enjoy) 'feedforward'. However, these same people may not have a positive reaction to the word 'feedback'.

Along with reframing, tone of voice is particularly important when giving advice to a colleague. Because they're your colleague and you work with them regularly, they'll pick up very quickly on the nuances you are subconsciously communicating. Try to show concern in your tone, rather than anger (e.g. if they've done something to upset you); or frustration (e.g. if they keep doing something that annoys you); or perhaps disappointment (e.g. if you feel they have let you down). 'Concern' is a feeling that is readily communicated and understood between close colleagues—it quickly leads to a mutual exchange of feelings.

Guidelines for giving feedback—strike that, let's call it 'advice'

And if you've ever considered starting off a conversation with someone with "Don't take this the wrong way" (which by now you'll be aware

---

187 M Goldsmith, 2004, "Leave it at the Stream", *Fast Company*, Issue 82 May, p 103.

does not work), here are some guidelines for giving advice that will greatly enhance the chances of your message being received, and received in a positive way:

Ask if it's okay to provide some advice

For example, "George, I was a little concerned about our conversation yesterday with John prior to the meeting. I'm no expert on the subject, but I do have some personal experiences to draw from. Is it OK if I offer some advice?"

Note: we will build on this example as we progress through these guidelines. In the example, imagine that you listened in on a conversation yesterday between George and John. You have been concerned about George for some time because of the words he uses when offering advice to other colleagues. He uses lots of 'you' words (often in the past tense) and whilst very well intentioned, his use of words often puts others off. So we're setting out to see if we can get the message across that George may have better relationships if he changes the words he uses. Follow the example and see how we go.

Give advice irregularly

If you are continually giving advice to a colleague, they will start to ignore what you are saying (even though they will continue to listen because they are a colleague). Pick the important things that can make a real change for your colleague, rather than nit-picking. In our example, the really important thing is to get George to change some of the words he uses as it can sometimes come across as demeaning.

Act as a sounding board

Once you've gained your colleague's approval to discuss the topic, ask how they see the situation. Get them to check their assumptions and why they see the situation the way they do. For example, "To me John seemed to get quite upset. And I think he reacted not only to what was said, but also to how it was said. He obviously disagreed with the opinion being given and I think there was more to it than that. What are your thoughts George?"

Test some tentative assumptions your colleague may have

We all make assumptions and we arrive at the best decisions when these are tested and found appropriate or found wanting and then we go down another path. For example; "Although the suggestions sounded OK and logical to me, John didn't seem to hear them—he reacted quite strangely. Could there be another reason?" Pause and listen: George will most likely discuss other possible things happening in John's life—however, we need to shift the conversation back to the words he used, (i.e. the process not the content). "What if the suggestions were put to John in a different way—using different words, or perhaps even through asking questions? How might that work? What questions would work?"

Expand their frame of reference

One way of doing this is to ask more questions such as "What else?" or "Tell me more" or "For example?" A further useful technique is to provide some of your own experiences that may demonstrate another way, for example, "I think explaining it to John in another way, perhaps one that is less intimidating such as asking questions could work. I also remember going to a training conference where it was suggested dropping the word 'you' when giving someone else some advice. Shortly afterwards, I had to give my colleague some really tough news and guess what? It worked! How could the advice to John be rephrased by eliminating 'you'?"

Provide process advice

I'm sure you will now be aware that in the 'George' example so far, we've actually been managing the conversation process. Whenever

George started to discuss content we listened, then through questioning brought him back to the process. We now need to help George understand the importance of managing the process in his own conversations. For example, "George, sounds to me that you like the idea of eliminating 'you' but are a little sceptical about how it might work. Would you like to try it out on me? I'll be John and you can give me the advice without using the word 'you'. Let's see how that might work".

Brainstorm solutions

Once you have your colleague engaged in the conversation there may be an opportunity to brainstorm some other ideas that could help. Remember your opinion is not the only one and can always be improved through sharing with others.

Words to avoid

It's also worth repeating here some of the words to avoid that you're now familiar with, as it's particularly tempting to drop back into old habits when giving advice to a colleague:

- Avoid 'but', 'yes, but' and 'however' and 'although'. We've discussed these in detail in Part 3. With colleagues, use the 'yes, and …' alternative which is particularly relevant.
- Look out for 'You need to …' (very tempting as you probably have the answer all worked out for your colleague). We've discussed the problem with 'you' in Part 3. We raise it here because with a colleague, we tend to feel that we really need to help and so it's tempting to jump straight in with "You need to …" or "You should …"

Techniques to avoid

Also, you may have heard during your career of giving criticism or advice via the 'feedback sandwich'. This does not work. The idea behind this technique is that:

1. You start off by focusing on the strengths—what you like about the person or what they've done. This is the first slice of bread in the sandwich, perhaps with a good dollop of butter.

2. Then you provide the criticism—things you didn't like—the things you think they should change. This is the 'meat' in the sandwich, the filling that's quite distasteful.

3. Lastly, you round off the feedback by reiterating the positive comments you gave at the beginning and the positive results that can be expected if the criticism is acted upon. You've now added the final piece of bread to sweeten the sandwich.

Sounds feasible? Unfortunately, it's been found that people ignore the positive strengths mentioned in Step 1. As we've shown elsewhere in this book, they know the 'but' is coming (Step 2). It's that criticism in the middle that bites. In Step 2 the brain has gone into 'fight or flight' mode and is not prepared to listen to anything else that follows no matter how positive. And so the final positive statements (Step 3) are soon forgotten.

Our own experience, in receiving this type of message, is that it seems disparaging so the sandwich is inedible. As Andrew O'Keeffe puts it:

> *The problem with the feedback sandwich is that humans have an instinctive need to classify. We classify in order to make sense and our classifications are binary in nature—on a variation of 'good' or 'bad'. So at moments of receiving feedback the listener is compelled to classify; is the feedback positive or negative? The feedback sandwich becomes a mixed message because it confuses the classification instinct.*[188]

---

188 A O'Keeffe, 2016, "Why the feedback sandwich doesn't work", *The National Learning Institute*, 31 August, http://nationallearning.com.au/why-the-feedback-sandwich-does-not-work/, (accessed 29 March 2018).

Receiving 'feedback'—how leaders can remain positive

And on the other hand, how do we manage the conversation when a colleague starts to give us advice (which they will probably frame as 'feedback')? How do we cope when a colleague starts giving information, advice or criticism that may be hard to accept? As an example, think about what you've already read in this chapter. There'll be some advice you keep and some that you'll throw away. This will be similar in a conversation with a colleague. However, our best guess is that no matter what, while listening to your colleague you'll start to recall the things you've thought about while reading this chapter and that in itself will be enough for you to think rationally about what your colleague is saying, no matter how effective or ineffective the words being used.

When first hearing some criticism from a colleague, engage your rational brain and rather than responding, ask some further questions such as:

- "When I hear xyz, what does that mean?" Notice we did not suggest "When you say xyz what does that mean?" rather "When I hear xyz ..."
- "Are there some other examples I should be aware of?"
- "What else?"
- "Tell me more."

It's known that we all react to criticism (or even well intentioned advice given in a negative way) for three reasons:

- It may seem (to us) wrong or unfair.
- We may dislike the person giving it.
- It may rock our sense of identity or security.

Douglas Stone[189] suggests (once we're away from the conversation) to write down the nitty gritty of the message:

---

189 D Stone and S Heen, 2014, "Thanks for the feedback: The science and art of receiving feedback well", Viking, New York, p 145.

- What is this feedback about?

  and …

- What is it not about?

Answering this two-part question will enable you to reframe the message into some positive advice—which you can choose to take onboard or throw away. From previous chapters you'll also recognise the importance of writing down your answers.

Remember all advice has some truth in it, even if only to reveal how others think. Before dismissing it, ask yourself, "What is the nugget that I can pull out of this?"

Before leaving this chapter, we should also look at what might be considered 'the other side of the coin', that of giving praise.

Criticism and praise—are they similar?

Are they the flip sides of the same coin? It seems not. We've seen the impact that criticism can have on colleagues, now what about praise? Before discussing how to give praise to a colleague, it is first necessary to look at the research on the impact of praise—much of it started with children. So before focusing on adults, let's start there.

"You're a good girl", "Gee, you did that well", these are probably things all parents have said to their children at some stage. The general view is that praise is good for children's development while criticism is not. However, research over the last decade or so has found that praise can also be damaging, particularly for younger children.

Researchers have found that praise for young children (perhaps up to the age of two to three, depending on their maturity) whatever way it is given, is good for their development. However, as children mature, they start to distinguish praise given for their abilities such as intelligence (which they intuitively perceive people either have or do not have and therefore cannot be changed) compared to praise given for their level of effort or the strategies they use. These, they realise, can be changed.[190]

As an early writer on the subject Haim G Ginott said:

Praise, like penicillin, must not be administered haphazardly. There are rules and cautions that govern the handling of potent medicines—rules about timing and dosage, cautions about possible allergic reactions. There are similar regulations about the administration of emotional medicine.[191]

Now, what about praising adults, is it similar to praising children? It seems so. We all like praise. We feel good as a result, but what else does it do? According to Clifford[192], both praise and flattery (flattery is described as 'praise that may be given without foundation') have more impact on our liking of the giver than on our behaviour. So praise, even of a particular achievement, will be remembered for making us feel good and for who gave it rather than exactly what is was for.

However, there may be situations where you can use praise to influence the performance of others. If so, the following guidelines will assist your influencing ability:

- Tell the person in specific, descriptive terms the behaviour s/he did correctly/well AND the impact of that behaviour.
  Example:
  "Chris, I really like the great job you did on the report to the executive committee last week. I was especially impressed with the

190 J Taylor, 2009, "Parenting: Don't praise your children", *Psychology Today*, 3 September, https://www.psychologytoday.com/au/blog/the-power-prime/200909/parenting-dont-praise-your-children, (accessed 29 March 2018).

191 B J Bushman, 2018, "Praise, like penicillin, must not be given haphazardly!" *Psychology Today*, 22 Jan 2018, https://www.psychologytoday.com/us/blog/get-psyched/201401/praise-penicillin-must-not-be-given-haphazardly, (accessed 20 June 2018).

192 C Nass with C Yen, 2012, "The man who lied to his laptop", Penguin Group, New York.

analysis of the numbers and the explanation of the impact on the business presented verbally and also in the written report."

- Tell the person how you feel about the behaviour or how the behaviour will affect others—be specific.

  Example:

  "I'm confident the senior team will be able to make an informed decision on our project because of the quality of the information provided."

- Encourage more of the same behaviour.

  Example:

  "Thanks for doing such a thorough job, Chris. Keep up the good work."

The bottom line ...

Guidelines for giving feedback and advice

If you have to give a colleague some advice the guidelines are:

- ask if it's OK to provide some advice;
- give advice irregularly;
- act as a sounding board;
- test some tentative assumptions your colleague may have;
- expand their frame of reference;
- provide process advice (avoid getting caught in the content); and
- together, brainstorm solutions.

And when you receive advice or 'feedback' from a colleague:

- Stay rational (bring this chapter to mind).
- Get more specifics by asking questions such as "When I hear ... what does that mean?", "Are there some other examples I should be aware of?", "What else?", "Tell me more"
- Write down answers to "What is this feedback about and what is it not about?"
- Finally, when either giving advice or receiving criticism from a colleague, keep in mind Bud's story—we're pretty certain that Bud's friend would have been supportive, critical and honest.

When giving praise ...

- Whatever your situation, giving praise makes you feel good and the person to whom you are giving it feel good, so do keep it up. It also has an important side benefit—in giving praise you need to look for the positives in others' behaviour—and that's what this book is all about.

4.7 The conversation you're having when you're not having a conversation

> **HEALTH WARNING**
>
> This chapter comes with a health warning. It includes 'How to be assertive where the stakes are high and it's either win or lose'.
>
> Use the suggestions here on 'strong assertiveness' at your own risk.

What is assertiveness? We all have our own ideas and definitions. It's a word that we often use in day-to-day conversation to describe our own or another's behaviour. One dictionary definition of being assertive is to "state with assurance, confidence or force; state strongly or positively."[193] And in terms of the words we use when being assertive, they vary quite considerably. There are degrees of being assertive, from using mild 'I-word' statements of requests for example, "I would like to have …" through to much heavier personal demands such as "I need …" or "I must have …'.

If you read again the dictionary definition you'll see that all the words used are positive—'assurance', 'confidence', 'strongly', 'positively'— with the possible exception of one—'force'. Very strong assertiveness (perhaps forceful) is sometimes confused with aggressiveness which is quite different. True assertiveness is not crossing another's boundaries. Assertiveness acknowledges and respects the boundaries of others. Aggressiveness is disrespectful of boundaries. How can you tell the difference? Here it's the 'you' word that gives it away—"You must …",

---

193 "Assert", WordReference.com, http://www.wordreference.com/definition/assert, (accessed 10 March 2017).

"You will …", "I need you to …"—all of these statements are asking for what we want without considering the needs of others. Excessive use of 'you' is a sure-fire indicator of aggressiveness.

Before we move on to looking at how to be assertive in a positive way, it's worth doing some self-reflection to identify our natural style. A quick and easy way to do this is to answer the following questions:

When I am faced with making a choice put forward by a colleague and I have a very definite idea of the answer (or I'm sure of the action that should be taken) and **he/she has a strong and different view**, how often do I:

1. **Give in** and accept the other's decisions?
2. **Ask** for what **I want**?
3. **Tell others** what action to take?

What is your personal view on being assertive? For example, do you think that 'giving in and accepting other's decisions' is the best approach? Or do you often think "Maybe I should have put my view forward, I'm really not happy with this result", or "I knew it wasn't going to work out—I should have been more forceful."

On the other hand, if you consider that 'telling others what to do' is the best option, it may be that your style will come across as very strongly assertive or perhaps even aggressive (depending on the words used and the tone of voice).

Because assertiveness can be perceived as a negative trait, most often we use assertiveness to describe someone else's behaviour not ours, and the results it has on their relationships, e.g. "He's so assertive and really puts people off". We therefore need to delve a little deeper to get a better handle on what is meant by 'assertiveness' and how it can be used positively. 'Being assertive' is such a common phrase that we all have an intuitive idea of what it is and what it means when it comes to building and maintaining relationships. **Figure 19** begins our illustration of how assertiveness impacts relationships.

The bottom left-hand corner of the graph shows the degree of assertiveness on a scale from 0 (no assertiveness) to 100 (full-on assertive). The *Relationships* axis ranges from –20 to 100, to allow for the instance of a score of 0 on *Assertiveness* (i.e. a person never displays any assertive behaviour) which leads to a negative impact on their relationships.

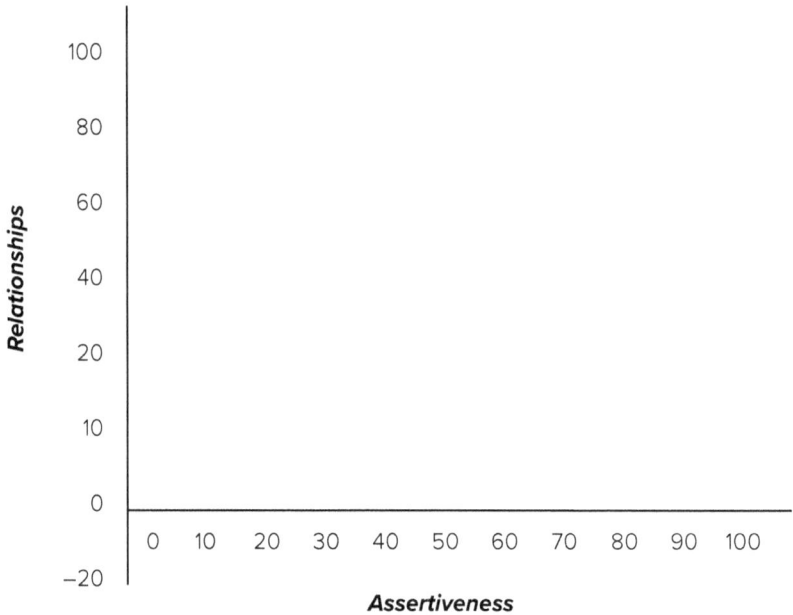

Figure 19: Relationships and assertiveness.

Research[194] supports the view that many of us consider that displaying no or little assertiveness results in poor relationships; at the other extreme, too much assertiveness affects our relationships badly; and a moderate amount of assertiveness has a positive impact on our relationships.

---

194 M Zeidner, G Matthews and R Roberts, 2009, "What we know about emotional intelligence: How It affects learning, work and our mental health", MIT Press, Cambridge.

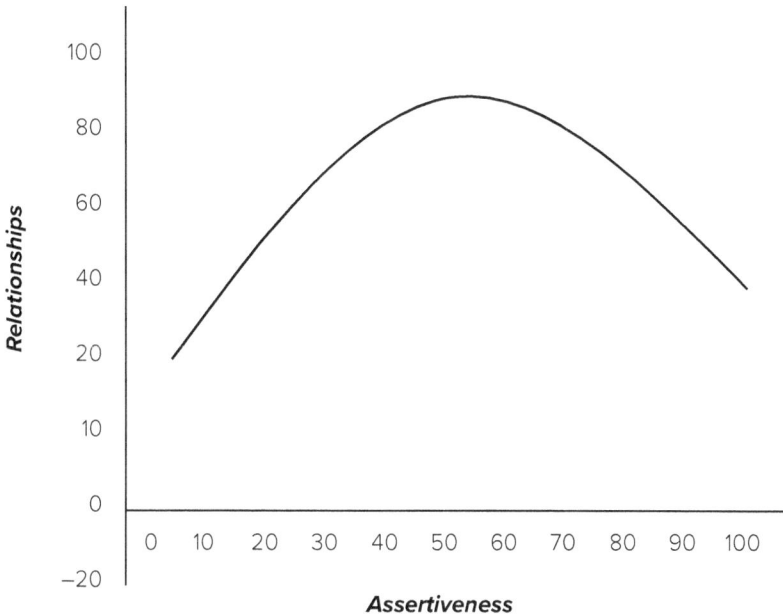

Figure 20: The impact of assertiveness on relationships.

Repeating the exercise with one change, i.e. to replace the *Relationships* axis with *Personal Outcomes* demonstrates the risk in taking an assertive approach (i.e. the result you might get *other than* building or maintaining a relationship). **Figure 21** illustrates two of the most likely outcomes—the result can be win-lose, meaning you get what you want and the relationship is damaged (or lost), or the situation is lose-lose, the relationship is damaged or lost and you do not get what you want. That is, when we ignore relationships and focus on our own needs, it becomes either a win/lose or a lose/lose situation:

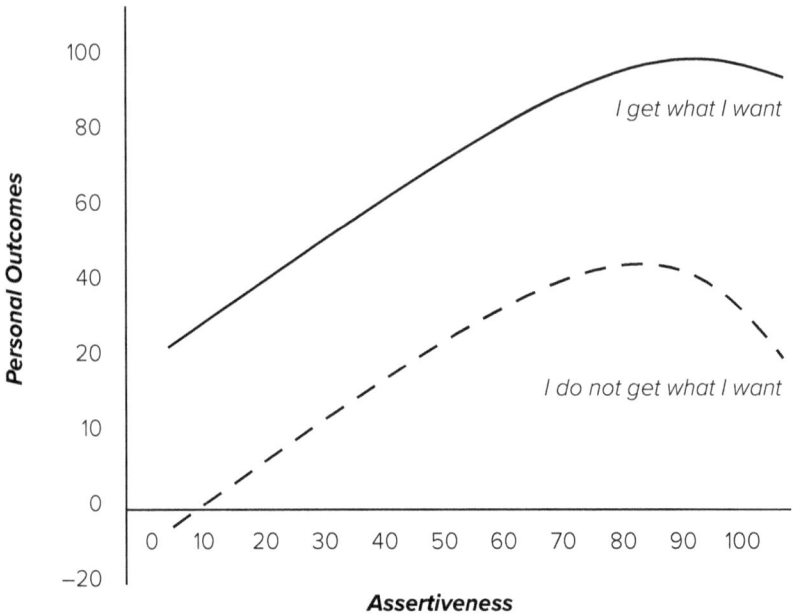

Figure 21: The impact of assertiveness on personal outcomes.

Let's now turn to a personal example, where full-on assertiveness was used to achieve a desired outcome.

Some years ago, the son of co-author Bob was returning to Australia from Switzerland where he had been visiting Bob on a cycling holiday (at that time Bob was living in Switzerland). Bob took him to the airport in Zurich and being a frequent flyer, checked him in. Everything went well—boarding pass issued, baggage checked—then Bob started to check-in the bike. The attendant said there would be an extra fee for the oversize bike box. Bob thought that was fine and that the fee would be perhaps 100 francs, maybe 120 francs) which would be OK. Then she said "That will be 600 francs, please" You can imagine Bob's shock (it was almost a third of his ticket cost).

This is how the conversation went:

Attendant: "That will be 600 francs."

Bob: "I'm not paying it."

Attendant: "I'm sorry, that's our new fee. That will be 600 francs please."

Bob: "I'm not paying it."

Attendant: "That's in our price list, oversize bags such as bikes—600 francs please."

Bob: "I'm not paying it."

Attendant: "I'm sorry, that's our new fee. I must follow procedures—600 francs please."

Bob: "I'm not paying it."

Attendant: "I can't book the bike in without the 600 francs fee."

Bob: "I'm not paying it."

Attendant: "I'll have to refer this to my supervisor."

Bob: "I'm not paying it."

Supervisor: "I'm sorry Mr. Selden, but those are our new fees, the cost is 600 francs."

Bob: "I'm not paying it."

Then ensued a further long series of explanations from the supervisor (including looking up their Procedures Manual), to which Bob only replied at every question or statement from the Supervisor: "I'm not paying it."

What's happening here? You will notice:

- Bob only responded with a strong assertion (*"I'm not paying it"*)—this was clearly his identified need.
- At no stage did Bob enter into a discussion about the airline's reason and logic. Had he done so, he would have had no grounds to argue—that was their fee and it was clearly outlined in their pricing schedule and procedures (note: this was a new fee). Bob's response: "I'm not paying it."

- Bob stayed entirely in 'his world' (his wants and needs)—he did not enter 'their world' (their procedures/price lists). His response: "I'm not paying it".

This was definitely a win/lose (personal outcome) situation and relationships did not enter into it. Who had what to gain or lose?

Potential gains		Potential losses	
Bob	The Airline	Bob	The Airline
No fee	600 francs	600 francs	600 francs
Son's bike shipped	Happy frequent flyer	Bike not shipped	Unhappy frequent flyer
Happy son	Happy traveller (customer)	Very unhappy son	Lost customer (to another airline)

You could say Bob's stance—"I'm not paying it"—was a gamble. And you'd be right. Because the relationship with the airline (for Bob) was not a big deal (he was already at their highest frequent flyer level) he was prepared to be assertive and suffer the potential consequences of his son's bike not being shipped.

Here's the Health-Warning mentioned at the start of this chapter: If you decide that it's a time where personal outcome is more important than the relationship, then it will always be a win/lose situation. You either get what you want or lose out, perhaps hugely, depending on how you have weighed up the potential losses or gains and how much they also mean to the other party.

In case you are wondering, Bob did not pay the 600 francs and his son's bike was shipped on the same flight as his. In this instance, his sustained assertiveness worked.

Guidelines for leaders who wish to be more assertive

The following four guidelines are ones that can be applied by all executives when they wish to be more assertive. We then go on to show how these general guidelines can be tailored to suit a particular executive's natural style of assertiveness.

1. Always state your wants, needs or desires with an 'I' statement (there's more on 'needs' in chapter **4.9: When does a conversation become a negotiation?**).

2. Keep your 'I' statement clean. If you want to soften the assertion, give your reasons only. Reasons are your personal opinions such as why you like or dislike something.

3. Avoid discussing logic. Logic is more scientific; it requires observable or tangible proof that something is right or wrong and can be checked by both people. You can reason with someone but you can't engage in discussing logic with them. Once you start discussing logic, your assertion collapses immediately.

4. Avoid using language that reduces the importance of what you're saying. For example, the word "just" implies that something is insignificant: "I just thought ..." or "This is just an idea ..." They tend to give the listener a warning that what's to come is trivial and irrelevant.

Earlier you would have scored yourself on answering the three questions, How often do I:

1. **Give in** and accept other's decisions?—PASSIVE
2. **Ask for what I want?**—MILD ASSERTING
3. **Tell others** what action to take?—FULL-ON ASSERTING

These describe a continuum of assertiveness and can be identified with certain words or phrases:

PASSIVE	MILD ASSERTING	FULL-ON ASSERTING

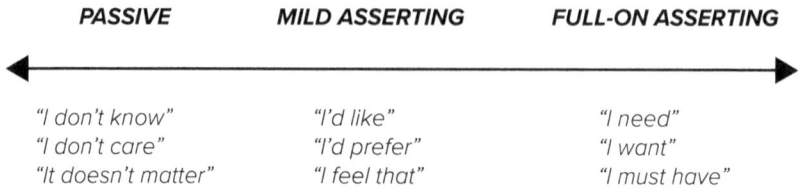

"I don't know"	*"I'd like"*	*"I need"*
"I don't care"	*"I'd prefer"*	*"I want"*
"It doesn't matter"	*"I feel that"*	*"I must have"*

Figure 22: The continuum of assertiveness.

Having read the discussion this far, where do you now consider yourself to be along this continuum in most day-to-day conversations?

If you find that you've scored yourself **more towards the passive end**, then you can become more assertive:

- Pay attention to what you think, feel, want and prefer in this conversation. Be clear on your needs.
- Practice saying what you want, particularly on things that are not that important to you or that will not damage the relationship. For example, if you see a new movie or TV show with a friend and they put forward a view (they may have really liked it), take the opposite view.
- Remember to practise your 'I' statements, "I'd like", "I'd prefer" or "I feel".
- Maintain strong and consistent eye-contact. People who assert strongly maintain eye-contact. Practice this in ordinary conversations to see how long you can maintain eye-contact before looking away—wait till the other person looks away first.
- Be very clear when stating what you want or expect. Avoid qualifiers such as 'I think', 'I suppose', 'Perhaps we could …' Replace these with clear statements of intent such as, 'I propose', 'I recommend', 'I believe'.

Remember also that your ideas and opinions are as important as anyone else's. This really helps you to be more assertive. It starts with an inner attitude that you value yourself as much as you value others.

If you find that you consider you're **already reasonably assertive**, but there are times when you would like to be much stronger:

- Be very clear on what your needs are.
- Weigh up the pluses and minuses of taking a strongly assertive stance in this situation.
- State your needs with a strong 'I' statement. Also use the word 'need' appropriately.
- Avoid being drawn into the other person's reasoning and logic—stay with your needs.
- If necessary, state reasons to support your needs, then return immediately to repeating your needs statement. For example, "I need this information today. I'm pleased when I get information on time".
- Maintain strong eye-contact.

Practice these in a non-consequential situation, for example if you have to return something to a store and the item is perfectly OK (i.e. there is no real need to return it other than having changed your mind).

If you find, or perhaps you've had some comments from others, that at times you seem to be a little overbearing or even somewhat aggressive, chances are that you're a little bit further to the right than 'Full-on Asserting' on the graph. This is most likely caused by using the 'you' word too often and too strongly when you want something from someone else. Despite what others may have told you, it has nothing to do with your personality, it's the words you may be using. Try these tips:

- Be very clear on what your needs are.
- Drop the 'you' word entirely from your statement of needs, for example avoid statements such as "You should", "You will", "I think you should", "I need you to".
- Involve the other person in the conversation, for example, "How would that work for you?" or "What are your thoughts on the

subject?" Also, use collaborative statements such as "I would like us both to leave here able to commit to what we agree to", "Let's see if there's a way for both of us to get what we need", "What's your point of view on …?", "My concern is …", "Would it make sense …?"

- Practice triangulation by using your hands—an object, paper, book etc. to direct your gaze away from the other person and encourage them to do similarly.

- Listen—get into their world by working with their reason and logic. Note: using logic here is a good strategy for a leader who may be seen as overly assertive (perhaps aggressive) as it enables both of you to agree on observable or tangible proof that something is right or wrong. It can also be checked by both people thus providing an immediate area of agreement.

The bottom line …

Assertive conversations—Health-Warning

Deciding to be assertive can result in either a win or lose situation, particularly when it comes to relationships. Be mindful of the importance of relationships when deciding to be more assertive, one should be aware of the physical and mental energy that this takes.

Those who try the strong assertiveness techniques discussed here for the first time may find that it takes a lot of energy to push out their wants/needs and refrain from discussing reason and logic (which is so much easier). This degree of energy is described as 'push' energy. You are pushing out (from within yourself) and quite often pushing against a contrary argument or contradictory opinion held by the other person. Be aware of this and stick with it. This is a technique that requires time and practice.

4.8 Creating an image

Although not strictly a challenging conversation, this chapter on presentations is included because:

- they are often seen as difficult;

- they should make a connection with your audience through the use of such techniques as rhetorical questions and metaphors; and
- everyone at some stage will have to give a presentation—if you're a CEO or senior executive, then you've probably given many already.

Through social science research we've known for some time that the use of rhetoric, imagery and metaphor can positively impact how the audience perceives and acts on the message.[195] However, a recent study has now taken this one step further. The results of the research by Loren J Naidoo and Robert G Lord,[196] suggest that not only does the use of such tactics impact audience behaviour, used well they also have a positive effect on perceptions in terms of the charisma of the speaker (**Figure 23**).

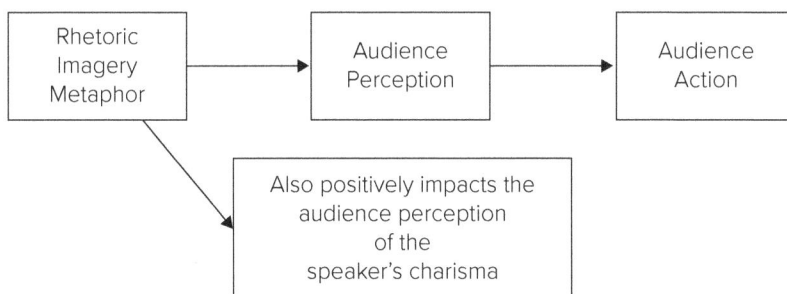

Figure 23: Audience perceptions and influence on the speaker.

195 B Selden, 2008, "Creating an image: Can a speech do it?", *Management Issues*, 29 August, http://www.management-issues.com/opinion/5164/creating-an-image-/, (accessed 29 March 2018).
196 J Naidoo and R Lord, 2008, "Speech imagery and perceptions of charisma: The mediating role of positive affect", *Leadership Quarterly*, Vol 19, 19 June, p 283–96, https://www.sciencedirect.com/science/article/pii/S1048984308000271, (accessed 29 March 2018).

Listen to some of the rhetoric, imagery, and metaphors candidate Barack Obama used in his now famous electoral race speech in March 2008 …

I am the son of a black man from Kenya and a white woman from Kansas. I was raised with the help of a white grandfather who survived a Depression to serve in Patton's Army during World War II and a white grandmother who worked on a bomber assembly line at Fort Leavenworth while he was overseas.

I've gone to some of the best schools in America and lived in one of the world's poorest nations. I am married to a black American who carries within her the blood of slaves and slave owners—an inheritance we pass on to our two precious daughters.

In a poll taken shortly after this speech[197], Obama was shown to be leading Hilary Clinton in the Democratic nomination race by 53 to 41 per cent. The behavioural impact stats are there, but did the speech impact people's perception of Obama's charisma?

After winning the Democrat nomination, press reports concerning the advice being given to Obama at the time included; "Get specific—lay out concrete plans", "Describe your experience in government—make Americans comfortable with you as their CEO", "Hammer your opponent above and below the belt".[198] None of this advice has anything to do with charisma—it is all about facts, logic and detail.

The other Presidential candidate Republican John McCain, used very little rhetoric, imagery and metaphor, but a lot of reason and

197 P Steinhauser, 2013, "CNN Poll: 53% who watched speech give president thumbs up", *CNN*, 12 February, http://politicalticker.blogs.cnn.com/2013/02/12/cnn-poll-53-who-watched-speech-give-president-thumbs-up/, (accessed 29 March 2018).

198 B Selden, 2008, "Creating an image: Can a speech do it?", *Management Issues*, 29 August, http://www.management-issues.com/opinion/5164/creating-an-image-/, (accessed 29 March 2018).

logic in his speeches. For example, in his address to the Los Angeles World Affairs Council in March 2008 only his opening paragraph gives any imagery or metaphor concerning McCain as a person; "... we should still shed a tear when all that is lost, when war claims its wages from us."[199]

The remaining 34 paragraphs all talk about reason and logic, saying nothing about the character of the man. As one press report concluded; "McCain appears dependent on a teleprompter, delivering even the most personal passages with an odd detachment. In his telling, his difficult five-and-a-half years as Vietnam prisoner of war might have happened to someone else."[200] However, McCain did do well in less formal settings such as town hall meetings and one-on-one conversations. But his discomfort behind the podium, and his preference for sticking with reason and logic whilst showing little emotion, was a distinct disadvantage as he struggled for national media attention.

Initially the race between the two presidential candidates was well and truly led by Obama. Audiences loved his charisma. However, as the election race went on, the gap between the two narrowed. Audiences were now listening for what was behind the message in terms of the reason and logic that would affect their day to day lives.

The research by Naidoo and Lord supports those poll results. They say that "high speech imagery will result in higher state positive affect in followers, compared to low speech imagery"[201]. So it appears as if Obama's advisors, once the initial speech was given, were now on the

199 Cited in S Holland, 2008, "McCain works to answer age and health questions", *Reuters*, 27 March, https://www.reuters.ocm/article/topNews/idUSN2619832720080327, (accessed 29 March 2018).

200 H Yeager, 2011, "John McCain's oratory leaves much to be desired", *Huffpost*, 25 May, https://www.huffingtonpost.com/entry/john-mccais-oratory-leav_n_95329.html, (accessed 29 March 2018).

201 B Selden, 2008, "Creating an image: Can a speech do it?", *Management Issues*, 29 August, http://www.management-issues.com/opinion/5164/creating-an-image-/, (accessed 29 March 2018).

right track—he'd developed an appropriate charisma in the eyes of the voting public through rhetoric and imagery, now it's time for reality—give them the reason and logic.

Whilst Obama's followers were encouraging him to get specific—give them the detail—look again at some of the words they themselves used to get their message across to Obama; "lay out concrete plans", "make Americans comfortable with you as their CEO", "hammer your opponent above and below the belt". Yes, in advising Obama to "get more specific—give them the details"—the advisors themselves were using numerous and powerful metaphors to get their message of "give them the details" across.

How leaders can use imagery and metaphors, and combine these with reason and logic

What are the messages in Naidoo and Lord's research for executives? There are three:

- Firstly, when speaking publicly, use **personal imagery** and **metaphors** so that the audience can see and feel your character.
- Secondly, whilst such imagery always works well, it is most powerful when the **situation is critical**, or the audience perceives **they are in a crisis**. People want the big picture and in particular, to hear and feel how the speaker has lived through similar times him or herself.
- Finally, the detail, the reason and logic, is best handled **one-on-one** and in **small group settings**. However, if you have a clear message to give in your presentation (which involves reason and logic), this will mean taking a very structured approach of explicit communication as to how the big picture will translate locally or to each person in the audience.

If you have to give presentations, that's the big picture. Now what about the detail? As this book is all about words, we'll start with some suggestions of which to use and which to avoid and conclude with a suggested format that includes metaphors, phrases and words that could be useful for your next presentation.

Of course key amongst those words to avoid, is 'don't'. What other commonly used words turn people off during a presentation? Tread carefully in your search for words. For every list of 'magic words' and 'power phrases' you might discover, you're apt to find an equally long list of overused terms to be avoided. Words like 'guaranteed' or 'unique' or 'quality' are so pervasive that your audience will tune them out altogether. Clichéd buzzwords like 'cutting edge' and 'industry-leading' or superlatives like 'world class' and 'once-in-a-lifetime' are better left unsaid.

Here are some examples of commonly used words and phrases that have lost their original meaning or impact. We've given some suggestions for replacing them.

Words or phrases that have lost their impact include:	Could be replaced with:	Or, a metaphor that may have a better impact:
Excellent (or excellence)	Outstanding	This is first-rate First class Top notch Blue ribbon Five star (although this too may be starting to lose some of its impact)
Awesome	Astounding	Breath taking Mind blowing Hair raising Heart stopping
Unique	Exclusive, special, unrepeatable	One off One of a kind They broke the mould when they made her
Like (used as a filler)	Remove entirely. Use silence as a short spacer between sentences.	

Words or phrases that have lost their impact include:	Could be replaced with:	Or, a metaphor that may have a better impact:
You know (often used at the end of a sentence)—similarly "Know what I mean?"	Remove entirely. Use silence as a short spacer between sentences.	
Basically	Remove entirely. Use silence as a short spacer between sentences.	
Filler words such as "um", "right", "OK", or "So …".	Remove entirely. Use silence as a short spacer between sentences.	
Obviously	Clearly, It is clear to me	Crystal clear
No problem	It can work, I'm willing	Door is wide open, I'm open
To be honest	I am willing to say more	Warts and all
Second to none	Number one	Gold medal position
At the end of the day	What's most important, ultimate objective	The finish line
Truth be told	As matter of fact	The nub, the gist, the essence, nitty-gritty
Let me share with you	I would like to say	May I highlight something
Think outside the box	A shift in thinking, a new way to see it, creative approach	Let your imagination run wild, hatch a new plan
Guaranteed	Committed, promised	It's a winner, brilliant
Moving forward	Next steps	The road ahead, the journey, the pathway
Reaching out (to you)	Contact, connect	Starting point
Quality*	Standards, level of performance	Gold standard

Table 13: Words or phrases that have lost their impact.

*Quality has been included in this list of words to avoid, to demonstrate the degree of difference of meaning the same word may have across different cultures. See the range of possible meanings below:

Country	Possible meaning
USA	It works
Japan	Perfection
Germany	Fit for purpose
France	Style
Australia	Service relationship

Be careful to avoid such cultural potholes. With 'quality' we have a commonly used word that has different interpretations between cultures. With words such as these it would be useful to explain your interpretation of what you mean when you use such words to ensure everyone has the same understanding.

And here are some words that are possibly on the cusp of losing their impact:

- innovative;
- sustainability;
- empower; and
- amazing.

Probably the best way to look at some positive words to build into your presentations is to use an example of what you mean then build in some metaphors as you construct the presentation. A good way of getting the best from the remainder of this chapter is to think now about the topic of your next presentation (or the last one you've made). As you think about your topic, use the following suggestions to develop some of the better words or metaphors to use.

For inspiration before you start, have a look at some of the metaphors and imagery that Martin Luther King Jr used in his famous 'I have a dream' speech:

"A lonely island of poverty in the midst of a vast ocean of material prosperity."

"But we refuse to believe that the bank of justice is bankrupt."

"… the quicksands of racial injustice to the solid rock of brotherhood."

"… storms of persecutions and staggered by the winds of police brutality."

"… a beautiful symphony of brotherhood."[202]

One of the reasons that Martin Luther King, Jr's speech is considered one of the most powerful speeches in US history, is King's masterful use of the metaphor as a rhetorical device. Take a moment to review these brilliant metaphors. Even though you may not have heard or read his speech in its entirety, it's possible to glean the intent and impact King was intending.

King's metaphors
"A lonely island of poverty in the midst of a vast ocean of material prosperity."
"But we refuse to believe that the bank of justice is bankrupt."
"… the quicksands of racial injustice to the solid rock of brotherhood."
"… storms of persecutions and staggered by the winds of police brutality."
"… a beautiful symphony of brotherhood."

You may have noticed in the above excerpts from his speech that King has used a pair of related metaphors to brilliantly depict cause and effect. For example, in another part of his speech he compared the Emancipation Proclamation to "a great beacon of hope" and

---

202 M L King Jr, 1963, "I have a dream", *U.S. National Archives and Records Administration*, https://www.archives.gov/files/press/exhibits/dream-speech.pdf, (accessed 20 June 2018).

"a joyous daybreak"[203]. He was making the point that just as a beacon or daybreak can bring light and hope, the Emancipation Proclamation brought enlightenment and optimism to millions of slaves.

Below we've explored the two related metaphors with our interpretation of the point King was emphasising:

A metaphor to describe the things that are happening/ not happening ...	A linking metaphor to show or describe the situation as it is now ...	The point being made ...
island of poverty	(island) vast ocean	The injustice of inequality between black and white Americans.
bank of justice	(bank) bankrupt	There is hope. This is a just society. Change is possible.
quicksands	(quicksand) solid rock	People of race will stick together to overcome all obstacles.
storms	(storm) winds of police brutality	The inequitable treatment of Afro-American citizens.
symphony	(singing or playing group—symphony) brotherhood	People of similar background will work together to overcome and the result will be something worthwhile.

We trust some of King's imagery has given you inspiration. We're not suggesting at this stage that you use the sophisticated 'two part' metaphor that King used in your next presentation. That's probably

---

203 ibid.

a little challenging. Merely begin with an easy metaphor to describe your intent.

Author Cam Barber[204] like many presenters, uses the metaphor of a road journey. When you drive on the roads, you know where you are on those roads. Each road has a name and/or number. Each town has a name. Each house has a number. If you are at house No. 100, you can go back to No. 50 or forward to No. 150. You can look at the signposts for directions. You can also look at your GPS for the structure of the roads in detail. In other words, it's easy to navigate the roads. You cannot get lost.

But when you give a presentation how can your audience know where they are? How can they know the structure of your presentation? How can they know what is coming next? They'll know because you put up signposts for them at the beginning and all along the route, so they're sure to make the final destination with you without getting side-tracked or lost.

Use the example in the following table to consider ways to harness the power of descriptive words or metaphors. The table has two columns. The first: 'Presentation phase' is a logical way of structuring the presentation to build to a strong conclusion. The second is 'Signpost language'. Think of these signs as directional aids to keep you and your audience on track so that you both arrive at your destination at the same time and with the shared knowledge and experience of the journey.

In the following example we've used one theme, 'relationships', for our metaphors throughout the presentation. Using a theme is not essential although it can be very effective so long as it resonates with the audience.

---

204 C Barber, 2012, "A short speech—create a 3-minute speech that rocks", *The Vivid Method*, 28 October, https://vividmethod.com/a-short-speech-create-a-3-minute-speech-that-rocks/, (accessed 29 March 2018).

Presentation phase:	Signpost language: Potential words, phrases or metaphors
Introduction	Here's an example of how one speaker used a metaphor in his opening remarks to deal painlessly with a very painful topic for his audience. After he acknowledged the group, he began: "Flying in for this meeting, I sat next to a woman with a very unusual ring on the middle finger of her left hand. When I commented on it, she said it was her wedding ring. I asked, 'Why do you have it on the wrong finger?' Replied the woman, 'I married the wrong man.'" After the laughter died down, the speaker then metaphorically linked the story to his point. "Given the disappointing results we have all been experiencing in the market lately, it is fair to ask, 'Are we in a relationship with the wrong person— the wrong strategy?' I believe so." Having eased his group into his topic and totally captured them with his off-beat opening, he then went on to present his arguments and alternative strategy ideas.
Opening metaphor/ framing	*Analogy of strategy with relationships*
Overview of the presentation	"This afternoon I'm going to explore the relationship between our product mix and our strategy to see how we might save this relationship, after all, they've been together a long time and I'd like to see them succeed, wouldn't you?"
Metaphors used	*Product mix and strategy as a longstanding relationship, one that still has value*

Presentation phase:	Signpost language: Potential words, phrases or metaphors
Finishing a section	"It's probably fair to assume that some of you have been in relationships that didn't work out as well as expected—I know I have. The points I've raised here … are clear indicators of why our strategy needs some counselling if this relationship is to flourish as it once did."
Metaphors used to finish a section before moving on	*Indicators that relationships is not flourishing— summary of evidence presented indicating need for change*
Starting a new section	"Now that we've seen what's causing this potential break-up in the product mix/strategy relationship, let's look at some ways we can get them back together and engender once again the excitement we experienced when they worked so well together previously."
Relate the new section to the one just finished	*Signalling the connection between measurements and changes about to be proposed*
Analysing a point	"Where does that lead us and how should we foster the relationship?" "Let's consider this in more detail and see how the partnership might work …" "What does this mean for them, for us?"
Use of metaphor (or theme) to reinforce these points	*More details of how the product mix and strategy could change to improve performance— questions also used*
Paraphrasing, clarifying and giving examples	"A good example of how our marketing strategy and product mix can really hit it off is …" "As an illustration, when they are really working in harmony, sharing the load and working toward the same outcomes …" "To show how this new relationship could really gel …"
Use of examples that will resonate with audience	*Visual imagery and explanation of what success could look like*

Presentation phase:	Signpost language: Potential words, phrases or metaphors
Summarising and concluding	"In conclusion, if we were to listen in on the conversation between the marketing strategy and the product mix, what would we hear? What would they be saying to one another? Would they be describing a match made in heaven? (Pause) I'm sure we'd hear things like … Together, let's reinforce that message."
Linking conclusion with the opening metaphor	*Imagery of success once it is actually achieved*

Table 14: Phases of a presentation.

You'll have noticed in the example given that the speaker has used 'we' in his opening remarks. Why was he justified in jumping straight to 'we' without going through the 'I' and 'you' phases first as was discussed earlier in the book? Was there a shared understanding of the issue or problem? Look at his words once again, "Given the disappointing results we have all been experiencing in the market lately". Clearly this is common knowledge to his audience and is the reason for this meeting, hence his legitimate use of 'we'—we have a shared problem.

However, in his next statement he reverts to 'I'—"Are we in a relationship with the wrong person, the wrong strategy? *I* believe so." He's now giving his personal opinion which is yet to be tested, justified and accepted by his audience. He needs to gain the audience's acceptance so at the moment it's only his opinion as to the reasons for the poor market results.

He will then go on to lead his audience through his reasoning (with facts and logic) and engender their support with rhetorical questions and metaphors. He is thereby sticking to the appropriate use of 'I', 'you' and 'we'.

Can you also see how he followed the conversation process?

1. Open a channel—create a welcoming space
2. Commit to engage—create value for the audience
3. Construct meaning—find common ground
4. Converge on agreement—search for areas of agreement
5. Evolve and build understanding—what's changed—Actions? Beliefs? Ideas?
6. Act or transact—what will happen next?

As a leader, consider how you can use metaphors to guide your audience through your next presentation—whether it be a presentation to the senior team, the board, or employees—with a clear and visual road map and signposting so that everyone arrives home 'tired but happy'.

The bottom line ...

When speaking in public:

- Use personal imagery and metaphors so that the audience can see and feel your character.
- Give people the big picture. They want to hear and feel how the speaker has lived through similar times. Give personal examples.
- Remember: the detail—the reason and logic—is best handled one-on-one and in small group settings. However, if you have a clear message to give in your presentation, take a very structured approach of explicit communication as to how the big picture will translate locally or to each person in the audience.

4.9 Tactics to use when a conversation turns into a negotiation

When you leave home for work, do you feel ready to face the day knowing that you will likely have a number of successful negotiations? Chances are the word 'negotiation' never enters your head.

We often think of negotiation as a formal process conducted behind closed doors by high powered executives, politicians or world leaders.

Yet everyday all of us negotiate. You may have to agree with colleagues on the content of a report or presentation; with the board Chair over a disputed decision; with a contractor on the terms for services; or with a neighbour over the state of a fence. All of these conversations are negotiations—where the two (or more) of you; your colleagues, or someone else, have to agree on a decision to take action.

Unfortunately, we often do not recognise these situations as negotiations nor ourselves as negotiators. As a result, we may enter these discussions less prepared than we could be. The result? Sometimes a less-than-successful outcome.

There have been hundreds of books written on the subject of negotiating and how to negotiate successfully. Yet it was only when Roger Fisher and William Ury wrote their seminal work, *Getting to Yes: Negotiating Agreement Without Giving In*[205] in 1991 that our breakthrough understanding of successful negotiating really took off. The key to this understanding, for which we are grateful to Fisher and Ury, is that successful negotiating, at its core, depends on being very clear about one's underlying needs, identifying and clarifying the needs of the other party, and then together, developing a range of options that will satisfy both party's needs.

You may find this chapter a little different to others. We invite you to join us on our journey of understanding the core principles of successful negotiating, as we intend to use a number of examples you may encounter daily in your personal life, as well as executive team meeting examples to illustrate. If you're not familiar with the underpinning principles of successful negotiating, it may be akin to learning a new language. For that reason, as you read through this chapter, we encourage you to think about how our suggestions can work in both your personal and business endeavours. In this way, you'll recognise:

---

205 R Fisher and W Ury, 1991, *Getting to Yes: Negotiating an agreement without giving in*, Random Century Limited, London.

- when the situation becomes a negotiation (rather than remaining a discussion); and
- the appropriate, strategies, techniques, tactics and indeed skills, to apply.

Tips for leaders to improve success in all negotiations

To help make all our daily negotiations more successful (for both you and the other person) it's important to use the right words, follow a good negotiating process and take on the attitude that "I am a negotiator". In terms of the right words—we've covered these earlier in the book—it's merely a matter of using them appropriately and following a sound negotiating process—the key is to be prepared to negotiate. To do so, you'll need to be clear on the following (**Figure 24**):

- State your case clearly and appropriately—"What is it that I really *need* from this negotiation?" Try and quantify what it is you want, i.e. amount of time, money, resources, services, etc. that will satisfy your needs.
- Organise your facts—"How will I support my case?"—"What facts do I have that will support what and why I want what I do?"
- Control the timing and pace of your discussion (the six phases of a conversation also apply in all negotiations).

TIPS TO IMPROVE NEGOTIATION SUCCESS

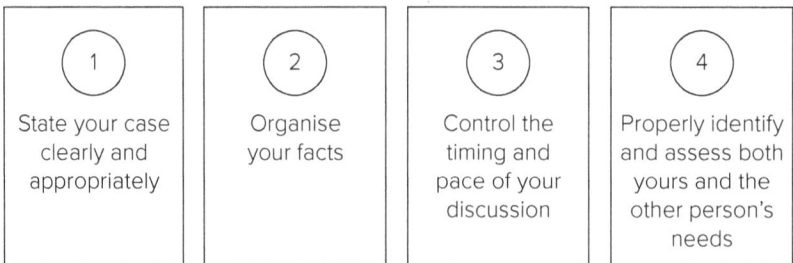

1	2	3	4
State your case clearly and appropriately	Organise your facts	Control the timing and pace of your discussion	Properly identify and assess both yours and the other person's needs

Figure 24: Tips to Improve Negotiation Success.

- Properly identify and assess both yours and the other person's needs. These needs are non-negotiable, i.e. how you want to feel as a result of a successful negotiation (more on identifying 'needs' shortly).

How do you carry out these four points successfully? Firstly, leaders require an understanding of some of the key principles of successful negotiating. You can assess your knowledge of negotiating by answering 'True' or 'False' to each of the following five questions:

1. I should ask for twice the amount I need?
2. My aim is to prevent the other person from saying "No"?
3. A small concession will relieve the pressure on me?
4. A "Win/Win" result is always possible?
5. Admitting to an error or omission is a sign of weakness?

The following answers will provide some useful tips for your day-to-day negotiating situations and those you find yourself involved with in meetings and working with teams.

Should I ask for twice the amount I need? False.

If you do, you'll undoubtedly have to back down and will lose an important opportunity to influence the other person. Research clearly indicates that negotiators who make large concessions end up worse off[206]. The secret of successful negotiating is to firstly identify your needs then work out a range of options that will satisfy those needs. Start the negotiation by asking for the options that best meet your needs (the negotiation experts call these options 'wants', i.e. what we want—we're using 'options' and 'wants' interchangeably here).

A good example of how this works, is in the popular reality TV show 'Shark Tank' where new entrepreneurs present their case to four

---

206 D Malhotra, 2006, "Four strategies for making concessions", *HBS Working Knowledge*, 6 March, https://www.scribd.com/document/255287033/4-Strategies-for-Making-Concessions-1, (accessed 29 March 2018).

potential investors ('sharks'). In almost every case where the entrepreneurs ask for the investment in the form of 5% or 10% share in the business plus $xx of investment, the sharks (who are interested) will counter with 35% or 40% or sometimes 45% share in the business plus the amount of dollars asked for. Invariably, the entrepreneurs, who really want the investment, accept one of the offers, and so lose the potential influencing power from their new venture (they've given away far more of the business than they intended). Whereas, entrepreneurs who are realistic in their request, may offer a 20%, 25% or 30% share, and are often answered with a much smaller counter increase in the offer from the sharks, e.g., 30%, 35%, or 40%.

What are needs?

'Needs' are those (often) hidden things that drive us to achieve. They cannot be seen or touched, but they are always felt. They are often hard to describe, such as the need to act in good faith or act based on company values in making a decision.

Needs should be clearly distinguishable from 'wants'. Wants are the things that we get that satisfy our inner needs and our view that things are being managed the way we would do it. This distinction between needs and wants is very important. To understand this clearly is to understand effective negotiating.[207]

Needs are never negotiable. After all, they are what drive us to want 'things'. Wants on the other hand are always negotiable. For example, you might like a hug (want) to gain affection (need) from your partner or perhaps child. Sometimes you will settle for a peck on the cheek (an alternative option to the original want) or holding of hands (another alternative to the original want) or even a pat on the back (another alternative want) to satisfy your need for affection.

---

207 For a clear distinction between needs and wants in economics see https://study.com/academy/lesson/the-difference-between-wants-vs-needs-in-economics.html, (accessed 30 May 2018).

In a business situation, you might like the affirmation (want) that satisfies your status as a worthwhile executive (need). Sometimes you will settle for a "Good point, Joan" from the CEO (an illustration of the original want) or other colleagues supporting your proposal unanimously (an alternative option), or the CEO suggesting that you consult someone else for advice on a critical issue (another alternative option). All of these, 'the affirmation from the CEO', 'support of your colleagues' and 'taking advice' are genuine 'options' that will satisfy your underlying 'need' to satisfy your thinking about your position as a worthwhile executive.

Some further examples of 'needs' and 'wants'

This concept of 'needs' and 'wants', is so important to the success of every negotiation, that we have provided some further examples:

Example 1: As a leader, I have a need to feel assured that another colleague is **acting in good faith**. My 'need' for this could be satisfied by some of the following 'wants':

- the colleague's willingness to step out of the conversation if there is any perception of a conflict of interest;
- the colleague's transparency demonstrated through a willingness to disclose extra information when asked even though there is no requirement to do so;
- the other colleague's willingness to repeat and explain a point in more detail until everyone has the same level of understanding; and
- acceptance of external advice to test a point of view.

Important note: Your original *need to feel assured* that the leader is acting in good faith is always non-negotiable. How you satisfy that need (through a variety of wants or options) is always negotiable.

Are there additional wants or options to the ones we've mentioned you can think of?

Example 2: As a senior executive, **I need to feel that the CEO is acting ethically** in a particular matter.

Here are some wants (ways of receiving assurance) I could ask for:

- external testing of data or advice provided by the CEO;
- discussion with the CEO one-on-one;
- discussion with other members of the management team without the presence of the CEO

Important note: Your original *need to feel that the CEO is acting ethically* is always non-negotiable. How you satisfy that need (through a variety of wants or options) is always negotiable.

Are there additional wants or options to the ones we've mentioned that you can think of?

How do you decide on what your needs are?

If your needs are not readily evident, then the best way to be clear about your needs is to ask yourself the question "Why?" as you think about what you want. Keep answering it till you find something that you can't see or touch. For example, if you decide that you want more information you could pose yourself a series of questions:

Question: "Why do I want more information?"
Answer: "To understand the risks more clearly."
Question: "Why do I want to understand the risks more clearly?"
Answer: "To be sure I can balance the rewards with the risks."
Question: "Why do I want to balance rewards and risks?"
Answer: "I *need to feel secure* that I have behaved with good faith, considered all the options.

Notice in this final answer the word 'feel' appears as does 'need': "I need to feel secure". In most cases when you find an answer to "Why?" that includes the word 'feel', you'll know that you've uncovered your need. So, in this example, by continually asking "Why?" you've identified your need to feel secure. Having identified your need 'to feel secure' there could be several further potential options to satisfy your need. For example:

- ask for more information;
- review that information and ask more questions;
- seek external advice;
- listen to alternative views;
- attend a relevant meeting.

All of these options (wants) may assist in satisfying your need to feel secure about acting in good faith. And through reflective questioning and relevant discussions, you may uncover further options.

Shortly we'll describe:

- a variety of *words* a leader can use in an effective negotiation,
- to identify a range of *wants*,
- that will enable you to satisfy your *needs*.

But first, back to that true/false quiz …

Is your aim to prevent the other person from saying "No"? False.

Getting a 'No' from the other person can be very useful because it gives you the opportunity to ask, "Can you give me your reasons?" This leads to uncovering the other person's real needs and some options that will satisfy them, options which you can probably supply.

One aim of negotiating is to create a large list of options that will satisfy your needs and do the same for the other person. In this way, you are likely to come up with some options that will satisfy both of you. Some questions that will help you to develop these options are:

- "What other options might be available?"
- "When I hear 'that can't be done' may I ask what if the opposite were true?"
- "If there were no limitations (to what's being suggested), what would a successful solution look like to you?"

- "From what I've heard, it appears that it may not be possible to ... at this time. What could make it possible?"
- "In an ideal world, what options would satisfy your needs?"
- "Can you give me an indication of how that might work?"
- "How could I help to ...?"

Will a small concession relieve the pressure? False.

If you make a small concession, chances are you are negotiating options rather than needs. Additionally, the other person may think you are weakening and will put more pressure on you. Far better to state or restate your needs and then explore as many options as possible to satisfy them. As part of this negotiation, you may come back to the offer that was just rejected, or you may find some even better options. Either way, you have gained a lot more information and not weakened your case.

As Roger Fisher and William Ury, point out: "Soft negotiators ... want to avoid personal conflict, make concessions readily and reach an amicable resolution. They are often exploited and feel bitter afterwards."[208]

So instead of making a small concession, ignore the current option and refocus on finding options that will satisfy your needs. For example, "I need to have (express here your inner *need*, not one of your wants). What options can you suggest that will help me in satisfying my *need*?" Note: in this example the word 'need' has been used twice. Once you've established your need (if possible before negotiating), write it down as a simple and clear statement. Then state and restate this need as you negotiate.

For example, if the CEO is negotiating with the board about a capital expenditure request, the board may need more time to consider the request. So the Chair could state their need as follows: "When does

---

208 R Fisher and W Ury, 1991, "Getting to Yes: negotiating an agreement without giving in", (2nd Ed), Century Business, Sydney, p xiv.

the decision have to be made? I've really had a tough week and I need more time to review this request with the board so that we can feel completely confident (*my need*) about our decision."

The CEO might suggest a break in the meeting and an informal discussion over lunch. The Chair could then say, "I'm not sure that is going to be enough time, what other options are there?"

A 'win/win' result is always possible. False.

It's desirable, but not always possible. Sometimes even the best negotiators have to 'agree to disagree'. The way to improve your ratio of win/wins is to focus very clearly on your own real needs (not positions or wants) and the needs of the other person. Searching for many different options to satisfy both people's needs generates more win/win solutions.

For example, there's a story about two cooks arguing over an orange. There's only one orange left in the fruit bowl and both cooks have determined that they want it and cannot possibly do without it. They become so aggressive about the situation that at one stage they even come to blows. Eventually they decide that since they cannot agree over who should have the orange, they will cut it in half. Having cut the orange in half the two cooks turn away, both completely unsatisfied with the outcome. Although each got half the orange, it's a clear case of 'lose/lose'.

As you've probably gathered by now this could become a win/win if both cooks were to focus on needs rather than options. Why did each need the orange? All it would have taken was for the cooks to take time out from screaming at each other, "I want it!", and to have instead asked each other one simple question, "What do you want the orange for?" This question would have uncovered that the first cook needed the juice from the orange. The second cook on the other hand, wanted the rind and flesh of the orange for her cooking. As is often the case, something so simple could have saved so much agony.

Note: more experienced negotiators instead of asking "What do you want the orange for?" would have asked one another, "What do you need the orange for?"

Is admitting to an error or omission a sign of weakness? False.

Research shows that disclosing such information demonstrates honesty. In psychological terms, it breeds what is called 'reciprocity' (which we have mentioned previously)—if you do something for me then I'll do something for you. People are far more likely to be honest with you when you are honest with them. Pulling the wool over someone's eyes may provide a short-term result at the expense of a long-term relationship. Such research also has another important result for leaders. In an exhaustive study of print medium sources, Koathari, Li, and Short found that positive disclosure can have a positive impact on risk:

> ... the firm's risk, as proxied by the cost of capital, stock return volatility, and analyst forecast dispersion, declines significantly. In contrast, unfavorable disclosures are accompanied by significant increases in risk measures.[209]

The power of admitting to an error or an omission often lies in the impact that the word 'sorry' can have on the other person. Saying "I'm sorry" and admitting to error can be a breakthrough in the negotiation, particularly when emotions are running high. Saying "sorry" works because it helps soften entrenched positions where powerful, unstated personal needs are blocking the willingness to move forward (we mentioned the power of saying "sorry" earlier in the book).

---

209 S Kothari, L Xu and J Short, 2009, "The effect of disclosures by management, analysts, and business press on cost of capital, return volatility, and analyst forecasts: A study using content analysis", *The Accounting Review*, Vol 84, No 5, p 1639, http://aaajournals.org/doi/abs/10.2308/accr.2009.84.5.1639?code=aaan-site, (accessed 10 April 2018).

Some final points on effective and successful negotiating strategies and techniques for leaders:

- Be prepared to think as a negotiator would—ask for what you want.
- Make sure your wants will satisfy your needs—avoid getting locked into bargaining over who is 'right'. Search for as many 'wants' as possible that will satisfy your needs.
- Argue to learn, not to win. To meet your own needs, it's necessary to learn as much as possible about the other person and their needs. The more you learn, the better chance you have of getting a good deal (i.e. the best decision, one that both people can accept).
- Make proposals regularly during a negotiation. Proposals move the negotiation forward. Use proposals such as:
  - "If you could support 'x' … then I might consider …"

The other person's response to these proposals will give you a lot of information to work with. For example, ask questions such as:

  - "Can you explain your reasons for …?"
  - "What are your priorities?"
  - "What else is there that you think I should know?"

- And remember to reciprocate—be willing to give as much information as possible—in this way, both you and the other party will be able to develop far more potential options to satisfy each other's needs.

The bottom line …

Know when you are in a negotiation vs. a discussion

- Leaders need to distinguish between a discussion and a negotiation, then take a positive negotiating perspective.
- To be effective as a negotiator, it's critical to identify one's own needs, then work hard during the negotiation to uncover and clarify the needs of the other party.

- Brainstorming as many options that might satisfy one's own needs, is an excellent method of preparing for a negotiation.
- Encouraging the other party to 'brainstorm' some options that may satisfy their needs through appropriate questioning during the negotiation, can lead to a satisfactory result for both.

4.10 How to overcome conversation stoppers and improve conversation deepeners

This final chapter in Part 4 includes many of the words, phrases or conversational habits that did not fit neatly into other chapters. However, they are important for improving the integrity of your conversations which ultimately help to develop the kinds of relationships that are so important to executives. We've split the chapter into two parts, what we've termed 'conversation stoppers' and 'conversation deepeners'.

How to counter someone who talks over the top of you

During a discussion on diversity in technology at the South by Southwest Music, Film and interactive Conference (Austin, Texas 2015), Google executives Eric Schmidt and Walter Isaacson were criticised for talking over US Chief Technology Officer Megan Smith.[210]

An audience member asked: "Given that unconscious bias research tells us that women are interrupted a lot more than men, I'm wondering if you are aware that you have interrupted Megan many more times?"[211] Ironically the audience member was the head of Google's Unconscious Bias Team, Judith Williams.

According to a study by Adrienne Hancock and Benjamin Rubin at the George Washington University, women do get interrupted more

---

210 A Marcotte, 2015, "Google chairman gets called out by his own employee for interrupting a female panelist at SXSW", *Slate Group*, 17 March, http://www.slate.com/blogs/xx_factor/2015/03/17/eric_schmidt_at_sxsw_google_chairman_called_out_for_interrupting_female.html, (accessed 29 March 2018).
211 ibid.

than men.[212] Surprisingly, when doing so, men and women interrupt women in equal numbers. While women will readily relate to this phenomenon of being interrupted, we're sure there will also be many men reading this who also find being 'talked-over' frustrating.

There are at least two strategies leaders can take in such instances:

Be assertive.
OR
Go with their story and steer them to yours.

If you decide to take the assertive approach, remember from Chapter 4.6 that there are three clear guidelines on assertiveness:

1. Always state your wants, needs or desires with an 'I' statement (and of course avoid 'you').
2. Keep your 'I' statement clean:
   'Can I please have a moment to finish what I'm saying?'
3. Avoid discussing logic—restate your reasoning:
   'I've clearly heard that point, now here's what I believe'

And should you decide to take the assertive route, be mindful that it may affect the relationship to some extent. You'll recall from our discussion on assertiveness that it requires a good deal of 'push' energy and is likely to provoke a 'push back' from the other person.

On the other hand, should you decide to work with their point and guide them towards yours, psychotherapist Diane Bath who frequently deals with people expressing their frustration at being talked-over, suggests five tactics.[213] These are summarised as:

---

212 A Hancock and B Rubin, 2014, "Influence of Communication Partner's Gender on Language", *Journal of Language and Social Psychology*, 11 May, Vol 34, No 1, p 46–64.

213 F Barth, 2015, "5 steps for dealing with someone who won't stop talking", *Psychology Today*, 22 April, https://www.psychologytoday.com/blog/the-couch/201204/5-steps-dealing-someone-who-wont-stop-talking, (accessed 29 March 2018).

1. Listen: make sure you know what the person is talking about and their key point or message. If they are an incessant interrupter, then just interrupting them back will only exacerbate the level of emotion in the conversation. Both voices will rise in volume and stances will become more erect, you have now entered the 'stand up and fight' mode.

2. After listening for a short time and formulating what they are trying to communicate, ask them for permission to interrupt …

   > "May I interrupt you there?"
   > OR
   > "Can I please have a moment to finish what I'm saying?"
   > OR
   > "Excuse me Peter, I didn't get to finish what I'm saying. I'd like to add that …"

   Note: in these last two examples the words 'what <u>I'm</u> saying' are used rather than 'what <u>I was</u> saying'. This ensures that the other person hears (subconsciously) that you are still speaking in the present tense and is therefore more likely to accept the interruption as a natural flow to the conversation.

3. When you interrupt, be ready to say something about what you hear them saying. If it's possible, try to find something positive about what they're saying or about them. This shows that although you are trying to stop them, you have listened. For example:

   > "Wait, I'd like to finish my thought now" then add what you were going to say about them.

4. Add some experience of your own that will confirm that you understand what they're experiencing. For example, a similar

event, a similar feeling or a funny story—anything that gives you a chance to share your own experience and that you can tie it to theirs. Although they are interrupting you, this tactic cultivates common ground and is more likely to encourage reciprocity.

5. Finally, stop the conversation if it goes on too long. After all it's your time they are using. For example:

> "I need to move on now. Can we finish this conversation tomorrow (or when you have time)?" And at this point you may also need to revert to the assertive approach mentioned earlier.

Because interrupting happens to all of us from time to time, we've probably used one of the following inappropriate phrases, sentences or questions. Our suggestions will provide an opportunity to improve your responses:

Inappropriate response to the interrupter	A better way to stop the interrupter
"You're speaking over me, please don't."	"May I have a moment to speak?"
"You're talking over me."	"May I please have a moment to finish what I'm saying?"
"You always butt in."	"May I comment on what's been said so far?"
"You are always cutting me off."	"Please listen to what I am proposing."
"You talked over me when I was trying to make an important point. I feel like you haven't really heard what I've tried to say about the situation."	"I really need to explain my view of the situation. When I've finished explaining, I'd like to hear your view."

You'll notice the use of 'you' that makes these first statements/ questions inappropriate and how using 'I' changes the tone, yet still remains assertive.

Note: 'may' and 'can' although often used interchangeably in everyday conversations, have quite different meanings. 'May' is a request to be allowed to do something, whereas 'can' refers to your ability to be able to do something. For example, "May I interrupt?" asks for permission whereas "Can I interrupt?" is asking the other person "Do I have the skill to interrupt (you)?" However, 'can' does seem stronger; for example, "Can I interrupt you there?" appears almost as an assertive declaration rather than "May I interrupt you there?" which is more passive (and perhaps polite). Because of its apparent strength and although not always grammatically correct, we'd recommend using 'can' in most cases.

How to handle questions that aren't really questions

"Don't you think …" or "Don't you think you should …?" are typical examples that can be described as vague statements of negation (more polite or gentle than simply saying 'no')."

Although this type of statement is phrased as a question (including the upward inflection at the end), it is not. It's a directive. It's a statement of the speaker's opinion and often given as contrary to what the other person has just put forward or suggested. Our experience is that these are not particularly destructive to the conversation; however, they can become annoying if heard continually. A suggested way of handling these is to:

Answer with a question:
"Am I hearing that … I should do … is that correct?"
"Tell me more …"
"Can you give me an example of what you mean?"

Once you've heard their point, follow with another question to direct the conversation back to you. For example:

"How does that relate to what I'm proposing?"
"How would that work with what I'm suggesting?"
"How would you see my idea working with what you're suggesting?"

These follow-up questions force the speaker to consider carefully your point of view and not dismiss it out of hand. Notice each question includes yours (the speaker's) proposal or suggestion. This will lead to a constructive discussion between the two of you because the other person has to provide an opinion of how their idea will combine/work with yours.

Overcoming one-word adjectives such as 'awesome'

Is it our imagination or are descriptions of things of beauty or terror becoming much shorter and less imaginative? For example, the word 'awesome' has become an overused adjective intended to denote something as 'great' but instead winds up meaning 'lame' and reflects poorly on the person using the word, which is a definite conversation stopper.

One way of enriching the subsequent conversation when hearing one-word exclamations such as 'awesome' is to ask:

"When I hear 'awesome' I'm not sure what it actually means. Can you explain why this … is awesome?"
OR
"Why is this … awesome?"

Overcoming common stoppers that may not seem like stoppers at the time

Negations

Here are some examples of negative phrases that are common conversation 'stoppers':

"That sounds great. I'll let you know."

"No, it's fine (or OK, good, right etc.)."

"I really like that, but …"

These (and others that you can probably recall) are all negations. The best way of dealing with these is to respond as follows:

"That sounds great. I'll let you know."	→	"What part of it sounds great to you?"
"No, it's fine (or OK, good, right etc.)."	→	"Why/how is it fine?"
"I really like that, but …"	→	"What is it that you really like?"

You'll notice all these responses pick up the positive part of the speaker's statement and reflect it back to the speaker as a question. This forces the speaker to focus on the positive aspects of the topic or subject. If you are practising the 'and' technique we covered earlier in the book, you might say:

"That sounds great. I'll let you know"	→	"and, what part of it sounds great to you?"
"No, it's fine (or OK, good, right etc.)."	→	"and, why/how is it fine?"
"I really like that, but …"	→	"and, what is it that you really like?"

Conversation stoppers you should avoid

"Let me see what I can do"—now there's nothing wrong with this statement apart from the fact that it closes off further discussion. Depending on the situation, this may be quite appropriate. So what is the downside? If you find yourself using this statement regularly, then there's a very good chance that you are taking on many problems that could or should belong to someone else to solve. If this does resonate with you, then one way of overcoming this is to ask questions that will get the speaker involved in the solution such as:

"How do you intend to handle this?"
"What are the next steps you'll be taking?"
"Who do you intend to discuss this with?"

Avoid 'qualifiers' or 'performatives'

Avoid using:

'Let me be honest' or 'Let me be perfectly honest with you' or 'To be honest' or 'I'll give you my honest opinion' or 'To be brutally honest' or 'Let me be truthful' or 'To be frank'

Do these mean that you haven't been honest with me in the past? Or that I should disregard everything else that you say because this is the truth? You could be quite sarcastic and respond, 'Finally, some honesty!'

It's been found that people turn off and stop listening; they hear these 'qualifiers' and find the speaker untrustworthy. So if any of these statements that employ the word 'honest' or 'truth' are amongst your usual sayings, we suggest dropping them.

There are many of these types of phrases that we use regularly, the experts call them 'qualifiers' or 'performatives', and they can become quite habitual. Often we do not realise we are using them. Yet when reading them in text they seem quite straightforward for example, 'As far as I know …', or 'With all due respect'. However, when spoken they are almost always followed by a statement that signals bad news or even dishonesty, for example 'as far as I know it's not possible to do that.' This heightens uneasiness in the listener.

James W Pennebaker, Chair of the Psychology Department of the University of Texas was quoted in the *Wall Street Journal* as saying these phrases are a form of dishonesty:

> *Language experts have textbook names for these phrases—"performatives," or "qualifiers." Essentially, taken alone, they express a simple thought, such as 'I am writing to say …' At first, they seem harmless, formal, may be even polite. But coming before another statement, they often signal that bad news, or even some dishonesty on the part of the speaker, will follow.*[214]

Below is a list of common qualifiers and why they might be conversation stoppers; or why they might be merely annoying, or perhaps why they could even be dangerous. We've grouped them into three categories—phrases or questions that:

1. may be harmful to the conversation or hazardous to the ongoing relationship;
2. are less dangerous but should be avoided wherever possible; and
3. are not harmful nor dangerous but may be heard as ineffectual by the listener.

---

214 J Pennebaker, 2014, "Why verbal tee-ups like 'To be honest' often signal insincerity", *Wall Street Journal*, 20 January, https://www.wsj.com/articles/no-headline-available-1390243667, (accessed 29 March 2018).

Conversation stopper	What they really mean and why they should be avoided
1. These phrases/questions may be harmful to the conversation or hazardous to the ongoing relationship:	
"Can I be … ('frank', 'direct', 'honest')?"	See our earlier discussion on 'honest'. Avoid.
"No offense, but" or "I hate to be the one to tell you this …" or "Don't take this the wrong way" (often followed with 'but')	What follows these statements is going to be hurtful or offensive. Always own your own opinion, not others. You could say for example "I've heard that … " or "I've seen that …"
"With all due respect"	*You're setting me up to be disrespected.* People see straight through this. This is a phrase that is often used by politicians.
"Frankly"	*So, you think I'm a dummy or less intelligent!*
"I want you to know …"	Often taken by the listener as overbearing.
"I hear what you're saying …"	You'll recall this from our earlier chapters; "I hear what you say but I disagree with it so totally that I am not even going to bother considering it. In fact, I have already forgotten it. Here's what I think …" Drop this phrase from your conversation entirely.
"I'm not trying to hurt your feelings, but …"	The only part of this phrase the listener will hear is "hurt your feelings". If it is bad news and you do need to apologise for it, you could say "I'm sorry. This is tough news for me to give".

Conversation stopper	What they really mean and why they should be avoided
"Confidentially ..." OR "Can I tell you this in confidence?"	This is similar to 'honesty'. Be careful as this phrase puts pressure on the listener. Do you want to go to this extent?
"Actually ..."	Interrogation experts suggest when people answer a question such as, "What did you do on the weekend?" those who prefix their answers with 'actually' are more likely to be lying about what follows. (We heard a five-minute community presentation recently where the speaker used 'actually' 23 times!)
2. The following are less dangerous, but should be avoided wherever possible:	
"I may be wrong, but" OR "If I didn't know better"	Means "I am right". Try to avoid these as they sound demeaning.
"I'm just saying ..."	Generally used as a defence mechanism when you question the speaker about their opinion. Although it's an 'I' statement it will be seen as defensive. Better to use "I believe", "I suggest", "I recommend", "I propose".
"I don't mean to be rude, but ..."	Once again the only word the listener will hear is "rude". Do you really want to be seen as rude?
"Promise me you won't get mad, but ..."	What you really mean here is "You're going to get really mad."
"It's really none of my business, but ..."	"I'm going to butt in to something that's none of my business." So why not avoid it all together?

Conversation stopper	What they really mean and why they should be avoided
"It really doesn't matter to me, but ..."	If it doesn't matter, then why say it?
"Nothing personal!"	Of course it's personal! Why else would you say it?
3. Nothing too wrong with the following, they just seem ineffectual:	
"It is what it is"	This is superfluous.
"I am thinking that ..." OR "As far as I know ..."	Nothing really wrong with these, only that they are qualifiers and weaken the statement to follow. If you need to show strength, change to "I propose" or "I recommend" or one that's a little softer, "I suggest".

Table 15: Avoiding and overcoming 'conversation stoppers'.

Conversation stoppers can be any of the following:

- using qualifiers which at best weaken your statement and at worst may make you seem dishonest;
- accusing the speaker of negative intent (even if they haven't finished speaking);
- taking over the conversation;
- changing the subject (too often);
- refusing to let someone speak (remember, most of us regularly interrupt the speaker before he or she finishes);
- going off on tangents;
- teasing and sarcasm;
- arguing;
- lack of curiosity (disinterest can bring a quick halt to any conversation);

- questions that make people feel judged, shamed or instructed; and
- questions that aren't questions, but directives ("Don't you think you should …?").

Conversation deepeners

When leaders become polarised in their views, what can draw them back to the middle, back to a space where they might be able to engage in more productive conversation? A study by Phillip Rogers and associates offers some interesting insights into how people come to moderate their views.[215] The study found that people tend to hold simple causal models in their heads. They typically know less about some things than they think they do. This is where the power of questioning comes in—it is often more helpful to ask a question than to spend time telling a colleague all the reasons for your opposing point of view, particularly when the competing views are extremely different.

And what kind of question is the most powerful? A mechanistic one; the study showed that asking a mechanistic, or 'how' type question and allowing a person to explain how their decision, policy or solution would work in practice, helped them to moderate their view. For example, rather than telling a colleague why something is wrong, ask them "How would that work?" or "How could that work in practice?"

Listening to someone explain their view is a more positive approach leading to a better conversation than trying to prove someone wrong with the power of your reason or logic.

Harvard Professor and cognitive scientist, Steven Pinker, describes the 'curse of knowledge' as "a difficulty in imagining what it is like for

---

215 P Fernbach, et al, 2013, Political Extremism is supported by an illusion of understanding, *Psychological Science*, 25 April, http://pss.sagepub/content/early/2013/04/24/0956797612464058, (accessed 29 March 2018).

someone else not to know something that you know."[216] It is one of the best explanations we have heard, for why people communicate poorly. Is your home cluttered with instruction manuals written by engineers who can design devices but somehow cannot explain how to use them?

It may simply not occur to a person who knows a topic well to explain jargon, spell out the logic or supply the necessary detail (not all the detail, just the relevant and necessary detail to fill in the missing chunks of knowledge). The difficulty is that the 'curse' is what prevents us from noticing the communication problems it creates. Avoid jargon, abbreviations and technical terms.

Using finance as an example, those who construct financial instruments have become so proficient at their work that they can easily forget everyone else may not be a member of their club. The curse of knowledge ensures that people will overestimate how standard a term has become and how widely it is understood. Users of acronyms tend to forget that the few seconds they may save for themselves comes at a cost in lost understanding among others in the conversation.

Remember the chunks. When we know something well, we are unaware of how abstractly we think about it. We forget that other people have not lived our experience or had our training. According to Steven Pinker there are two ways that thoughts lose their moorings: chunking and functional fixity.

Chunking: Human working memory can only hold a few items at a time. The brain solves this problem by packaging small chunks into larger and larger packages. Each chunk has information packed inside it, an acronym is an example. The use of multiple acronyms allows us to group chunks into bigger concepts that are more easily remembered. And chunking is not just a memory tool; it is the lifeblood of higher intelligence. So, chunking can be both a blessing and a curse.

---

216 S Pinker, 2014, "The Sense of Style: The Thinking Person's Guide to Writing in the 21st Century", Allen Lane Penguin Books, p 59.

It's very useful for leaders to chunk larger pieces of say a project, into smaller chunks so that the key points are easily remembered, and the entire concept is understood. However, it becomes less useful when the chunks are described by acronyms which are uncommon to others.

Functional fixity: This is the second way thoughts lose their meaning when communicated. A failure to realise that your experience (your 'chunks') may not be the same as that of other leaders, goes part of the way toward explaining why we baffle each other with jargon, technical terms and acronyms. However, it's not the only way we create confusion. Why do we create confusing terms and jargon in the first place? Because the more familiar we become with something, the more we think about it in terms of what it does rather than what it looks like and what it is made of. When we get fixated on the function of a thing and forget about everything else, 'functional fixity' has occurred.[217]

For example, there's a famous experiment (posthumously published by Karl Duncker in 1945[218]) where people are given a candle, a book of matches, and a box of thumbtacks and asked to attach the candle to the wall so it won't drip. Consider how you might attach the candle to the wall?

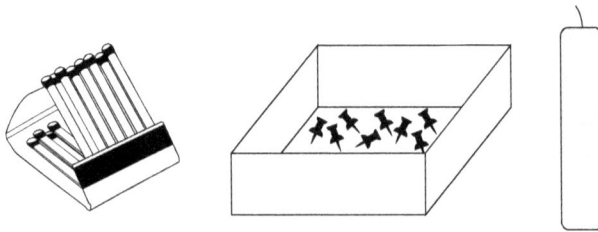

Figure 25: The candle problem.

217 ibid, p 71.
218 J Faletto, 2017, "The candle problem from 1945 is a logic puzzle that requires creative thinking", *Curiosity*, 4 August, https://curiosity.com/topics/the-candle-problem-from-1945-can-only-be-solved-by-creative-thinkers-curiosity/, (accessed 10 March 2018).

Most people are stymied. They can't figure out a solution because they think of the box as a container for tacks rather than a physical object with handy features like a flat side surface and perpendicular sides that could hold a candle tacked to the wall.

The solution to this challenge is to empty the box of thumbtacks, use the thumbtacks to nail the box to the wall, put the candle into the box, and light the candle with the match.

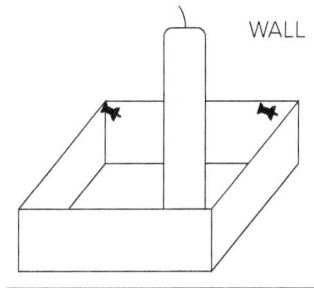

Figure 26: The candle problem—solution.

So if we combine our 'fixation for function' with 'chunking' and stir in the 'curse' that hides each chunk from our awareness, we can start to understand that people communicate things the way they are thinking, rather than in a way more appropriate to gaining the understanding of others. Think about the term 'culture'. So many things are rolled into that term. We started this book by 'chunking' that term into parts such as selection, induction, rewards and leadership behaviour to gain an understanding of how leaders can think about shaping culture and setting tone.

Since a third of our brains are dedicated to vision and other significant sections to touch, hearing, motion and space, we need to beware of abstractions and use concrete language that allows us to form visual images and make meaning. This is the reason metaphors and stories are so powerful for creating real understanding in a conversation. Consider these two examples of abstractions from Steven Pinker which have been made much simpler:

Example 1:

Management actions at and in the immediate vicinity of airports do little to mitigate the risk of off-airport strikes during departure and take-off.

vs.

Trapping birds near an airport does little to reduce the number of times a bird will collide with a plane as it takes off or lands.

Example 2:

We believe that the ICTS approach to delivering integrated solutions, combining effective manpower, canine services and cutting-edge technology was a key differentiator in the selection process.

vs.

They chose our company because we protect buildings with a combination of guards, dogs and sensors.[219]

Which language in these two examples makes more sense? When understanding improves, so does the quality of communication.

How leaders improve conversations by using 'conversation deepeners'

Here are some quick tips for improving conversation deepeners. We trust you'll recognise many of these from earlier in the book and now have an understanding of why we've included them again as 'conversation deepeners':

- Let the speaker know you're listening by nodding, making eye contact, and asking questions to make sure you understand him or her.

---

219 S Pinker, 2014, "The Sense of Style: The Thinking Person's Guide to Writing in the 21st Century", Allen Lane Penguin Books, p 73.

- Draw people out by asking open-ended questions that invite expansive answers:
  - "What else?"
  - "Tell me more?"
  - "How might that work in practice?"
- Explore the language people use and the thinking behind their statements:
  - "That sounds interesting, why would you suggest that?"
- Ask questions that are constructive, resource-seeking and forward-moving. For example, ask about hopes and positive achievements, rather than mistakes or regrets:
  - when it's implemented?"
- Ask someone to say more about the things she/he finds meaningful:
  - "Tell me more"
  - "For instance?"
- Ask questions that invite the speaker to go beyond 'black and white' thinking by exploring complexity:
  - "What is it that you find most interesting about this proposal?"
  - "Who else have you discussed this with, and what was their impression?"

The bottom line ...

Conversation techniques, question and word choices

Having read this far, no doubt you are now starting to consider or perhaps re-consider some of the words you are using and some that you may be thinking of dropping. In addition to what you've decided thus far, you may now like to consider to:

- Review our discussion on assertiveness to mitigate people talking over you. The key points can be found in chapter 4.6: The conversation you're having when you're not having a conversation.
- Include in your conversational repertoire some 'opening up' type questions to deepen a conversation with someone who regularly pushes their opinion

in the form of a question such as "Don't you think (that) ...". A number of the more powerful ones we use are:
  - "Am I hearing that ... I should do ... is that correct?"
  - "Can you give me an example of what you mean?"
  - "How does that relate to what I'm proposing?"
  - "How would that work with what I'm suggesting?"
  - "How would you see my idea working with what you're suggesting?"
  And the most powerful (and our all-time favourite):
  - "Tell me more ..." (you can see that this is not really a question, but an 'invitation').
- Encourage further meaning or understanding from people who often use one-word adjectives such as 'awesome' by asking:
  - "How so?"
  - "Why is this (awesome, exciting etc.)?"
- Avoid some of the conversation stoppers such as "I'll let you know", "Let me see what I can do", or "Let me be honest (with you)".
- Help others moderate their view (or perhaps explore the practicality of their views) by asking 'how' type questions such as:
  - "How would that work?"
  - "How could that work in practice?"
- Help people better understand your point of view (or functional expertise) by:
  - avoiding jargon; and
  - chunking the explanation of your suggestions or recommendations.
- Overcome 'functional fixity' by explaining your expertise in terms that others can understand. As someone said recently, "Tell it as if you're talking to your elderly uncle or aunt who was born decades before the internet".

4.11 Concluding comments on managing challenging conversations

Every leader must discuss difficult issues from time to time. There will also have to be tough conversations after a serious event, such as a breach of security or a major issue with safety or quality. There are also those challenging conversations leaders will need to have with one another from time to time or with senior managers or the CEO. The right approach to these conversations can have a positive impact on the outcome. The right approach is achieved through being cognisant of the six phases of conversation, and in the case of challenging or difficult conversations, being able to navigate carefully and skilfully through each phase.

In Part 4, we've demonstrated how word choice and phrasing can help guide leaders to set a positive tone, even when the topic or issue is quite challenging. This has been through the consideration of different perspectives in order to create new solutions that engage others both intellectually and emotionally. Conversational concepts, covered in detail earlier in the book, such as mirroring, framing, triangulating, metaphors, and clean language have provided the tools to examine a range of different perspectives.

Whatever the situation, leaders are encouraged to raise sensitive issues promptly, and to talk about them honestly and openly. Sensitive issues can inflame passions so it is vital that difficult discussions remain balanced and fair. The suggestions covered in Part 4 for handling some of the challenging conversations leaders will face from time to time, will give leaders the means to judiciously deal with sensitive issues and bring about positive outcomes.

CONCLUSION

What tone is being set at the top in your organisation?

Our journey of discovering the powerful impact words have for leaders, started with the story of World Bank star economist, Paul Romer, who was stripped of his leadership role because of his use of words:

> *It's possible that I was focusing too much on the precision of the communications and not enough on the feelings my messages would invoke.*[220]

Romer's words are but one of the many examples we've called on to illustrate the power of words and what can happen when the impact of a leader's words does not match the desired intent. Whilst the intent may seem quite logical and factually based when spoken or written, it is often how the recipient *feels* about the message that will determine whether it has the desired impact. Isn't this what setting the tone is all about—delivering a message that has the desired impact on behaviour versus creating a set of unintended consequences?

---

220 A Mayeda, 2017, "War over words erupts as World Bank start economist loses management duties", *Sydney Morning Herald*, 26 May 2017, https://www.smh.com.au/business/the-economy/war-over-words-erupts-as-world-bankd-start-economist-loses-management-duties-20170526gwdj97.html, (accessed 26 May 2017).

Setting the tone starts with words because human beings transfer information and feelings to one another by putting their thoughts into words. Leaders translate their expertise, their thinking and judgements into words. This includes their thinking about values, strategies, goals and risks which is delivered to those throughout the organisation with words, both verbal and written. Words and the conversations they create are the most powerful tools available to leaders for shaping behaviour, which impacts decisions and actions, and in turn forms the 'way we do things around here', i.e. the culture of an organisation. Therefore, for leaders facing increasing expectations in relation to their responsibility for setting organisational culture and building trust, the importance of using words, which align intent and impact, is critically important.

We've signposted throughout *Setting the Tone from the Top*, ways poor word choice can result in reputational risks, and how those risks can have as much impact as strategic, operating and financial risks. A mere rumour, a hint of impropriety or a single social media post gone viral can damage or worse, destroy corporate and brand reputations in an instant along with shareholder value. Through social media, for example, a leader's inappropriate or poorly chosen words can go viral in a nanosecond, undermining efforts to build a consistent message and tone from the top.

However, being an effective leader is about more than avoiding negative publicity—it's about taking positive actions that set a positive tone and generate high quality decisions and ethical behaviour. We have shown many examples where the positive and affirmative language that leaders use has a positive impact on the tone that is set for the entire organisation. Many of our examples have included powerful metaphors, so it is apt to conclude with one to punctuate this point; 'water flows best downhill'. At the top of the hill, some points for leaders to consider in *Setting the Tone from the Top*:

- Are the conversations among senior leaders positive and affirming? Are they setting the 'right tone'?
- What changes could, or should leaders make in the language they are using?
- As a leader how can you influence your colleagues and staff through your positive and affirmative language?
- As a leader, what do you think you might do more of or less of, to have those beneficial conversations that are so important to setting the tone from the top?

The key tenet of this book is about conversations and how they impact relationships with colleagues, staff, senior management, the CEO, the board, the media, and other important stakeholders. The quality of these relationships impacts behaviour, which in turn shapes culture. And it all starts with words:

Words are not things—they are representations and symbols we use to view, to think about and process our perceptions of reality and they are the means of sharing these perceptions with others. Yet few leaders understand how vital conversation is to the health and productivity of their company culture.[221]

We believe conversation is one of the most vital ingredients in setting the tone from the top. Leaders who want to role model, inspire and promote ethical behaviour need to understand the impact of their conversations and word choice on culture and therefore the integrity of their organisation.

We have seen significant falls in trust in the leadership of corporations as well as governments around the world. Trust in the leader is one of the major deciding factors for people when choosing whether

---

221 J Glaser, 2013, "Conversational intelligence: How great leaders build trust and get extraordinary results", Taylor and Francis Inc. Brookline, MA, p 9.

to work for a company or stay with a company. Without trust, it is difficult to build a culture of integrity, one where ethical standards are understood and adhered to in practice. Some of the situations we have highlighted in the book, along with business conversations we have observed, indicate that perhaps the quality of those conversations and their impact on relationships are not valued as highly as they should be. Relationships have been eclipsed by things thought to be more pressing, more immediate, dare we say, like "making the numbers". But there is a ripple effect; leaders need to deeply consider the unintended consequences of what they say on decisions and policies which in turn impact behaviour, relationships and outcomes.

As author and speaker Brian Tracy says:

"The glue that holds all relationships together, including the relationship between the leader and the led, is trust, and trust is based on integrity."

Leaders who want to embed a culture of trust and integrity in their organisations can do so with every conversation.

SUGGESTED READING

In addition to the many other influences on our thinking, we've found the following books useful and recommend them to you:

A Damasio, 1994, *Descartes' Error: Emotion, reason and the human brain*, Grosset/Putnam, New York

N Doidge, 2007, *The Brain that Changes Itself*, Penguin Group, London

D Eagleman, 2015, *The Brain: The story of you*, Canongate Books, London

A Edmondson, 2019, *The Fearless Organization: creating psychological safety in the workplace for learning, innovation and growth*, Wiley & Sons, New Jersey

P Ekman, 2001, *Telling Lies: Clues to deceit in the marketplace, politics and marriage*, Norton, New York

S Finkelstein and D Hambrick, 1996, *Strategic Leadership: Top executives and their effects on organizations*, West Publishing Company, St Paul MN

S Finkelstein, J Whitehead and A Campbell, 2008, *Think Again: Why good leaders make bad decisions and how to keep it from happening to you*, Harvard Business School Publishing, Boston

R Fisher and W Ury, 1991, *Getting to Yes: Negotiating agreement without giving in*, Penguin Books, New York

E Fox, 2012, *Rainy brain, sunny brain: How to retrain your brain to overcome pessimism and achieve a more positive outlook*, Basic Books, New York

J Haidt, 2013, *The Righteous Mind: Why good people are divided by politics and religion*, Vintage Books, Random House, New York

R Heifetz, 1994, *Leadership without Easy Answers*, Belknap Press of Harvard University Press, Cambridge, MA

P Howard, 2000, *The Owner's Manual for the Brain*, Bard Press, Atlanta GA

D Kahneman, 2011, *Thinking Fast and slow*, Farrar, Straus & Giroux, New York

G Lakoff and M Johnson, 1980, *Metaphors We Live By*, University of Chicago Press, Chicago

J Lawley and P Tompkins, 2000, *Metaphors in Mind*, Developing Company Press, London

C Nass, 2010, *The Man Who Lied to his Laptop*, Penguin Group, New York

D Pink, 2011, *Drive: The surprising truth about What Motivates Us*, Penguin Group, New York

S Pinker, 2014, *The Sense of Style: The thinking person's guide to writing in the 21st Century*, Penguin Group, London

S Pinker, 2007, *The Stuff of Thought: Language as a window into human nature*, Penguin Books, New York

R Sapolsky, 2017, *Behave: The biology of humans at our best and worst*, Bodley Head, Penguin Random House, London

S Scott, 2002, *Fierce Conversations: Achieving success at work and life one conversation at a time*, Berkley Penguin Random House, New York

M Seligman, 1994, *Learned Optimism*, Griffin Paperbacks, South Australia

AUTHOR BIOGRAPHIES

Melinda Muth

Melinda is an educator and consultant who specialises in personal and team effectiveness, principally with senior executives and leadership teams. She is a facilitator and guest speaker in a variety of executive education programs in Australia and has worked in Asia and the USA. She is a Facilitator and Fellow of Australian Institute of Company Directors, leader of the Governance Development practice with Peakstone Global and a Director of Streamwise Learning.

She has held a number of executive leadership roles including Director of Business Development and Marketing with Deloitte along with board roles as Chair of Australian Scholarships Foundation, CuriousWorks and Director of HCA Philanthropy, HeartKids NSW, the Quest Foundation, the Union University & Schools Club and Indigenous Community Volunteers where she was Chair of the Audit & Risk Management Committee. She is a member of the Academy of Management, the Australian Human Resource Institute and the Harvard Club of Australia.

Her credentials include a Bachelor of Science in Design, magna cum laude, from the University of Cincinnati, an MBA from the Harvard Business School and a PhD from the Australian Graduate School of Management (UNSW) for research on the impact of boards on firm performance. Her doctoral thesis focused on the dimensions of board structure and director networks that impact firm performance.

Bob Selden

Bob is a Senior Consultant for Family Business Central, an organisation that assists families to manage the "family" so that the family can manage the "business".

He's the author of 'What To Do When You Become The Boss', a best-selling book (currently 75,000 copies sold and published in four languages) for newly promoted managers. The book reflects Bob's experience over many years as a line manager and organisational development consultant. Bob's coached senior executives at one of the world's premier business schools—the International Institute for Management Development in Lausanne Switzerland and all level of managers at the Australian Graduate School of Management, Sydney, Australia.

Setting the Tone from the Top came about through discussions with fellow author and long-time colleague, Melinda Muth following a presentation Bob gave on 'the power of words in conversations across different generations' at an AICD conference in Melbourne in 2017.

Bob has qualifications in psychology from Macquarie University and organizational development from Charles Sturt University. He currently lives in Palmerston North, New Zealand with his wife Anita, is a keen cyclist, and smiles a lot!

Index

www.ingramcontent.com/pod-product-compliance
Lightning Source LLC
Chambersburg PA
CBHW071325210326
41597CB00015B/1358